THE ARISTOCRATIC IDEAL
IN ANCIENT GREECE

Attitudes of Superiority from Homer
to the End of the Fifth Century B.C.

by

Walter Donlan

Coronado Press   1980

ISBN 0–87291–140–3

COPYRIGHT NOTICE
©Walter Donlan 1980

All rights reserved. No part of this publication may be reproduced, stored in a retrieval system, or transmitted, in any form or by any means, electronic, mechanical, photocopying, recording or otherwise, without the prior permission of the Coronado Press

Set in 10 on twelve point Press Roman
Published in the United States of America
by   Coronado Press
      Box 3232
      Lawrence, Kansas, 66044
      USA

To my father and mother

ACKNOWLEDGMENTS

To list the names of teachers, colleagues, friends and students whose advice and criticism have enriched my understanding of the evolution of the Greek aristocratic ideal would be an impossible task. Suffice it to say that they have helped me to avoid many more errors of judgment and emphasis than inevitably appear herein.

Warmest thanks are owed to my fellow teachers in the Department of Classics at Penn State for providing, over the years, an atmosphere of comfortable friendship and generous encouragement.

Much of the research for this book was made possible by a Faculty Research Fellowship, awarded by the Institute for the Arts and Humunistic Studies of the Pennsylvania State University in 1974. Several grants for research and typing were also generously made available to me from the Liberal Arts College Fund for Research at Penn State.

Permissions from The University of Chicago Press to quote from Richmond Lattimore's translation of the *Iliad*, from Harper and Row to quote from Lattimore's translation of the *Odyssey* and from Harvard University Press to quote from H. G. Evelyn-White's Loeb Classical Library translation of Hesiod, *Works and Days* and *Theogony* are gratefully acknowledged.

Finally, special thanks are due to John E. Longhurst of Coronado Press whose critical eye, editorial skill and keen wit prove that the spirit of humanism is still alive.

CONTENTS

Introduction ix

Chapter One   The Ideal of the Warrior-Aristocrat 1

Chapter Two   The Old Ideal under Challenge 35

Chapter Three   The Crisis of Identity: Theognis and Pindar 77

Chapter Four   The Aristocratic Ideal in the Classical Period 113

Chapter Five   Aristocratic Life-Style in the Fifth Century 155

Notes to the Text 181

Index 213

INTRODUCTION

MODERN INTERPRETERS of the intellectual and cultural history of ancient Greece turn instinctually and inevitably to the artists and thinkers whose achievements have ranked them high above the mass of ordinary men. More often than not these great figures represented the convictions and prejudices of a narrow group within the society as a whole. In the surviving treasures of Greek art one is tempted to see the plastic or graphic extension of the same point of view. The gleaming stone temples house statues of gods cast in the image of highborn men and women; sculpture and painting depicted gods and heroes in attitudes of serene aloofness or noble youths and maidens in graceful action or elegant repose. The bitter drudgery of a hard life eked out from stony soil was seldom celebrated in literature and art. The unspectacular lives of the countless thousands of "ordinary" people, and their attitudes and values, sparsely recorded and difficult to recover, resonate hardly at all in the researches of modern scholars.

The tendency to define the essence of a culture in terms of its highest refinement can lead to a distorted view of the dynamics of that culture. In one of the most influential books written in this century about the cultural ideals of Greece, the late Werner Jaeger could say,

> All later culture, however high an intellectual level it may reach, and however greatly its content may change, still bears the imprint of its aristocratic origin. Culture is simply the aristocratic ideal of a nation, increasingly intellectualized. (*Paideia* I, p. 4).

But is this true?

We must remind ourselves that the Parthenon, which still crowns the ancient citadel of Athens, was the product of Athenian democracy's proudest hour, and that the enormous gold and ivory statue of Athena, which once dominated its interior, carried the helmet, spear and shield of the citizen-soldier. The very gold that sheathed her body was part of the treasury of the people, the *dēmos,* to be used in an emergency as the sovereign people voted it. Athena herself was no remote queen nor a symbol of the lofty intellect, but the patron of the potters and other artisans who labored daily in the city below. According to the ancient myth her gift to Athens was the olive tree, whose oil filled the potters' jars and provided a cash crop for the farmer-soldiers who manned the ranks; her animals were the owl and the snake, homely creatures which represented the life forces of a simple agrarian community.

It is necessary, too, to recall that the god at whose festivals the Athenians watched the tragedies and comedies of the great playwrights was not the aloof, aristocratic Apollo, but Dionysos, a cthonian, a rural vegetative god, who, despite the antiquity of his worship, was often regarded as a late interloper to the Olympian pantheon. Athena and Dionysos were part of the Greek ideal; in origin and essence they are not representative of a specifically aristocratic ideal.

We must be very careful, therefore, not to confuse the aristocratic ideal with the ideals of the whole of the Greek culture; they are not one and the same, although at many points they coincide. When it is realized that the aristocratic ideal is essentially the product of a particular class and not a national ideal, its development and the forces and stresses which shaped it are more easily apprehended.

The Greek aristocratic ideal did not, as Jaeger and others have assumed, give Greek culture its definitive form. Rather, it was itself shaped by opposing forces in Greek society, and it developed and changed in response to pressures on the social class which was its focus. We can go further and say that the resultant pattern of social and intellectual attitudes, usually identified as the Greek aristocratic ideal, was not a static or constant phenomenon, but that it evolved, at times by almost imperceptible shifts, into a final phase which was, in very many respects, quite different from its early stages.

This book is neither a constitutional history nor a formal study of political institutions of Greek states, but an exploration of the patterns of social attitudes and values of one subgroup — the aristocratic class. Nor have I attempted to substitute for the traditional view of Greek society a new theory of social development, but merely to shift the perspective somewhat, to show how totally the aristocratic pattern of thought was a class phenomenon and to indicate its dependence on the often fast-moving and important social and cultural changes experienced in the Greek world during the period from 800 to 400 B.C.

In short, I wish to present the Greek aristocratic ideal as a "defensive" standard, whose proponents were constantly and consistently aware of the challenges to their values posed by the larger society, and who reacted by altering their own scheme of values. The aim, which in time became increasingly self-conscious, was both to prove the superiority of the upper class and to impose a particular set of values on the society as a whole. That this attempt was successful, to some extent at least, is indicated by the fact that modern observers of ancient Greece have continued to confuse the "Greek ideal" with the "Greek aristocratic ideal."

Finally, it is hoped that those whose main interests lie outside the area of Greek studies will gain some insight into the process of Greek social evolution. Hellenic society provides a fruitful model of study for the social scientist, first because of the very high level of self-consciousness and historical awareness that possessed the ancient Greeks, and secondly, because we are far enough removed to be objective in our assessment of the social drama, and to trace its evolution over a lengthy period of time.

In some ways this is an "old-fashioned" book. As its subtitle affirms, it is a study of *attitudes* — primarily the "thought-world" of a remarkably homogeneous upper stratum, contrasted, where possible, with the outlook of those who were not of the privileged few. Attitudes are primarily a function of reflection; as such they are most apparent in the literary sources. Other evidence for human attitudes are the surviving monuments — from temples to safety pins — and demographic information gleaned from these and other sources. Where it was feasible, I have made reference to this valuable material, which supplements (and sometimes corrects) the written record. However, such information is often difficult to assess, and reliable statistical or demographic data hardly exist. In like manner, other areas of ancient studies, such as political history, religious cult, prosopography, which are closely entwined with the evolution of the aristocratic ideal, are used to supplement the literary expression of social attitudes, without losing sight of the restricted purpose of this study: the isolation of the sociopsychological currents that accompanied the main flow of events in the Greek world from 800 to 400 B.C.

◊

One last word: As every student of ancient Greece is painfully aware, a disproportionate amount of the available literary data comes from Athenian writers, and is related to social and political problems in

Athens. Such an emphasis is unavoidable, but we can be reasonably sure that the attitudes discernible in our Attic sources are representative of attitudes of Greeks in other communities.

Ω

CHAPTER ONE

The Ideal of the Warrior-Aristocrat

THE ULTIMATE ORIGINS of the Greek aristocratic ideal lie buried in the obscurity of Greece's prehistory; but in the poems of Homer, at the dawning of the historical era, we find the elements of the ideal already articulated. The great epics, the *Iliad* and *Odyssey,* composed about 750 B.C., reflect the culture of an "Heroic Age."

There continues a lively debate among scholars about the historical validity of the "world of Homer." For some, the epics, which were the products of centuries of oral development, reflect the institutions and material culture of the Mycenaean era, which ended with the widespread destruction of numerous centrally controlled, highly bureaucratic, "palace" complexes around 1200 B.C. (the time of the Trojan war). For others, they depict the society of a subsequent Dark Age, between 1100 and 900, while others see the epics as more or less contemporary records of the time of final composition, the eighth century B.C. A number of scholars reject these alternatives, maintaining that the poems are fictional amalgams of material background, institutions, and values, drawn from the whole period, from late Mycenaean to after 750 B.C., and therefore useless as historical or social evidence.

Whether the society portrayed in Homer was a "real" one, mirroring an actual society, in space and time (as I believe), or not, there can be no disagreement about one fact. The cultural standards and attitudes found in the *Iliad* and *Odyssey,* that make up what is called the "Heroic Ideal," had a profound effect on the conceptual universe of all subsequent generations of Greeks from the late eighth century on. Historically "real" or not, the epic system of values was very real to the Greeks of the Archaic and Classical periods (and beyond), who had no doubts about the literal existence of the events, characters and behavioral standard depicted in the epics. For them, Achilles, Odysseus, Hector,

---

N.B. NOTES TO THE TEXT appear last, with running heads to indicate to what page(s) they refer.

and the other heroic figures spoke and acted just as Homer (about whose existence there was no doubt either) said. And, for the post-Homeric Greeks, especially for those of higher status, the norms of individual behavior contained in the Homeric warrior-ideal constituted a paradigm which they assumptively accepted as right and proper. The evolution of the Greek aristocratic ideal, formed on the model of the ideals embodied in the Homeric epics, is the story of how the upper-class Greeks conformed to, deviated from, or altered this fundamental set of normative values in response to changing social realities.[1]

The historical culture itself, the source from which this warrior "code" arose, is only dimly perceived by us. I believe, with Finley and others, that the institutional background of the *Iliad* and *Odyssey* is essentially the experience of Greeks on the mainland, Aegean islands, and the coast of Asia Minor in the tenth and ninth centuries B.C. While many of the culture's features (architecture, weaponry and modes of fighting, use of metals, etc.) are Dark Age retrojections into a dimly remembered Mycenaean past, the political, economic, social and ideological systems belong to this period. The social system was one of chiefdoms, of a not advanced type, which exhibited many elements of an egalitarian, non-stratified tribal structure. The economic base of the culture was stockbreeding (cattle, sheep, goats, swine), along with agriculture (grain, vine, olives). These Greeks lived in small, unprepossessing, mud-brick villages, usually unwalled, with farm plots and pasturage outside. The central societal institution, however, was not the clan-village, but the household, *oikos*, a patrilineal corporation, consisting of the male *oikos*-head, his immediate family, dependents and slaves. The *oikos* was almost completely self-sufficient economically, and enjoyed much political autonomy also. Heads of wealthy (in flocks, land and treasure) and powerful lineages were called *basileis*, a word that is commonly rendered as "kings." Although the Homeric *basileus* was anachronistically vested with some of the trappings of the powerful Mycenaean overlord, the *wanax* (a title that is occasionally applied to some human leaders and to the gods, in Homer), the texts show the Homeric *basileus* to correspond to the model of the tribal chief in all respects. The chief of the most dominant lineage was the paramount, also called simply *basileus*, a "first among equals," to whom other *basileis* and their corporations were tied in a complex system of reciprocities, rather typical of primitive chiefdoms.

It is of fundamental importance to stress at the outset that the epic system of values was formulated within the kind of social organization that anthropologists term "simple" or "primitive." This does not imply that the Greeks of the Dark Age were intellectually or artistically "savage" (one need only refer to the high technical and aesthetic standards of Geometric pottery — or to the epics themselves). It is simply that the ethical superstructure of a pre-literate tribal culture, characterized by a pre-market economy and a pre-state polity, is the valuative statement of the underlying structure. Thus, the "heroic ideal," like the social structure itself, was essentially tribal, reflecting the values of a society in which physical skill, courage, and leadership were the prized attributes, high rank was attained or maintained by accomplishment in an atmosphere of individual competition for prestige, set within the context of a rigidly prescribed system of obligation and counter-obligation. As the result of a variety of structural and historical causes (which cannot be explored here), the dominant ethos of the high-ranking Homeric individual revolved around success in war; accordingly, the main concern of the epics is the great deeds of men in battle or contest.[2]

With the evolution of more complex social structures after 700 B.C., especially with the emergence of the state form, the *polis* (the rudiments of which can be traced in the epics), the focus of activity of the ruling stratum shifts in conformance. Nevertheless, the standard of success, the agonistic impulse, and, indeed, the tribal form itself, exhibit a remarkable tenacity throughout Greek history. Despite the enormous changes that took place within Greek culture during the four centuries covered by this survey, the upper-class Greeks of the late fifth century B.C., in their reflections concerning human behavior and the relations between men, continued to take as their assumptive starting point the complex of received beliefs embedded in the heroic ideal.

Because the purpose of this study is the relatively narrow one of tracing the evolution of the aristocratic ideal, it will be necessary to abstract, somewhat artificially, the ideal from its social matrix. I hope this will not present too many conceptual difficulties to the reader, who is asked to keep in mind that, although detailed discussion of the social forces behind attitudes and changes in attitudes must be severely limited, those forces were the operative causes of the world of thought that we are describing.

Before the various aspects of the heroic ideal are described in detail, a brief explanation of a tool useful in the study of social concepts is in order.[3] In the Greek language (as in English) there are certain "key" words, highly charged with social and ethical implications. Very important among these are the groups of adjectives and nouns that signify "good" and "bad" — fundamental notions in any social order. A study of these and similar terms, observed over a long period of time, affords valuable clues to the shiftings of cultural values. In Homer, for example, the chief epithets of approbation, *agathos* and *esthlos,* which are inadequately translated as "good," refer mostly to excellence in some physical sphere and are almost always related to warcraft. Thus one is said to be *"agathos* at the war-cry," or *"esthlos* in close fighting."[4] Hence, frequently the best translation in Homer for these two adjectives is simply "brave." Not surprisingly, the word that indicates "bad" *(kakos)* is often best rendered in the epics as "cowardly."[5] These words later operate within a more broadly social or ethical-moral sphere, but in Homer there is practically no trace of these broader significations. According to the value system of the Homeric fighter a man was judged "good" or "bad" by the standards of physical prowess, and their attendant psychological states.

The Homeric hero in war was inspired by a single purpose: to win personal glory and honor *(timē, kydos)* for himself by means of valorous deeds performed on the field of battle. Accordingly, the goal of every activity, practically without exception, was the recognition of self by peers as a good warrior. This ideal operated even in areas where, according to the modern sense of values, different motivations would seem to apply. The acquisition of wealth, for example, which was a major preoccupation of the epic warriors, and about which they talked endlessly, was not prompted by greed: such a motivation belongs to market economies. The possession of great wealth was a conspicuous sign of success — visible proof of prowess and leadership. It was also the means by which prestige and rank were enhanced, since it enabled the holder to give valuable gifts to guest-friends *(xeinoi)* and to reward followers, thereby insuring and increasing loyalty and dependency.

The wealth of the early Greek world was in flocks and land, the property of the *oikos,* controlled by the *oikos*-head. Aside from normal natural increase, wealth was acquired or added to in the form of booty from war raids (animals, captives, metal, luxury objects); the warrior-chief shared in the general distribution of spoils, and, as leader, was awarded an extra share as his special prize *(geras).*[6] As a general rule, therefore, one grew rich, stayed rich or became richer, by fighting; the successful warrior was a wealthy man, and, conversely, a rich man was a successful warrior. The clear and definite impression of the Homeric age's attitude towards wealth is that it was regarded both as the tangible proof of a man's excellence and a means of increasing reputation and standing, not as a primary goal in itself.

One rather odd (to us) form of non-landed wealth in the epics, cumbersome bronze tripods or cauldrons, is explainable only in terms of display and exchange. These and other treasures were "laid up" *(keimēlia)*, not as misers' hoards, but as proof of status and attainment. Equally significant are the elaborate rituals of gift giving, in which the exchange of such objects of value confirmed the standing of the warriors and served to cement social relations among them. In short, the "social" motives for the acquiring of goods had greater force than purely "economic" motives. When, according to legend, Ajax went mad with rage and frustration because Odysseus, not he, was awarded the arms of the dead Achilles, it was not on account of the value of the prize, but because these would have been the outward signal to all the world that he was, indeed, the heir to the fame and glory of Achilles.[7]

This emphasis on the visible proof of success demonstrates the importance of opinion in determining status as a warrior; how one "seemed" not what one "was" was the index of a man's worth. In fact, one "was" what one seemed to others. Homer allows his warriors many moments of self-doubt as they ponder whether to stay or to run; always it is how they will appear to others which determines their decision to risk their lives.[8] There is not one character in Homer who possesses perfect internal security. The Homeric warrior cannot say: "I know my own worth, and I do not care what others say about me," since he could, in fact, see himself only in terms of what others said about him. Past success counted for little; men who displayed great courage over long periods of time might suddenly be accused of outright cowardice because of a momentary hesitation.[9] Seldom, if ever, does a warrior defend himself by appealing to past performance, for worth is always measured by the present moment, and the individual Homeric hero appears never to be in disagreement with this imposed necessity for constant justification. A.W.H. Adkins has put the matter succinctly: "The Homeric hero cannot fall back upon his own opinion of himself for his self only has the value which other people put upon it."[10] And because of this total dependency on honor which can only be realized in terms of public opinion — "what people say" — all other appeals to action fade before the need to prove oneself. Thus Hector, the greatest of the Trojan heroes and the bulwark of his city, even when he was urged by those most closely connected to him, his family, not to expose himself to certain death in combat with Achilles, could reply only in terms of his heroic honor.[11] Fear of failure, that is, loss of public approbation, is the reverse of the need for appearing successful, and acts as an equally powerful motivating factor of personal behavior. For this reason Homeric society has been termed a "shame culture" as opposed to a "guilt culture."[12]

External valuation extends to other areas, too. For example, how one looked in the simple physical sense was not separable from the true self. Thus it can be said of a stranger that "He looks like a *basileus.*" Needless to say, this is said only of someone who was a *basileus.*[13] The importance of physical appearance is underscored in the *Odyssey,* where, to hide his identity, Odysseus is disguised by Athena as a beggar. Yet, even after he slew the suitors, having revealed himself as the absent chief, his wife, Penelope, appears unable to recognize him because of his "evil rags."[14] No less significant in this regard is the fact that the only "commoner" who plays a role in the *Iliad,* the obstreperous Thersites, is described as physically repulsive. This is sufficient, apparently, to stamp him as socially inferior.[15] We shall see that external appearance as an index of human worth, already firmly established in Homer, continues as a constant theme in the developing aristocratic self-conception.

The emphasis on physical prowess and the honor which it wins does not preclude, but presupposes, intelligence and resourcefulness. Cunning in stratagem and trickery, along with facility in public speaking, were desirable attributes. Nevertheless, it is clear in Homer that intelligence is not separate from physical ability but is integral to it. The ideal is a combination of physical excellence (which includes good looks as well as strength) and mental agility. Some, like Odysseus, who is most often called "resourceful" and "of many counsels," or the wise old Nestor, have the latter ability to a higher degree; others, like Ajax, are primarily men of action, not noted for skill in planning and persuading. The intimate connection between body and mind is readily seen in the characterizations of heroes. Hector praises Ajax for his "stature, strength and wisdom" (*Iliad* 7.288-89). Diomedes is called by Nestor "mighty in battle, and in counsel *(boulē)* best among your age group" (*Iliad* 9.53-54). Hector kills a warrior who is described as better by far than his father "in all sorts of *aretai,* both in swiftness of foot and in fighting, and in intelligence *(noos)* among the first of the Mycenaeans" (*Iliad* 15.641-43). Priam tells the god Hermes (disguised as a human) that he is "admirable in form and beauty *(eidos),* and wise in *noos*" (*Iliad* 24.376-77). Conversely, Elpenor is said by Odysseus to have been "not overly courageous in war nor sound in wit" (*Odyssey* 10.552-53).

Odysseus gives a capsule description of himself that sums up the nexus of attributes considered necessary for the complete hero. He tells his men that they had escaped the brute strength of the Cyclops "through my *aretē* (i.e. courage and skill), my *boulē* (counsel, advice) and my *noos* (intelligence)" (*Odyssey* 12.211). The most succinct statement of the composite ideal is Peleus' charge to Phoenix to teach the young Achilles "to be both a speaker of words and a doer of deeds" (*Iliad* 9.443).[16] There is, however, also an awareness that few, even among heroes, achieve the ideal of the perfect combining of body and mind. Once Odysseus rebukes Achilles:

> you are stronger than I am and greater by not a little with the spear, yet I in turn might overpass you in wisdom *(noēma)* by far . . .
> (*Iliad* 19.217-19, Latt.)[17]

Elsewhere Homer had Odysseus lecture a rude young Phaeacian—saying first that the gods do not give gifts to all men alike "neither in stature nor yet in brains or eloquence." The hero goes on to say that one man is inferior in appearance *(eidos),* but a superb speaker, and wins honor thereby; another has *eidos* like the gods but no ability in speaking,

> as in your case the *eidos* is conspicuous, and not a god even would make it otherwise, and yet the *noos* there is worthless.
> (*Odyssey* 8.167-77, Latt.)

These examples, which evidence a certain tension between the realms of the physical and the mental, reinforce our impression that the Homeric world set little stock by mere brute strength or even that it commended simple physical ability, but sought its highest ideal in the combining of skill (with the attendant proper mental attitude, courage) and intelligence.[18] Even in the mental sphere, however, the emphasis is on action. The notion of introspective intellectuality is simply nonexistent in Homer. The thinking portion of the hero's make-up is directed toward the deed: tactical planning, trickery, persuasion in council. Naturally, excellence in these things, as in the other areas of activity, leads to the primary goal of personal fame, either at the moment, or, very importantly, after death.

The conception that excellence was a function of both body and mind, so vividly expressed in the Homeric poems, sank deep into the Greek consciousness, and remained integral to the self-perception of the aristocrats of the Archaic and Classical periods that followed. However, the tension, already observable in Homer, between "mere" appearance and the reality of accomplishment, and between physical and mental ability (which leads to the more abstract formulation of the dichotomy between action and thought) was to have a profound effect on the aristocratic ideal.

When we probe more deeply into the warrior-ideal we find aspects of human behavior that differ markedly from those of the later Greek aristocrats. A case in point is the muted sense of identity with, and responsibility to, the wider community. In general, private considerations tend to override public concerns in Homer. The hero feels his responsibility to self and expanded self (family, friends) much more heavily than to any larger group (tribe, community). When the Achaean chiefs appeal to the sulking Achilles' sense of loyalty to the whole of the Achaean army he can respond only in terms of his offended honor.[19]

Among the Trojans, fighting on home territory, identification with the community is naturally more pronounced. But even here the focus is relatively narrow. They fight "for their children and for their wives" (*Iliad* 8.57). Hector tells his allied forces that they were summoned "to save the wives of the Trojans and their little children from the war-loving Achaeans" (17.223-24); of course, their reward for this service will still be glory for themselves (line 232). Agenor, in his challenge to Achilles, says that the Trojans "will stand before our beloved parents, our wives and our children, to defend Ilion" (21.587-88, Latt.).[20]

Appeal may, in fact, be made to a larger circle of relationships and responsibilities. Hector seeks to inspire the Trojans to valor:

> He has no dishonor when he dies defending his country *(patrē)*, for then his wife shall be saved and his children afterwards, and his house and property shall not be damaged.
>
> (*Iliad* 15.496-98, Latt.)

He urges a Trojan warrior to fight: "we must kill them, or else sheer Ilion be stormed utterly by them, and her citizens *(politai)* be killed" (15.557-58, Latt.). Paris is told by Hector (3.50) that Helen is

> to your father a big sorrow, and your city *(polis)* and all your people *(dēmos)*.[21]

In a moving simile from the *Odyssey* the homesick Odysseus weeps,

> As a woman weeps, lying over the body of her dear husband, who fell fighting for her city *(polis)* and people *(laoi)* as he tried to beat off the pitiless day from city *(asty)* and children.
>
> (*Odyssey* 8.523-25, Latt.)

Poulydamas, one of the Trojan counsellors, having observed a disturbing omen, urges Hector to proceed cautiously. Hector's reply (*Iliad* 12. 243),

> One bird sign is best, to fight in defense of our country *(patrē)*,

is the closest the epic comes to expressing the notion of loyalty to the community as an abstract ideal. It is Hector, above all, who appears as a spokesman for responsibility to the community, but even his frame of reference is restricted. And it is instructive to note that the ruling family of Troy, including the patriarch, Priam himself, views the loss of Hector in personal terms.[22]

Naturally, the fact that loyalty to a larger group *can* be appealed to means that a concept of broader social obligation existed, but the main motivation remains personal and familial. In the final analysis, even Hector is concerned mostly with his own fame; his family comes next, Troy last (*Iliad* 6.447-65). The wider community, which to a later generation of Greeks will become the main focus of manly activity, does not yet exist. As M.I. Finley says, "the community could grow only by taming the hero and blunting the free exercise of his prowess, and a domesticated hero was a contradiction in terms."[23]

The reasons for this ambiguity are to be found in the nature of the political organization of Homeric society. The segmental tribal design, made up of numerous small, autonomous corporations (*okoi* and lineages) headed by chieftains jealous of their independence, tended to be centrifugal and atomistic. In such a polity loyalty was concentrated in a narrow sphere of kin and followers, hence the great importance of "friendship," *philotēs*, as a value and as a motive for behavior. The "immature" chiefdoms which integrated these groups were politically fragile and subject to dissolution (as in Odysseus' chiefdom at Ithaca). The *polis*-form, which begins to become visible in the eighth century, eventually provided a focus of communal solidarity as kinship and corporation loyalty yielded to a sense of the unified community of citizens. Even then, however, *oikos* and lineage retained much of their autonomous and divisive nature, with the result that even the Classical *polis* was rent by factional conflict among leading families for hegemony. The evolving aristocratic ideal had to face this ethical dilemma which surfaced after 700 B.C. in the form of tension between narrow class interest and the ideal of fealty to a collective whole. Such a straitened frame of reference, centered on self and the small circle of kin and close associates, as opposed to the larger sphere of cooperative responsibility, influenced the whole of the Homeric individual's pattern of activity.

A whole range of emotional responses, which we associate with "chivalric" behavior – truth-telling, honesty, mercy towards a fallen foe or for the defenceless – or the more "tender" aspects of human relations, like affection, pity, kindness, are certainly not lacking in the Homeric scheme of values. The epics do not reflect a world of unrestrained barbarity, despite the violence and bloodshed which are the constant background of the poems. But such traits have little priority, and go quickly by the board if they conflict with the aims of success. In the Judaeo-Christian system of ethics heaven is the guardian of these virtues, but in the Homeric world the gods evince little concern for "personal" morality; ethico-religious restraints on uninhibited human behavior are minimal, and the sphere of divine interest in human-to-human behavior is quite narrow. There are passages in the epics where it is taken as a self-evident fact that the gods punish men when they commit acts which transgress the rights of other men. But such passages are rather few in number, and there is little sense that fear of heavenly retribution provided much motivation.[24] In the *Iliad* there is a simile which describes a destructive storm sent by Zeus:

> in a deep rage against mortals after they stir him to anger because in violent assembly they pass decrees that are crooked, and drive righteousness *(dikē)* from among them and care nothing for what the gods think ...
>
> (*Iliad* 16.386-88, Latt.)

Zeus and the other gods are also concerned with the keeping of oaths and the punishing of oath-breakers (*Iliad* 3.276-80, 298-301; 4.155-68; 19.258-65). Once the soldiery of both sides asks Zeus to impose the judgment of death on either Paris or Menelaus as the cause of the many evils brought by the war (*Iliad* 3.320-23).

In the *Odyssey*, which perhaps reflects a somewhat more "progressive" stage of ethical development, the restraining influence of the gods over the actions of men appears stronger. Nestor relates to Telemachus (3.132-34, Latt.) that Zeus "devised a sorry homecoming for the Argives, since not all were considerate *(noēmones)* nor righteous *(dikaioi).*" There are, in the *Odyssey*, several other references to the displeasure of the gods at men's injustice, but, on closer examination, they are all seen to occur within the context of the code of hospitality and the treatment of strangers and suppliants. "All strangers and beggars are

The Ideal of the Warrior-Aristocrat

from Zeus" is the formula used to express the religious injunction (*Odyssey* 6.207-208; 14.57-58). Odysseus tells a story that once a king of Egypt rescued him, as a suppliant, from the hands of the angry citizens of the land Odysseus' men had just plundered, for "he regarded the wrath of Zeus, the Protector of Strangers, who especially is angered at evil deeds" (14.283-84). It should be noted that the "evil deeds" *(kaka erga)* refer not to the rapine and slaughter committed by Odysseus' sailors but to the slaying of a suppliant. Odysseus' swineherd, Eumaeus, describes the suitors of Penelope, who are greedily devouring Odysseus' livestock, as men

> who do not have in their minds the vengeance of the gods, nor pity. The blessed gods do not love cruel deeds, rather they honor justice *(dikē)* and the righteous deeds of men.
>
> (14.82-84; cf. 20.214-16)

The "crime" of the suitors is precisely that they violated the societal norms of reciprocity and hospitality — dramatically symbolized by the mistreatment of the beggar Odysseus. Antinous, the most arrogant of the suitors, hurls a footstool at Odysseus as he is begging (a social sin that is repeated on two other occasions by other suitors). Odysseus puts a beggar's curse on Antinous (17.475-476); the other suitors are upset at the breach of socio-religious custom:

> What if he is somehow a god from heaven; and, indeed, gods, putting on all sorts of shapes, likening themselves to strangers from other lands, visit cities, watching over the violence *(hybris)* and lawfulness *(eunomia)* of men.
>
> (17.484-87)

The most vivid expression of this main province of divine interest in human wrongdoing is found in a dialogue between Odysseus and the Cyclops. Odysseus entreats him:

> Respect the gods, O best of men. We are your suppliants, and Zeus the guest god, who stands behind all strangers with honors due them, avenges any wrong towards strangers and suppliants.
>
> (*Odyssey* 9.269-71, Latt.)

The Cyclops, completely remote from any civilized human responsibility, answers:

> Stranger, you are a simple fool, or come from far off, when you tell me to avoid the wrath of the gods or fear them. The Cyclopes do not concern themselves over Zeus of the aegis, nor any of the rest of the blessed gods . . .
>
> (9.273-76, Latt.)[25]

His refusal to respond to the claims of religious custom shows the Cyclops as a creature outside the pale of correct human association, while the suitors, by negating the claims, show themselves as betrayers of the norms of proper social behavior. Thus their punishment may be seen as divine requital for their impiety.[26]

On a broader scale, however, religious sanctions on human-to-human behavior, which are powerful factors in later Greek ethical development, are not a major part of the heroic ethic. Once again the causes are to be sought in the structure of the social organization. Within the bounds of tribal corporations — family, household, lineage, clan — the relations between individuals and subgroups are maintained by social mechanisms that require no appeal to "higher" authority. Within such tightly knit segments anti-social acts like murder, adultery, robbery, theft, etc., are self-evidently bad, because they threaten group stability and must be put to right. Balance and redress operate within the confines of the social units concerned. Murder, for example, is a problem between the families of the killer and the slain; the instrumental goal is social harmony.

> And, indeed, a man accepts recompense *(poinē)* from the killer of his brother or of his dead son; and the slayer remains among his *dēmos*, having paid back much; and the man's heart and proud spirit are held in check because he has received recompense.
>
> (*Iliad* 9.632-36)

The alternative to peaceful settlement is blood feud or exile of the killer (See *Iliad* 15.430; 23.85; *Odyssey* 24.430-37). In the same way, an adulterer balances the wrong he has done by paying the adulterer's fine *(moichagria, Odyssey* 8.332). In such cases "justice" and a fair dealing," operating within the context of the reciprocal nature of primitive societies, need no divine superstructure for reinforcement.

It is in the dealings of stranger with stranger that divine concern with human behavior manifests itself most: the keeping of oaths, the rules for the treatment of strangers, suppliants and beggars, and the uses of hospitality (the violations of which are also a diminution of the gods' own *time*). Because these situations are beyond the control of tribal mechanisms of redress and amelioration, a "transcendent" morality is required.

The beginnings of a sense of divinely ordained "justice" within the community itself or as a universal conception governing all men, however rarely expressed, is significant. It reflects both the reality of wider contact among Greeks from different geographical areas (around 900 B.C., according to archaeologists), and also the needs of a society in structural flux. The main characteristic of the chiefdom form of polity is that it gathers separate and essentially autonomous groups under a kind of "centralized" government, with the paramount as head, thus making all the subgroups of the community interdependent. More formal and more complex institutions to settle disputes are required, because social problems involve a number of segments and disparate points of view, not amenable to the direct "justice" of kinship groups. The formal proceedings for adjudicating a dispute over blood price depicted on the Shield of Achilles (*Iliad* 18.497-508), with a gathering of the people, a "jury" of elders, and an "umpire," illustrate the beginnings of an institutionalized process of justice. At the same time, the unstable Homeric chiefdom has difficulty keeping the autonomous corporations "in check," and in times of social upset the delicate centralized system breaks down. At Ithaca, because of the paramount's long absence, no assembly of the people had been held for twenty years. When Telemachus, Odysseus' son, finally convokes an assembly, he is frustrated because the combined political power of the suitors (members of independent *oikoi*) overcomes the centralized process of arbitration. The only "solution" is a recourse to force – the slaying of either Telemachus or the suitors, and a narrowly averted civil war. Finally, as social stratification increases, together with decline of local kinship groups, the individual of lower status finds himself adrift and at the mercy of powerful men. For all these reasons the abstract idea of universal justice, promoted by the gods, finds expression.

In the Homeric poems these forces are at work, but in muted fashion. Thus, apart from infrequent mentions of social justice in the broad sense, and in the concern over the breakdown of public order in the *Odyssey*, which prompts cries to heaven (couched, we note, in terms of transgression of the norms of sociability, especially of hospitality), the concept of "righteousness" and of divine sanction for its observance is limited to situations that occur outside the limits of the tribal order. The "necessity" for imposing the restraints of divinely ordained right, which originates in the regulation of intertribal behavior, on the community itself, betokens an important social change, the significance of which becomes evident with Hesiod and the seventh century.

A key feature of the Homeric social system was a highly developed pattern of social behavior between eminent men from different tribal groups: an elaborate etiquette of gift exchange, stylized eating and drinking ceremonial, and modes of polite address. These formed a complex system of guest-friendship *(xeniē)*, which afforded individual protection in a hostile tribal world, fostered the expansion of "foreign" contact and increased the prestige of individuals and their *oikoi*.[27] In addition, the ceremonial aspect gave a kind of psychological protection to the ideal; everyone took part in a solemn charade which insured the validity of the heroic conventions. All heroes treat one another as heroes, even when they are enemies; the bond which linked heroic warriors together was the unity of the code, which transcended tribal and even ethnic boundaries. This common feeling helps to explain why the *Iliad* displays practically no cultural differences between Greek and Asiatic, despite the obvious real disparities which must have existed. By the same token, the Trojan war is hardly portrayed as a "national" war, and seldom is the motivation for the conflict ever felt as "patriotic." Rather the war is perceived as a private quarrel between two feuding high-ranking households. Later Greeks would make much of the fact that this was the first clash of Europe and Asia, East and West, Greek and barbarian, but the Homeric epics reflect almost identical societies on both sides. Homer seems scarcely aware of the fact that Greeks and Trojans would speak different languages.[28] Thus, even when it is projected on an "international" scale, unity of aristocratic culture is the important factor: Hector is as much a Greek warrior-aristocrat as Achilles and the motivations for their actions are exactly the same.

An example of this common identification is seen in the encounter between the Lycian Glaukos and the Greek Diomedes in *Iliad* 6.119ff. They meet on the field of battle as enemies; Diomedes is impressed with Glaukos' bravery, and, suspecting that he may be a god, asks him his lineage. Glaukos gives the history of his family, after which Diomedes cries that his ancestor, Oeneus, and Glaukos' grandfather, the hero Bellerophontes, had been guest-friends: "Therefore," he continues:

> I am your friend and host in the heart of Argos; you are mine in Lykia when I come to your country. Let us avoid each other's spears, even in the close fighting.
>
> *(Iliad* 6.224-26, Latt.)

The Ideal of the Warrior-Aristocrat

Then they exchange gifts and go off to seek other foes—another clear indication that the heroic ethos, with its complicated norms of social behavior, supersedes all other considerations as an impetus to action. A scene such as this also points up the greater importance that ties of friendship and personal loyalty within the fraternity of the warrior élite had over tribal and communal bonds. In this case Glaukos and Diomedes find the host-guest system a more compelling determinant of behavior than the requirements of mortal combat. What prompted Achilles finally to reenter the battle was his need to avenge the death of his companion Patroclus and not any sense of loyalty to the Greek army.

It is in light of these considerations that the Homeric treatment of lineage must be viewed. The ability to trace descent from heroes of the past was important in two directions. It acted as a spur to the individual, who felt that he had to live up to his own illustrious warrior-ancestors, and it helped to establish the warrior's credentials as warrior, identifying him as a member of the closed fraternity, enabling him to "trade" on his status. However, claim to personal excellence on the grounds of lofty ancestry was seldom possible. In the first place, ancestry was usually traced back no further than three or four generations—and the majority of the Homeric genealogies mention grandfather or simply father.[29] But, more importantly, success had to be won by the individual on his own account. Rarely does a warrior give his lineage in order to impress others with his eminence—and at times the point of a recited genealogy seems to be the necessity for the hero to meet the standards of excellence set by his forebears. Thus, after the long narrative of his ancestor Bellerophon, Glaukos says:

> But Hippolochos begot me, and I claim that he is my father; he sent me to Troy, and urged upon me repeated injunctions, to be always among the bravest, and hold my head above others, not shaming the generation of my fathers, who were the greatest men in Ephyre and again in wide Lykia. Such is my generation and the blood I claim to be born from.
>
> *(Iliad* 6.206-11, Latt.)

When Diomedes says, "I also boast that I am by birth the son of an *agathos* father" (*Iliad* 14.113), he appears to be claiming that he is a good man because of his ancestry. Actually, Diomedes sets forth his lineage as a compensation for his youth (line 112), specifically his uncertainty about his ability to offer counsel to the other, older, leaders. Having given his genealogy, he says:

> Therefore, you could not call me a coward *(kakos)* and a weakling by birth, and dishonor my spoken counsel, when I speak out well.
>
> (4.126-27)

What Diomedes means, having listed three generations of ancestors who were brave warriors, is that his pedigree, full of fighting men, makes his battle counsel meritorious. Although he has proved his worth as an *agathos* on his own merits, the fact that he could point out others of like ability in his family enhances his claims to these qualities. In this respect, a very important one, the Homeric warrior ideal differed from the later aristocratic ideal in which noble ancestry was appealed to as automatic evidence of class superiority.[30] The epic attitude shows the genesis of this idea, but for the Homeric warrior high descent was not a guarantee of worth, as may be seen from a passage in the *Iliad* where Agamemnon, fearful that Menelaus would be chosen by Diomedes for the dangerous spying mission in the Trojan camp, advises Diomedes:

> Do not, out of the reverence in your heart, leave behind a better man, and, yielding to reverence, take the worse, looking to birth — not even if he is more chiefly *(basileuteros)*.
>
> (*Iliad* 10.237-39)

Menelaus' higher birth status makes him no less the worse man *(cheirōn)*. For another indication that high birth was regarded mainly as a spur to achievement we may turn to the prayer of Hector for his infant son:

> Zeus, and you other immortals, grant that this boy, who is my son, may be as I am, pre-eminent among the Trojans, great in strength, as I am, and rule strongly over Ilion; and some day let them say of him: "He is better by far than his father," as he comes in from the fighting; and let him kill his enemy and bring home the blooded spoils, and delight the heart of his mother.
>
> (*Iliad* 6.476-81, Latt.)[31]

Moreover, should success be lacking, for any reason, ancestry counted for nothing whatever. Paris, despite his lofty birth, was despised by Greeks and Trojans alike, because of his softness. In addition, the sudden mutability of fortune in a world governed by physical force made the accident of birth less dependable. For an illustration of this we can turn to the fears of Andromache regarding the prospects of Astyanax after Hector has been killed:

The day of bereavement leaves a child with no agemates to befriend him. He bows his head before every man, his cheeks are bewept, he goes, needy, a boy among his father's companions, and tugs at this man by the mantle, that man by the tunic, and they pity him, and one gives him a tiny drink from a goblet, enough to moisten his lips, not enough to moisten his palate. But one whose parents are living beats him out of the banquet hitting him with his fists and in words also abuses him: Get out, you! Your father is not dining among us."
(Iliad 22.490-98, Latt.)

Although Odysseus' son Telemachus was the acknowledged heir to the rule of Ithaca, all knew that if one of the suitors prevailed Telemachus would lose not only the chiefdom but his property besides.[32] And the community at large was apparently quite content to sit back and watch the warrior-chiefs quarrel among themselves, without thought of interference. One may be born the son or daughter of a chief, but a pirate raid or kidnapping could reduce one's status to that of a slave.[33] At the funeral of Hector, Andromache considers the fate of the Trojan women who will be taken as slaves when Troy is ultimately captured; she laments her own misfortune and that of her child Astyanax:

and among them I shall also go, and you my child, follow where I go, and there do much hard work that is unworthy of you, drudgery for a hard master...
(Iliad 24.732-34, Latt.)

The prime requisites for political rule, as for military success, were personal prowess and ability to lead.[34] Thus, in the confused situation at Ithaca, the young Telemachus was physically (and psychologically) inadequate to cope with the suitors; the old chief, Odysseus' father Laertes, was powerless; and even Odysseus himself could not simply return and claim his office, but had to regain it by slaying the suitors. By the same laws of personal excellence it was also possible to raise one's social status. In an interesting passage in the *Odyssey*, Odysseus, disguised as a beggar, tells the fictitious story of how he, born the bastard son of a Cretan noble, with only a tiny inheritance, gained great fame, wealth and power because he was a good warrior.[35] And when Odysseus was preparing to fight the suitors he made two of his slaves, the swineherd Eumaeus, and the cowherd Philoetius, henchmen in his struggle to regain the chiefdom, promising that:

> If by my hand the god overmasters the lordly suitors, then I shall get wives for you both, and grant you possessions and houses built next to mine, and think of you in the future always as companions of Telemachos, and his brothers.
> (*Odyssey* 21.213-16, Latt.)

These are, however, the only hints of "upward mobility" in the Homeric poems. Although fame and position are won by virtue of a strong right arm, the epics reflect a society which had already begun to turn the corner from individual achievement, dependent solely on skill and prowess, toward the idea of a social class in which membership alone allowed one to claim excellence *(aretē)*. Although the self-image of the Homeric aristocrat centers on personal ability and the glory that can be won only by individual merit, it has already become clear that one must be a member of the "club" in order to compete. There are no sharply defined class distinctions yet; rather Homer tends to obscure the faceless mass of "ordinary" people. While they are not unimportant, they serve mainly as background to the exploits of the heroes. Homer never suggests that they are inferior;[36] nevertheless their role, both in war and peace, is played down. They are the *dēmos*, the people, or *laos*, the host, rather passively reflecting the greatness of the individual warrior-chiefs, who have already begun to appear aware of themselves as a distinctive group.

Again we can look to comparative anthropology for a clearer perspective. In anthropological terms, the "ranked" society of the tribal chiefdom had just begun to move in the direction of the "class" or "stratified" society of the archaic aristocratic state. In the "egalitarian" social structure which exists at the level of band or tribe there is equal access to status positions (and, of course, to economic resources as well). In such societies a great hunter or warrior will achieve status distinction, but this status is neither transferable nor inheritable. Each generation can (and must) achieve status on its own. We have seen clear evidence of this egalitarianism surviving in Homer. In "ranked" societies, usually signalled by the appearance of chiefs, rank is "built-in" as it were. The office of chief is often hereditary (as in Homer); chiefs, and their families, consequently have structured greater access to prestige. Usually those who work closely with the chief (his companions and followers), and their families, share in this ranking, constituting a kind of nobility (or, "proto-nobility"). In such an organization may be discerned the beginnings of an hereditary class sytem, in which an upward change in status becomes difficult to achieve. Although ranked societies exhibit differential access to prestige, access to goods remains equalitarian; that is, all free members of the community have equal access to the group's production. In Homer, for example, the spoils of war and raid are distributed evenly, sometimes by lot, to all the warriors. However, those of high rank, the leaders, are awarded an extra, or choice portion *(geras)*, as their due. This inequality amidst equality ("chiefly due") confers greater prestige and an edge of wealth (which can be used to reward, and thereby to increase, one's following), and has a redundant effect on the ranking system. A "class" society, on the other hand, restricts access to economic resources as well as to high status; not every type of person has an equal chance to acquire land, animals and other goods. Only in such a system is it possible to speak of "nobles" and "commoners," "the rich" and "the poor" as formally conceived social categories. Within the context of these schematic societal models, the social structure of the Homeric world conforms, as we have already observed, to the ranked chiefdom, which also exhibits a number of features of the egalitarian tribal scheme.

The purpose of this brief examination of evolutionary models, besides "fixing" Homeric society more firmly along the spectrum of these types, is to emphasize that the Homeric Greeks did not attain the level of the stratified or class society. Nor did the Greeks ever really evolve such a social system. As we shall see, the Greek aristocracy later developed a "class consciousness," and some of the mannerisms of a true ruling class. Economically and politically, in some parts of the Greek world, the élite managed to acquire for a time something like a monopoly of economic resources and status positions. Nevertheless, the state forms which eventually emerged from the declining chiefdoms of the late Dark Age retained to a remarkable degree elements of the early tribal system — especially a profoundly rooted spirit of egalitarianism.

Certainly, contrary to an often expressed view, the political system which forms the background of the epics is not a highly stratified feudal order of "barons" and "peasant masses." The common people are not regarded as social inferiors — there is, in fact, no birth or class nomenclature in Homer. The role of the people, though passive for the most part, does not imply submissiveness to their leaders. It must be remembered that the rank and file are also given the epithet *aristoi* (best), and that they, too, are called "heroes."[37] The crew that sailed with Odysseus on his voyage home from Troy were not all noble warriors; most of them were ordinary soldiers, but they had the love and respect of their captain, who called them his companions and friends.[38] The war-leader was still, in the old tribal sense, the "shepherd of the people," "leader of the host," and mutual dependency and respect are evident. High rank, with its attendant honors, was, in a real sense, still a gift of the community at large; conversely, if a leader abused his privileges, he was accountable to the people. This reciprocity is summed up in a famous conversation between Sarpedon, chief of the Lycians, and Glaukos, his second in command. Why, Sarpedon inquires of Glaukos, do the Lycians give us such great honor—first place at the feasts, choice meats, respect like the gods, and

> a great piece of land by the banks of Xanthos, good land, orchard and vineyard, and ploughland . . .

The question is a rhetorical one and Sarpedon answers it himself:

> Therefore it is our duty in the forefront of the Lykians to take our stand, and bear our part of the blazing of battle, so that a man of the close-armoured Lykians may say of us: "Indeed, these are no ignoble men who are lords of Lykia, these *basilees* of ours, who feed upon the fat sheep appointed and drink the exquisite sweet wine, since indeed there is strength of valour in them, since they fight in the forefront of the Lykians."
>
> (*Iliad* 12.310-21, Latt.)

There is more than an implication in these words that should they fail in their duties they would no longer merit the honors they received. The chiefs were not simply single champions fighting alone; their primary military function was to lead and inspire the warriors, who were not an insignificant rabble, but fellow tribesmen, able and willing to judge their leaders. The "man of the Lykians" does not say that his leaders fight for him, but that they "fight in the forefront." And when the commons do act they act decisively and as free men.[39]

Only once in Homer is there any sign of strain in the easy alliance between noble warriors and ordinary soldiers. In *Iliad* 2, Thersites, a commoner,[40] verbally abuses the supreme commander of the Greeks, and is beaten by Odysseus for his presumption. Generations of scholars have tried to extract from this incident far-reaching conclusions regarding the social organization of Dark Age Greece. Much of the controversy centers on whether or not a "commoner" had the right to speak in the assembly. Those who deny this possibility assert that otherwise

The Ideal of the Warrior-Aristocrat

Odysseus would not have humiliated him. But, as Homer himself says, Thersites had done this before—he was always abusing Odysseus and Achilles (whom he now defends); and the fact that he was allowed to finish his speech would seem to show that speaking out was not unthinkable. It seems easiest to say that Thersites had a "right" (probably not used much) to speak out, but that he overstepped the bounds of tribal custom not only by speaking his mind, but by urging a specific course of action—in this case to abandon the war and return home. In any event, this is the only sign of open societal tension in either epic, and it would be unwarranted to read into it anything beyond the simple fact that the Homeric soldier was a free man who usually obeyed his leaders and took their advice, but demurred when conditions seemed to warrant it.[41]

To what extent the ordinary people subscribed to the warrior-code is not easy to say, since their voice is so seldom heard. We may suspect that their outlook was different. The outburst of Thersites, for example, reveals a point of view that is clearly contrary to the ethic of the aristocratic warrior, and is worth quoting in full:

> Son of Atreus, what thing further do you want, or find fault with now? Your shelters are filled with bronze, there are plenty of the choicest women for you within your shelter, whom we Achaians give to you first of all whenever we capture some stronghold. Or is it still more gold you will be wanting, that some son of the Trojans, breakers of horses, brings as ransom out of Ilion, one that I, or some other Achaian, capture and bring in? Is it some young woman to lie with in love and keep her all to yourself apart from the others? It is not right for you, their leader, to lead in sorrow the sons of the Achaians. My good fools, poor abuses, you women, not men, of Achaia, let us go back home in our ships, and leave this man here by himself in Troy to mull his prizes of honour that he may find out whether or not we others are helping him. And now he has dishonoured Achilleus, a man much better than he is. He has taken his prize by force and keeps her. But there is no gall in Achilleus' heart, and he is forgiving. Otherwise, son of Atreus, this were your last outrage.
>
> *(Iliad* 2.225-42, Latt.)

The whole tenor of Thersites' speech is non-heroic—the only reference to the code is his statement that Agamemnon has dishonored *(atimēsen)* Achilles.

Aside from this, a number of further points can be made about the speech. First of all, for Thersites, the object of fighting was simply to amass booty. Second, he makes no bones of the fact that the spoils are won by people like him, the ordinary soldier. Third, he takes for granted that Agamemnon's motive for the war is greed and nothing more. Fourth, he confidently assumes that it is the mass of the army who are the mainstay of the expedition. Finally, and perhaps most importantly, he takes Agamemnon to task in the strongest terms for failing in his duty as a leader. When he says that it is not seemly "for you, being the leader *(archos)*, to bring the sons of the Achaeans into evil," he is stating the principle that the commander has a responsibility to lead properly; should he fail in this his troops have the right to repudiate him. This attitude, stated explicitly here, is very similar to the implicit recognition of it by Sarpedon in the passage quoted earlier (above, page 20). The poet seems anxious to point out to his audience that Thersites' views were not shared by the rest of the Achaean troops, for he had them say after Odysseus has beaten Thersites:

> Come now: Odysseus has done excellent things by thousands, bringing forward good counsels and ordering armed encounters: but now this is far the best thing he ever has accomplished among the Argives, to keep this thrower of words, this braggart out of assembly. Never again will his proud heart stir him up, to wrangle with the princes *(basileis)* in words of revilement.
>
> (*Iliad* 2.272-77, Latt.)

But Homer appears to be protesting too much here, and we may safely believe that in his total lack of sympathy with the heroic code of honor, and in making Agamemnon accountable for his failures of leadership, Thersites reflected the sentiments of the non-aristocratic host. There is, in fact, no good reason to suppose that the code of personal glory should operate at the lower level of society, although many historians tend to regard as self-evident that the cultural ideals of the warrior-heroes were accepted universally throughout the society.[42]

Otherwise, the few glimpses of ordinary life in the epics show a preoccupation with the daily crises of earning a living or the simple pleasures of life in an agricultural society. An important fact, often not sufficiently stressed, is that in societies based primarily on subsistence, or near subsistence, agricultural economy (as ancient Greece always was for the most part), the mere filling of the belly was the constant preoccupation of the vast majority of the population. In outlook, the great

The Ideal of the Warrior-Aristocrat

figures of the *Iliad* and *Odyssey* had moved far beyond that stage; glory, not food, was their chief concern, and it is this simple fact perhaps more than anything else that separates them from the mass of men. There is a passage in the *Iliad* which casts this difference into vivid relief. After the death of Patroclus, Achilles resolved to fight and was eager to begin. Odysseus, the man of practical reason (the most "ordinary-minded" of the heroes), insisted that the army have breakfast first. In anger Achilles retorts:

> Food and drink mean nothing to my heart but blood does, and slaughter, and the groaning of men in the hard work.
> (*Iliad* 19.213-14, Latt.)

Odysseus answers him from a wisdom that is far older than the ideal of glory in war:

> There is no way the Achaians can mourn a dead man by denying the belly. Too many fall day by day, one upon another . . . and all those who are left about from the hateful work of war must remember food and drink . . .
> (*Iliad* 19.225-31, Latt.)

While the host eats, Achilles abstains from mere food—Athena distils nectar and ambrosia, the sustenance of the immortals, into his breast to sustain his strength. But the theme of the empty belly is a constant motif of "lower class" thought throughout Greek literature, and one can observe its occurrence frequently, often in conscious opposition to the more exalted aristocratic ideal.

We may sum up the Homeric aristocratic ideal by saying that worth or excellence, *aretē*, was conceived of in the physical sphere almost exclusively, most specifically in terms of prowess as a warrior. The aim of the high-status warrior was public recognition of his ability. The Homeric proto-aristocrat endlessly competed with his fellows for prestige *(kydos, timē)*, with the goal of being recognized as "best" *(aristos)*; his greatest fear was failure and its accompanying communal humiliation. Responsibility and loyalty were directed towards his immediate family and the corporate household *(oikos)*, extending outward to a small circle of friends and companions *(philoi, hetairoi)*. Other attributes and qualities might be prized or considered desirable, but they were either adjunct to or proof of fighting skills and the *timē* these won. Wealth was a by-product of prowess, a sign of success, and a means of increasing one's influence. Mental excellence was important, but mainly as an aid to action. A handsome or prepossessing exterior was the obvious accompaniment of size and strength and of the status that they commanded. Descent from gods or from other great warriors was both proof of ability and incentive to excel further. All sociopsycological responses, such as loyalty, kindness, pity, mercy, affection, fair dealing, responsibility to others, were manifested to a greater or lesser degree, depending on the demands of the primary goal of aggrandizement of self, family, and followers. The sense of membership in an exclusive group of like-minded men, regardless of tribal affiliation, was prominent.

As the aristocratic self-conception was altered by time and circumstances these earliest components of the Greek aristocratic ideal appear in a state of considerable flux, with now one, now another set of values dominating. In assessing the heroic ideal it is difficult to exaggerate the "singlemindedness," as Finley calls it, in which

> everything pivoted on a single element of honor and virtue: strength, bravery, physical courage, prowess. Conversely, there was no weakness, no unheroic trait, but one, and that was cowardice and the consequent failure to pursue heroic goals.[43]

But this, it must be stressed, is a warrior's ideal, refined to an extraordinary degree. Just as Achilles' overly intense dedication to the requirements of heroic honor proved too extreme even for his fellow heroes, so also there is good reason to question the extent to which ordinary men shared the code. Certainly the degree of their dedication to the values of the military élite must have been considerably less. From the little evidence given us in the Homeric poems about the "man of the *dēmos*" we know that his conception of society emphasized the responsibility of the leader towards his followers. That this attitude prevailed in peace as well as war is shown by a speech of the "beggar" Odysseus to Penelope:

> your fame goes up into the wide heaven, as of some *basileus* who, as a blameless man and god-fearing, and ruling as lord over many powerful people, upholds the way of good government, and the black earth yields him barley and wheat, his trees are heavy with fruit, his sheepflocks continue to bear young, the sea gives him fish, because of his good leadership, and his people prosper under him.
> (*Odyssey* 19.108-14, Latt.)

The Ideal of the Warrior-Aristocrat

These remarkable lines, like the speech of Thersites and the dialogue between Sarpedon and Glaukos, give a glimpse of the leader as perceived by the ordinary person. If the *basileus* is "god-fearing," "upholds justice *(eudikia),*" and exercises "good leadership," his people *(laoi)* prosper. This triad of virtues plays a negligible role in the ethos of the aristocratic champions.[44]

At the same time we see little evidence that those outside the dominant group felt disposed to challenge its pre-eminence or to offer a "counter-ideal." In a world where physical might was the decisive factor the great warrior enjoyed a natural superiority, universally recognized and unchallenged. From this natural superiority flowed all the perquisites of wealth, status and respect, ungrudgingly given so long as there was no violent interference with the rights of those who ranked below. In the epics there are very few signs of disagreement between rulers and ruled; at most we can see fairly plainly that the heroic ideal of personal honor was not shared by all elements of the society.

Finally, all that has been said of the Homeric warrior-élite must be put firmly in a proper sociological perspective. I have called these chiefs and "outstanding men" *(exochoi)* "aristocrats," and their value system an "aristocratic ideal," mostly for want of better terms. Just as Homeric society was not "feudal" in the post-Roman European sense (despite certain analogies, which misled earlier scholars), so Homer's "rulers and counsellors" were but fledgling aristocrats, and their attitudes had not hardened into the code of a stratified "class." As Starr and others have pointed out, the epics themselves and the findings of archaeology reveal that the Dark Age aristocrat was no powerful "prince" or "baron." His economic superiority was only relative, his material life-style not vastly different from that of his fellow tribesmen. Because of the fragile nature of the chiefdom form itself the political authority of the *basileus* was severely limited. Despite the obvious self-awareness of these men as a group apart, in the absence of a true class society the Homeric "aristocratic ideal" could not have been a conceptualized ideological superstructure intended to differentiate a "nobility" from the "masses." We may thus conclude with Starr, that

> ... the Homeric world had not yet traveled all the way toward the elaboration of an aristocratic ethos, i.e., an obligatory pattern of life and values *consciously* conceived and shared by a limited group which considered itself "best" and the claims of which were generally accepted, even cherished, by other elements of society.[45]

That time had not yet come, but it was not far off.

◊

When we turn from Homer to the next important figure of Greek literature, Hesiod, we can note signs of social tension. Hesiod was a farmer, who lived and composed his poetry around 700 B.C., shortly after, or perhaps at the same time as, the final composition of the *Odyssey*. The "world" of Hesiod is an exactly contemporary one; Hesiod is a direct witness of his own time, which is later, perhaps by four, five or six generations, than the historical period reflected in the Homeric epics. His father, he tells us, pressed by poverty, had emigrated from Asia Minor to the mainland of Greece, settling near the town of Ascra in Boeotia, which Hesiod calls "bad in summer, horrid in winter, good at no time," and there took up farming. The living was not much better in Boeotia, and the picture of daily life that we get from Hesiod is one of unremitting toil for small reward. Still, Hesiod was not poor; he would rank as a fairly prosperous independent freeholder by the standards of the early seventh century B.C. in Greece. The life of harsh manual labor, the lot of the marginal farmer, has changed little since then. Countless millions have lived (and live) just as Hesiod described in his long poem, *The Works and Days*—few have looked at the world from the perspective of a warrior-chief. For this reason it is not surprising that there is no trace at all in Hesiod of the Homeric warrior ideal. Prowess and glory are foreign concepts to the farmer whose main concern is a full stomach and whose idea of wealth is a full barn. The *Iliad* opens with an invocation to the Muse to sing the wrath of Achilles. Hesiod heard the Muses, too; on Mount Helicon, as he was tending his flocks, they summoned him to compose, addressing him thus:

> Shepherds of the wilderness, wretched things of shame, mere bellies . . .
>
> (*Theogony* 26)[46]

The reproach of the Muses underlines the difference between the aristocratic outlook, obsessed with prestige, and the peasant's constant preoccupation with survival. Pride, honor, glory, immortality, self-doubt had small place in Hesiod's world; his message was simple: work hard and you will be "wealthy."

> If your heart within you desires wealth, do these things and work with work upon work.
>
> (*Works and Days* 381-82)

For the Homeric hero abundant wealth was a sign of eminence, for Hesiod wealth was a decent living and not having to borrow. The warriors of the epic moved in a world of elaborate courtesy, gift exchange and complicated personal obligations; Hesiod distrusted his neighbors, preached a stingy parsimony, and quarreled with his own brother over their inheritance. Homeric women were valued possessions, respected and fought over; for Hesiod woman is an evil. The Trojan elders, when they sight Helen, who was the cause of untold woe, say:

> Surely there is no blame on Trojans and strong-greaved Achaians if for long time they suffer hardship for a woman like this one.
> (*Iliad* 3.156-57, Latt.)

To Hesiod, Pandora, the primal woman, was a curse from the gods.[47] Examples could be multiplied, but these suffice to show how far removed was Hesiod's outlook from the "refined" view of Homer.

There is one important point of contact between the two worlds that helps also to underline the differences in outlook. On several occasions Hesiod talks about the *basileis;* these are not the high-souled, glory-obsessed warriors of Homer; rather they are local big-men, whom Hesiod calls "gift-devouring." They accept bribes and are interested only in their own might, not the welfare of the people. To his brother, Perses, who had cheated Hesiod of his inheritance, he says:

> For we had already divided our inheritance, but you seized the greater share and carried it off, greatly swelling the glory of our bribe-swallowing *basileis* who love to judge such a cause as this.
> (*Works and Days* 37-39)

Later in the same poem he comes to the theme again:

> There is a noise when Justice *(Dikē)* is being dragged in the way where those who devour bribes and give sentence with crooked judgements take her. And she, wrapped in mist, follows to the city and haunts of the people, weeping, and bringing evil *(kakon)* to men ...
> (*Works and Days* 220-23)

Concern over the greed of the leader and his responsibility to the people not to lead them into evil had formed the substance of Thersites' charge against Agamemnon. So, here the two poets meet in the authentic voice of the independent peasant and the common soldier.

Twice Hesiod speaks of the truly good rulers; but his descriptions do not match the Homeric ideal of personal glory and fame:

> All the people *(laoi)* look towards him while he settles causes with true judgements: and he, speaking surely, would soon make wise end even of a great quarrel; for therefore are there *basileis* wise in heart, because when the *laoi* are being misguided in their assembly, they set right the matter again with ease, persuading them with gentle words.
> (*Theogony* 84-90)

The chiefly qualities commended here are wisdom and fairness, dispensed with a gentle concern. Another description, highly reminiscent of the simile from the *Odyssey* quoted above (19.108-14), depicts the just leader as bringing his people into prosperity and peace:

> But they who give straight judgements to strangers and to the men of the land, and go not aside from what is just *(dikaion)*, their polis flourishes, and the *laoi* prosper in it: Peace, the nurse of children, is abroad in their land, and all-seeing Zeus never decrees cruel war against them. Neither famine nor disaster ever haunt men who do true justice; but light-heartedly they tend the fields . . . the earth bears them victual in plenty . . . their wooly sheep are laden with fleeces; their women bear children like their parents. They flourish continually with good things . . .
> (*Works and Days* 225-36)

As we have seen, Justice, the fair dealing between men and men, is much on Hesiod's mind, an ethical concept which is missing almost entirely from the *Iliad* and the *Odyssey*. Also, Justice is given very strong divine sanction by Hesiod; his Zeus, unlike the Zeus of Homer, is vitally concerned with justice in general and with the punishment of mortal wrongdoing. Justice, Law and Peace are the children of Zeus (*Theogony* 901-903). At the beginning of the *Works and Days* we are told that Zeus

> easily makes strong and easily crushes the strong man; easily he humbles the conspicuous and raises the obscure; easily he straightens the crooked and withers the arrogant . . .
> (Lines 5-7, translation mine)

In a passage that goes much farther than anything in Homer he says that Zeus gives punishment *(dikē)* to those who commit violence *(hybris)* and cruel deeds. Often a whole community *(sympasa polis)* suffers for the evil deeds of a *kakos* man, with famine, plague, destruction of their army, their walls, and their ships (*Works and Days* 238-47). He admonishes the leaders in the strongest terms:

O *basileis,* mark well this *dikē,* you also; for the deathless gods are near among men and note all those who oppress one another with crooked judgements and do not heed the anger of the gods. For upon the bounteous earth Zeus has thrice ten thousand immortals, watchers of mortal men, and they keep watch on judgements *(dikai)* and cruel deeds *(schetlia erga)* as they roam, clothed in mist, all over the earth.

(Translation mine)

Dikē sits beside her father, Zeus, and tells him of men's injustice

until the *dēmos* pays for the mad folly of *basileis,* who, evilly minded, pervert judgement and give sentence crookedly. Keep watch against this, *basileis,* and make straight your judgements, you who devour bribes; put crooked judgements altogether from your thoughts.

(*Works and Days* 248-64)

The social priorities of Homer and Hesiod are evident on a grander, theological, level. Homer's Olympus is a mirror of the heroic world on earth: the gods banquet, boast and quarrel like the mortals below — indeed, they mingle with the heroes and sometimes even battle with them. Hesiod's Olympus is an island of calm in a harsh universe. His great cosmological tale, the *Theogony,* recounts the slow, often grim, evolution from primeval chaos and savage passion to order and stability, where, finally, a Zeus mindful of justice sits on the throne. So, it is by opposites and contrasts that we perceive Hesiod's assessment of the aristocratic ideal. It should be clear by now that the heroic value system was the ideal of a small group, not of the society as a whole. On the few occasions when Homer allows the lower class outlook to show through, we see a non-responsive, almost negative reaction to the ideal; for Hesiod that ideal hardly exists.

In the considerable span of time that separated the world of the *Iliad* and the *Odyssey* from the contemporary experience of Hesiod, the social fragmentation already apparent in the epics had increased. The chiefdom form of polity, unstable by its nature, had not evolved into the centralized monarchy or the feudal state, but into a system of local aristocracies. According to the late Karl Polanyi, the tribal order, with its integrative institutions and bonds of reciprocity, was yielding to a "crude individualism."

The traditional political structure of tribal settlements had been viciously distorted by the "gift-devouring princes," who now failed to return the law and justice that was their responsibility. The empty forms of chieftainship remained; but meaning and content were gone. The tribal obligations expressed by those forms had faded. Justice became an abstract ideal to be pursued, and was no longer the institutional setting for the life of the tribe.[48]

The pessimism that came with the consciousness of "tribal decay" is vividly captured in Hesiod's famous description of the retrogression of humankind. In successive stages, from a "golden race," in primordial times, when men "lived like gods," without sorrow or toil, through a constantly degenerative process a "silver race" was replaced by a race of bronze, culminating in the present "iron race."

> Thereafter, would that I were not among the men of the fifth generation, but either had died before or been born afterwards. For now truly is a race of iron, and men never rest from labour and sorrow by day, and from perishing by night; and the gods shall lay sore trouble upon them.
>
> (*Works and Days* 174-178)

Interestingly, Hesiod breaks this regressive ordering of metal races by placing a "god-like race of hero-men" between the bronze and the iron race of his own day. These "demi-gods" *(hēmitheoi)*, "more righteous and better" *(diakaioteron kai areion)* than those who had preceded them, were the Homeric race of warriors who fought at Thebes and Troy, now dwelling in ease in the "Isles of the Blessed." This revealing bit of social history shows that Hesiod was grimly aware of the breakdown of the stable order of the tribal community, in which mutual responsibility afforded even the lowliest beggar some measure of security. In times to come, he predicts,

> The father will not agree with his children, nor the children with their father, nor guest with his host, nor comrade with comrade; nor will brother be dear to brother as aforetime. Men will dishonour their parents as they grow quickly old, and will carp at them, chiding them with bitter words, hard-hearted they, not knowing the fear of the gods. They will not repay their aged parents the cost of their nurture, for might shall be their right: and one man will sack another's city. There will be no favour for the man who keeps his oath or for the just or for the good; but rather men will praise the evil-doer

The ideal of the Warrior-Aristocrat

and his violent dealing. Strength will be right and reverence will cease to be; and the wicked will hurt the worthy man, speaking false words against him . . .
(*Works and Days* 182-94)

The preceding race of heroes, when the chiefdom form was still sufficiently viable to integrate the community and to ameliorate the divisiveness of atomistic individualism, was, for Hesiod, a nostalgic exception to what he sees as the inexorable decay of human morality.[49]

In spite of his pessimism, Hesiod is aware of the possibility of a new type of social ordering, in which "community" might once again prevail. But community henceforth is to be the association of neighbor and citizen, not the community of kinship. The reciprocity of a changing order must be accomplished outside of the paternalistic beneficence of the corporation head or the mutual assistance of the clan.

Call your friend to a feast; but leave your enemy alone; and especially call him who lives near you: for if any mischief happen in the place, neighbours come ungirt, but kinsmen stay to girt themselves.
(*Works and Days* 342-45)

In a world in which strife and competition are constant, when "neighbor view with neighbor, hastening after wealth" (*W&D* 23), and the *basileus* is likened to a hawk who terrorizes the powerless nightingale (*W&D* 202-12), then neighborliness and fairness must be strictly observed.

Take fair measure from your neighbor and pay him back fairly with the same measure, or better, if you can; so that if you are in need afterwards, you may find him sure.
(*Works and days* 349-351)

Nevertheless, neighbors do not always cooperate. A person in want may go begging "to other men's houses" in vain (*W&D* 395); "grieving in heart, with your wife and children, you may seek a living among your neighbors, and they do not care" (*W&D* 399-400):

For it is easy to say: 'Give me a yoke of oxen and a waggon,' and it is easy to refuse: 'I have work for my oxen.'
(*Works and Days* 453-54; cf. 477, 706)

When we consider the social forces at work at the end of the eighth century—the waning of kinship-community, the uncertainty of mutuality from fellow villager, the spirit of selfish competition, the increase of status and wealth differentiation, land scarcity and rising population — it is easy to understand Hesiod's insistence on the need for justice sanctioned by the gods, and his emphasis on individual moral responsibility.

Hesiod's concern with ethical relations is especially reflected in word usage. It was noted that in the epics the words for good *(agathos, esthlos)* and bad *(kakos)* referred almost exclusively to the sphere of physical excellence and bravery. In fact, the epithet of highest commendation, *agathos,* is used only of high-status warriors, never of the rank and file. In Hesiod, on the contrary, these words never refer to physical excellence, and often have a decidedly ethical-moral connotation.

For example, Hesiod pairs *agathos* with the adjective for "just" *(dikaios),* a combination not found in Homer.[50] In another place he says:

> A *kakos* neighbor is as great a plague as an *agathos* one is a great blessing; he who enjoys an *esthlos* neighbor has a precious possession. Not even an ox would die but for a *kakos* neighbor.
> (*Works and Days* 346-48)

It is plain that good and bad here are defined in terms of a simpler ethos which stresses service, cooperation and fair dealing, with no reference at all to the qualities that make a Homeric man *agathos.* Equally in the ethical sphere is this usage:

> Do not get a name either as lavish or churlish; as a friend of *kakoi* or as a slanderer of *esthloi.*
> (*Works and Days* 715-16)[51]

Again, in Hesiod the adjective *aristos* (best) has a force lacking in Homer, in a passage where "quiet" intellectual competence is given great value:

> That man is altogether best *(panaristos)* who considers all things himself and marks what will be better afterwards and at the end; and he, again, is *esthlos* who listens to a good advisor; but whoever neither thinks for himself nor keeps in mind what another tells him, he is an unprofitable *(achreios)* man.
> (*Works and Days* 293-297)

The Ideal of the Warrior-Aristocrat

Hesiod's notions of ability and success *(aretē)* and of the good man have no reference at all to the heroic conception of these. *Aretē* consists in being a successful farmer; the good man *(agathos anēr)* is one who is capable, efficient, prudent and cooperative within the narrow sphere of agrarian life.[52]

It is clear that the semantic differences in the uses of terms of approval and disapproval betoken a rift in social perceptions. We cannot, of course, make too much of these differences; given the disparity of subject matter, time, and perspective, between Homer and Hesiod certain differences are inevitable. Accordingly, the terminology of merit is used differently by different groups in the community. Hesiod does not record a radical change in values nor is he consciously rebutting the traditional claims of the *agathos;* he simply reflects the ethical norms of his portion of the society of his own time. If, in all respects, Hesiod saw the world through a peasant's eyes, most certainly he advocates no change in the political structure. In this sphere his sole concern is that the leaders respond to communal needs, hence his preoccupation with justice and the divine machinery which would ensure that justice.[53]

◊

In summary: the differences of outlook in Hesiod and Homer are attributable to a number of interconnected factors. Most obvious is the simple fact that a warrior-leader and a small or middling farmer will view their environment differently. Structural changes in Greek society, however, are of greater account in the differences in attitudes expressed. The transition from the tribal chiefdom to the "aristocratic" polity witnessed the passing of the kinship order and the economic and social stability that such an order represented. Social differentiation, competition, craft specialization, private property, indebtedness, social alienation, are all evident in Hesiod's assessment of contemporary life. What the material and technological causes were that led to the replacement of the security of a kinship society by the insecurity of a territorial society are too complex and too uncertain to speculate on here. Certainly, the slow evolution from an economy based primarily on stockbreeding to one that was principally agricultural, attained by Hesiod's time, was a key factor. A dramatic rise in population around the middle of the eighth century, the result, surely, of the increase in food production, seems to have led to a land shortage, and, in turn, to the export of surplus population in the form of colonization. An increase in foreign trade and in the manufacture of goods for export (also connected with the colonizing movement), the import of luxury items from the East, richer finds in graves and sanctuaries, attest to a general rise in prosperity, but most especially among the upper stratum.[54]

The beginning of the stratified society, in which access to fundamental resources is restricted to certain groups, signals important changes in ethico-religious values. According to a recent theory, when a society is marked by unequal distribution of wealth — individual ownership of property, debt relations, and economic stratification — supernatural sanctions governing human behavior are likely to emerge and to become prominent; hence, the apparent paradox that "the ethical systems of advanced literate cultures are supernaturalistic to a greater degree than those of preliterate cultures."[55]

As yet there is no sign that the two concepts of *aretē*, despite the increasing differences, had become polarized. One supposes that when an eighth- or early seventh-century aristocrat called himself a "good" man the term embraced essentially the range of qualities of the Homeric *agathos,* and that the same would be true, *mutatis mutandis,* of the peasant concept of the *agathos.* Where we do see active evidence of discontent or protest is when the contrasting points of view come into abrasive contact—as in the case of a Thersites, whose expressions of quarrelsome independence earn him blows from the spokesman of the traditional order, or in a Hesiod, when he is affected personally by the power of the "bribe-devouring" *basileis.* So long as the society as a whole remains relatively stable—with an aristocratic warrior-group which protects the weaker members of the community from outside aggression, and a peasant-group that recognizes the inherent "superiority" of its leaders, accepting protection with gratitude, and offering in return its loyalty and respect—and, so long as neither group attempts to exceed its place in the order, the friction points will be few. But once the delicate balance is broken: when, for example, the leaders fail in their responsibilities by using their power and wealth to oppress or to aggrandize themselves at the expense of the people, or when the larger mass of the populace begins to intrude itself into spheres of activity formerly confined to the aristocrats, assuming, say, an important military role, or attempting to gain political control, then the social fabric shows signs of wear, and active strife results. That is what happens during the next two centuries in Greece. Naturally, the expressed values of the competing groups will be reshaped radically in the process of adjusting to the social changes.

Ω

CHAPTER TWO
The Old Ideal under Challenge

AS A RESULT of the pressure of considerable social, economic and political ferment in the Greek world during the next two centuries, important changes occurred in the pattern of values professed by the aristocratic class. The main evidence for social attitudes during this period, which extends from about the first quarter of the seventh century to around 500 B.C., is literary. Unfortunately, the so-called lyric poets of the seventh and sixth centuries B.C. have come down to us in very fragmentary form, and we possess only a tiny quantity of this major artistic outpouring. Because the seventh century was the beginning of the historically self-conscious stage of Greek culture, the testimony of the direct literary remains is supplemented by the prose writings of later Greeks, especially the historians of the fifth, fourth and later centuries, who have preserved for us something resembling a coherent account of the events of the period. In addition to the "researches" of these historiographers and antiquarians, inscriptions on stone and bronze, a much fuller archaeological record, and a scattering of other sources have given us the data to reconstruct the main outlines of the evolution of Greek thought during the Archaic Age, as it is called.

Few periods of history before the modern era have experienced so rapid a pace of social and intellectual change as the Archaic and early Classical Ages, a rate of evolution that appears all the more remarkable because of the few advances in the technological sphere. In many ways it was a truly revolutionary age, but change was not, as it often is in human history, the result of new techniques. Aside from the momentous transition from bronze to iron, there were no "revolutions" in agriculture, industry or practical science; most technical skills (many of which were borrowed in the first place) were already known, and were merely refined. Even the extraordinary discoveries in natural science and mathematics achieved by the sixth- and early fifth-century Greek "physicists," were founded on the practical wisdom of the ancient Near

East—and became highly abstract intellectual constructs which had little material application. The enormous energy of the Greeks of the Archaic Age exploded in all directions save that of technology; the "revolution" was one of ideas, aesthetics and politics, in which technological innovation played only a subsidiary role.[1]

Small-farm agriculture, based on traditional farming techniques, had become the principle mode of production by Hesiod's time, and remained so, essentially unchanged, for centuries thereafter. The manufacture of goods, trade, shipbuilding, and other "industrial" activities became important economic factors after 800 and expanded rapidly after 700, but never came close to rivaling agriculture as a source of livelihood. It has recently been estimated that the percentage of the population of Greece engaged in agriculture was over eighty and may have been as high as ninety percent.[2] This does not mean that trade, commerce and manufacture were insignificant; however small the portion of the population that was involved, the pursuit of wealth by these and other means (e.g. mercenary service, piracy) was an important social phenomenon, to which we shall have occasion to refer later.

As a general rule, the small or medium independent farm was the base of economic existence in Greece. There were exceptions to this norm (as in Sparta), and in the course of the Archaic Age in many Greek states there came to be a concentration of land in the hands of a few wealthy landowners, which provoked social unrest. Nevertheless, individual possession of land (which essentially defined citizen status) was the standard pattern as well as the ideal. The enduring quality of this ideal is seen in the frequently raised cry for the redistribution of land — whenever inequality in land ownership became severe. The sociopsychological effects of this economic fact were momentous, for it meant that change during these turbulent years took place against the background of a generally static and stable rural economy and within the context of a value system based on an agrarian way of life and the ideology of ownership of land as the criterion of citizenship. Its chief manifestation was a prevalent notion of equality (realized in many variations and degrees, of course). There were other consequences: the gap between rich and poor never became a yawning gulf; there never developed a large and powerful merchant class, nor a class of permanently oppressed peasants; Greece knew neither plantations nor teeming urban centers. The social stratification that emerged with the evolution from the tribal design to the "aristocratic" state did not result in a formal class system. No Greek, however elevated his status, ever had a title before his name; no citizen of the many small *poleis* ever thought of himself as an "inferior."

In spite of their dominant position in the archaic polis, aristocrats could not automatically assume the mantle of class superiority. The aristocratic ideology had to conform to the social realities, which meant that from the very beginning its evolution was adaptive. In formal terms: "A code of ethics is merely an aspect of a social system. It is merely a mechanism of social control. As social systems evolve, so will their ethical counterparts." Or, to put it another way, "the social systems are the independent [variables], the ethical systems the dependent, variables."[3] The evolution of the social system itself is still not well understood, and the brief sketch that follows must, of necessity, be highly selective and simplified.

Around 750 B.C. a number of major processes are evident: a steep rise in population, the beginning of a long wave of overseas colonization, a sharp increase in trading activity, and the emergence of the polis or "city-state." They are all related, of course, although their causal connections are elusive. I have already suggested that the rise in population was the effect of greater productivity due to the change from a stockbreeding to an agrarian base. Colonization (which itself implies the existence of some kind of systematic organization) appears to have been primarily a response to surplus population and land shortage, but is also connected to the increase in trade and commerce. Most historians agree that by 700 B.C. there was a general rise in the level of prosperity throughout the Greek world. We know from the evidence of grave goods that the upper stratum had developed the taste for and the means to acquire expensive trade luxuries after 800 B.C. In addition, there is good reason to posit the existence of a "middle" group of fairly well-off farmers (among whom was Hesiod) and a fair number of moderately prosperous artisans and traders, gathered in the slowly growing urban clusters.

The polis, or "city-state," form of social organization was the principal political development of the period. Unfortunately, its origins and early form are poorly known. A polis was both more and less than a "city," more and less than a "state," as we use these terms today. It can be defined as "an independent group of people occupying an area with definite borders," but considering that the rather small geographical area which was inhabited by Greek-speakers eventually held 1500 of these units, ranging from small villages with surrounding populations in the hundreds to true urban centers, with corresponding diversity of institutions, simple categorization is impossible. The single, overreaching characteristic of all *poleis,* large or small, was the self-identification of its members with the group; the life of a "citizen," *politēs,* in its every aspect, was bounded by this identification. It is perhaps not too sweeping a generalization to say that all elements of the preceding tribal life, psychological as well as material, were subsumed in the polis. Thus, not only did the polis provide the systematic framework of a man's military, legal, political and property relations, it also determined his religious worship, his marriage customs and his recreational and aesthetic pursuits.[4]

The evolution from a kinship-and-loyalty tribal system to a territorial unit which undercut the traditional bonds of social integration and united town and countryside into a single entity with institutionalized political authority, did not occur uniformly. The story of Greek constitutional development is the story of hundreds of separate communities whose growth was determined by local and regional variables. In some remote areas the older tribal structure *(ethnos)* survived almost unchanged; some states, like Sparta, were curious hybrids combining elements of both forms. Despite this unevenness, a general model of political evolution is discernible. The tribal chief, *basileus,* whose nascent centralized political authority (as we have seen) had eroded in the face of competing claims by lesser chiefs, lost his preeminent leadership which passed to corporate control by the powerful lineages in the community. By about 700 B.C. the very office of *basileus* had virtually disappeared, except as one of a number of (usually annual) magistracies into which the powers of the chief had dispersed. There was no "ruler"; political leadership of the early polis was in the hands of men from dominant descent groups, large landholders, who held exclusive control of the political and military offices, cult associations, and the legal machinery. These were the "aristocrats," whose power base, as before, lay in their households *(oikoi)* and in the wider associations of lineage *(genos)* and phratry, corporations which figure more prominently in the polis than in the chiefdom.

The jealous competition for hegemony in the polis among the aristocratic lineages gave rise to long-standing rivalries and temporary and shifting alliances, leading to feuds, which often broke out into that internal warfare *(stasis)* which all Greeks dreaded, but which appears to us as a normal characteristic of polis life through the centuries. In their jockeying for position and prestige aristocratic lines naturally sought to increase their bases of wealth and influence, inevitably at the expense

The Old Ideal under Challenge

of non-aristocrats. Signs of class conflict, the result of political and economic exploitation by the ascendant aristocracies, are evident from the time of Hesiod on. Sporadically there arose in various Greek states individual strong men, usually men of wealth and ancestry, called *tyrannoi*, "tyrants," who opportunistically grasped political power for themselves and attempted to establish family dynasties. Ranged against their fellow aristocrats and playing on the discontent of the medium and small farmers, tyrants often appeared as defenders and "champions of the people" (as Aristotle calls them), whose acquiescence to their rule was necessary.[5]

If, as many scholars maintain, the appearance of tyrants points to reaction against aristocratic oppression of the populace, the role of the people in the tyrants' rise to power demonstrates no less the lower classes' potential for political leverage. To understand the evolution of the aristocratic ideal it is important to emphasize that at the very time men of wealth and family were trying to widen the gap between themselves and others — to become a true aristocratic class — those below this stratum were affected by the same dynamic processes at work in the society. The sense of individualism and self-awareness, restless vitality, probing curiosity (both the cause and the effect of the dramatic social changes we have sketched) touched all free men of the new polis.

At some time between 700 and 650 B.C. a change in military tactics had far-reaching consequences. The older style of fighting, like that portrayed in the *Iliad*, consisted of opposing groups, loosely organized, with a majority of the combatants armed haphazardly and lightly. The decisive fighting was done by individual warriors who were heavily armed and well protected, in many cases operating as cavalry. The outcome of a battle was decided, not by the lightly-armed mass, but by these individual aristocrats, successors of the Homeric warriors. In the new tactical system a large body of infantry, each soldier heavily armed with helmet, breastplate, shield and greaves* and wielding a long spear, stood in close formation, shield to shield, in deep ranks. This formation, called the phalanx, moved in unison and was able to overpower any existing opposing force. An individual, or knots of individuals, as well as the cavalry forces then in use, would be powerless against the concerted thrust of the bristling lances. So the phalanx and the heavily armed infantryman (*hoplitēs*, from *hopla*, arms) became, like any successful military innovation, the prevailing mode of warfare.

---

*Armor for the leg below the knee.

Clearly, the new phalanx was intimately bound up with the emerging polis; the military innovations and the socioeconomic structure developed in tandem. The phalanx presupposes, first of all, a rather large number of men. The principle of the phalanx is relatively simple: the deeper the formation the more pressure it exerts, and the longer the front line the more easily the enemy could be outflanked. So, the more hoplites a city could muster the more successful it was in warfare. Second, the phalanx requires that the large number of men necessary to man it have sufficient wealth to provide their own heavy equipment and the leisure and inclination to train together as a cohesive body.

The very existence of this new style of fighting implies that changes were taking place in the values of the society.[6] When the single warrior becomes part of a "team," the old ideal of personal glory must yield to the ideal of collective glory; the community rather than the individual becomes the focus of brave deeds. Another important social implication is the introduction of equality into the ranks. A relatively poor man of undistinguished family, whose property qualification may have been barely sufficient for the furnishing of his panoply, might find himself fighting alongside a wealthy man from an eminent family. The poor man could be the hero of the day, the "nobleman" the coward. Under the impulse of comradeship in arms and the sense of belonging to a civic unit, the scope for distinction on the basis of wealth or birth alone was reduced. In times of peace the noble would find his fellow hoplites demanding a share in the affairs of the polis which they defended in war, or at least insisting that they be treated fairly and not be subject to exploitation, either economic or political.[7]

Under the impact of the military innovations and the accompanying social awareness on the part of the "ordinary" soldiers, the old Homeric warrior ideal shows signs of change. Bravery and skill in battle are still the principle values of the soldiers, but it is a new and "non-heroic" kind of bravery that is celebrated by the poets. The essential requirement of success with the phalanx is that the hoplite stand firm in the compact ranks and not give ground; and so, in the literature after 700 B.C. the heroic individual fighter yields pride of place to the cooperative infantryman. A Spartan poet, Tyrtaeus, writing about 650 B.C., exhorts his countrymen, who had just begun to fight in the new formation:

> Let each man hold, standing firm, both feet planted on the ground, biting his lip with his teeth, covering with the belly of his broad shield his thighs and legs, his breast and shoulders . . . let each man,

The old Ideal under Challenge

Closing with the enemy, fighting hand-to-hand with long spear or sword, wound and take him; and setting foot against foot, and resting shield against shield, crest against crest, helmet against helmet let him fight his man breast to breast, grasping the hilt of his sword or of his long spear.

(Fr. 8.21-34, Diehl)[8]

It is only natural that a different emphasis is now placed on the potent Greek notion of *aretē*. In the poems of Tyrtaeus *aretē* is no longer the daring individual success, the flash of personal brilliance; the impulse towards cooperative action altered the older values, and *aretē* for Tyrtaeus is simply the ability to stand firm in ranks:

For a man is not *agathos* in war, unless he endure seeing the bloody slaughter, and standing close reach out for the foe. This is *aretē*, this the best and loveliest prize for the young man to win. A common good this, for the whole polis and all the *dēmos,* when a man holds, firm-set among the fighters, unflinchingly . . .

(Fr. 9.10-17D)

In Tyrtaeus' Sparta the soldier is exhorted to fight and die for his country, his polis, not for individual glory or for plunder, which enhance a man's status. Glory there was, but it could be stated only in terms of the community. Here again, the words of Tyrtaeus illustrate the shift in emphasis:

For it is a fine thing *(kalon)* for an *agathos* man to die, falling among the front-fighters, fighting for his fatherland . . .

(Fr. 6.7.1-2D)

The man who falls among the front-fighters and loses his dear life, bringing glory to his town and the people *(laoi)* and his father, struck many times in front through the breast and bossy shield and breastplate—him both young and old alike bewail, and the whole polis is distressed with grievous longing; and his tomb and children are famed among men, and his children's children and his family to come. And never does his goodly fame perish, nor his name, but even though he is under the earth he is immortal because he stood firm, acted bravely, and was fighting for his land and children when violent Ares struck him down.

(Fr. 9.23-34D)

Another early poet, Callinus of Ephesus in Asia Minor, a near contemporary of Tyrtaeus, speaks in identical terms:

> For it is an honorable and glorious thing for a man to fight for his land and children and wife against the enemy . . .

Callinus also says (in the same poem) that the man who dies at home:

> is not dear to the *dēmos* nor regretted,

but the good warrior:

> him both great and small lament if he die, for a stouthearted man, when he is dead, is a grievous loss to all the *laos*, and alive he is like a demi-god.
>
> (Fr. 1D)[9]

A side consequence of this altered ideal is the new belief that death for a "higher cause," that is, the polis, is a good thing. This is in sharp contrast to the Homeric belief that one's own life was particularly valuable. Homer's heroes never considered dying for a "cause," and a sentiment like this one by Tyrtaeus would seem impossibly extreme to the most valiant of the epic figures:

> Make life your enemy, and the black spirits of death dear as the rays of the sun.
>
> (Fr. 8.5-6D)

The idea of dedication to the community was not completely new in the seventh century; we saw its genesis in Homer, especially among the Trojans and Hector, the most communally oriented of the epic heroes. Nevertheless, Hector thought still in terms of the segmental tribe — his concern was for the close circle of family, not for the territorial community. Tyrtaeus calls the new *aretē* a *xynon esthlon*, a "common good," a concept that does not appear in the epics.

We recall that the Homeric warrior's primary goal was fame among men for great exploits. Glory is also sought by the new polis warrior, but it can be earned only by service to the state, and the peer group that awards it is no longer a small circle of similarly minded heroes, but the *whole* community. In the seventh century, then, the notion of personal greatness recedes, and the idea of civic approbation takes its place. One of the natural effects of this process was that valor, fame and glory became localized. Homer's heroes sought a transcendental "fame among men"; the polis fighter can expect a more homely reward:

> All honor him *(timaō)* both young and old, and he goes down to Hades having had much joy; growing old he stands out among the townspeople, and no one wants to harm him, in his honor or his rights, and all yield place to him on the benches, both the young, his age-mates, and those who are older.
> (Tyrtaeus fr. 9.37-42D)

With the major elements of the heroic ideal thus transmuted, it is not surprising to find that other qualities which formed an important part of the traditional ideal are similarly downgraded. Again we turn to Tyrtaeus, who says things which would have been incomprehensible to the epic hero, but which reflect perfectly the polis ideal. At the beginning of one of his poems he lists skills and accomplishments which were, in epic terms, proof of a man's goodness — skill in running and wrestling, great strength, fleetness of foot, bodily beauty, vast wealth, political power, eloquence — and says he would not praise a man that had these:

> not even if he had all fame *(doxa)* except savage valor.
> (Fr. 9.1-9D)

As Werner Jaeger says, Tyrtaeus "recast the Homeric ideal of the single champion's *aretē* into the *aretē* of the patriot..."[10]

It is important to stress that this is not so much a rejection of the code of the aristocratic warrior as it is a transvaluation. Essentially the Tyrtaean scheme subsumes all the excellence of the fighting man into the single cause of service to the whole community. The effect on the aristocratic ideal of this restrictiveness was bound to be drastic. For when all the citizens of the polis, aristocrats and non-aristocrats alike, are exhorted to dedicate their manly abilities to the common cause, and when honor is conferred, not as the consequence of individual superiority but for ability to further the common good, then a recasting of the old priorities is demanded. Put another way, when the aristocratic *aretai* cease to command universal approbation, that is, cease to be functionally valuable, and if the aristocratic group wishes to retain its superior position in the community's regard, then it must seek other ways of demonstrating its superiority.

Hesiod's poetry showed us a section of society which simply did not concern itself, except at the points of abrasive contact, with the ideals of an aristocratic group. Tyrtaeus' Spartan ideal shows essentially the same element of society encroaching on the aristocratic *aretai,* and dramatically reducing their scope. This means, of course, that now the areas of possible tension between groups are liable to increase, as the cultural values of the noble class become subject to closer and more critical scrutiny in contrast to the new criterion of usefulness to the society as a whole.

While Tyrtaeus and Callinus were speaking for the new civic awareness of duty to a common cause, other voices began to be heard, which more directly challenged aristocratic assumptions. Archilochus of Paros is the first truly individual figure in Greek literature. We possess only bits and fragments of this master poet, compared by later Greeks to Homer himself, but even these remnants show us a man of intense personal feeling who expressed himself in a new and important way. The facts of his life are obscure, and even his dates are uncertain. As well as can be established, he lived and wrote around 650 B.C. His father was an important member of the Parian aristocracy, who led a colony to the northern island of Thasos; his mother was a slave. Archilochus led a wandering life; he himself took part in the colonizing of Thasos; he may have been a mercenary, but that is not certain. What is certain is that he spent most of his life as a soldier:

> In my spear is my kneaded bread, in my spear my Ismarian wine. I drink leaning on my spear.
>
> (Fr. 2D)

He was both soldier and poet (fr. 1D):

> I am a squire of the lord of war, Enyalius, and I understand the lovely gift of the Muses,

a fighter, drinker, lover, of a swashbuckling kind — a match in these qualities to any Homeric figure. But, in all respects he was a man of the new Greece, the world of the polis and of the hoplite infantryman, of restless energy and psychological uncertainty. Archilochus' poetry (like that of Tyrtaeus) is full of epic phrases and formulas, but the thought is quite otherwise. His view of a soldier's life was almost totally the reverse of Homer's idealized world of personal glory and brilliance, for Archilochus not only rejected the epic conventions, he mocked them.

The Old Ideal under Challenge

The astounding difference in outlook may be seen in some famous lines, which were considered shocking even by later generations:

> Well, some Thracian is enjoying my shield which I left – I didn't want to and it was a perfectly good one – beside a bush. But I saved myself. What do I care about that shield? The hell with it, I'll get another one just as good.
>
> (Fr. 6D)

Nowhere in Homer do we find this sort of cynicism or ironic self-mockery. To the Homeric warrior, who lived in a constant agony of self-doubt about his own bravery, to abandon arms and flee was a sign of cowardice and failure; to have broadcast it, as Archilochus did, would have been unthinkable.[11] But Archilochus' poetry is full of such "anti-heroic" reaction. One by one he slights the cherished tenets of the epic ideal. On comrades in arms, he writes:

> A mercenary, Glaukos, is a friend – as long as he's fighting.
>
> (Fr. 13D)

On the glory of combat:

> Seven fell dead whom we caught in pursuit, we the thousand slayers.
>
> (Fr. 61D)

On posthumous glory:

> There's no respect or fame from townsmen when you're dead. It's the praise of the living we want – while we're alive. A dead man gets the worst of it – every time.
>
> (Fr. 64D)

In the epic scheme of values physical appearance was not only important, but decisive in determining status. Archilochus explodes that notion in these lines:

> I don't like a general who is big or who walks with a swagger, or who glories in his curly hair, cut-off moustache. Give me a man who's little, bandy-legged, feet firm on the ground, full of heart.
>
> (Fr. 60D)

There is no question of Archilochus' bravery; he was a soldier, and a good one. He simply removed the aura of romanticism from warfare, seeing the world as it really was and his robust, earthy view of life illustrates the new mood of realism which characterized the age. For Homer all things and all places were ideally good;[12] Hesiod, though, had no illusions about miserable Ascra, and Archilochus says much the same about Thasos:

> She stands, like the backbone of an ass, crowned with a savage wood.
>
> (Fr. 18D)

And in a fragment about his native Paros he says:

> Never mind Paros, and those figs, and the life of the sea.
>
> (Fr. 53D)

Paradoxically, this attitude of negative realism did not contradict the new spirit of communal patriotism. For all their heroic idealism the Homeric warriors were motivated mainly by their own self-centered desire for personal glory; according to legend Archilochus died defending his homeland, Paros.[13]

The difference between the Archilochean and Homeric expression of values seems immense — all the more so because Archilochus' diction, as well as many of his themes, were those of the Homeric epos. So severe a divagation from traditional standards is a testimony to the structural changes that had taken place in Greek society. The mood of pessimism born of the insecurity produced by the transition from a kinship to a territorial system that we observed in Hesiod has its counterpart in Archilochus' salty iconoclasm a generation or so later. But what Hesiod lamented, Archilochus accepted as natural. To some modern critics Archilochus was a rebel who completely disdained the norms of behavior he had inherited. It is perhaps more correct to view him as a transitional figure, not rejecting but modifying a scheme of values which, although still vital, could not stand unaltered in the face of new realities, uncertainties and ambiguities.[14] The very act of "rejecting" old certitudes demonstrates their continuity. A recent work on Archilochus expresses this point of view. Archilochus may have parodied and mocked the tradition, but he was not "anti-heroic; nor one died and mocked the tradition, but he was not anti-heroic; nor one who entirely rejected the 'honour' code that in one form or another has

The Old Ideal under Challenge

permeated Greek society . . . down to the present day. Archilochus continued and modified the cultural traditions embodied in the epic."[15]

To this assessment we may add a further thought. By 700 B.C. the epic ideal against which Archilochus pointedly ranged his own view of reality already had the character of a stylized ethos, which aristocrats, fully conscious now of social division, had appropriated for themselves. By mocking the "code" of the warrior-élite, Archilochus challenged one basis of the aristocracy's claim to superiority, not in a "partisan" way, as if he were some anti-aristocratic ideologue, but as an ironic critic of a concept which had become artificial and outmoded by the realities of societal change. The new generation of critics, forceful and outspoken in their opposition to the potent (but static) norms of upper-class behavior — and Archilochus was the first, not the only one — brought about a radical reshaping of the aristocratic ethos. A testament to the lasting quality of the sting administered to the enduring mirage of the Homeric ideal is the harsh attack launched against Archilochus by Plato's cousin Critias, a thoroughgoing oligarch, some 250 years later. Critias censures the unrestrained nature of Archilochus' own self-revelations: his slavish birth, his poverty, his intemperateness and sexual excesses, and, "what is even more disgraceful than this, [is the admission] that he threw away his shield."[16] This enumeration of character defects (which reveals, by the way, the fifth-century aristocratic version of the traditional norms) focuses especially on Archilochus' lack of restraint in both deed and word, a characteristic that will become one of the main props of the evolving aristocratic ideal.

In his own way Tyrtaeus mirrored the restructuring of traditional norms of manly worth, but, like the Homeric warrior (and the later aristocrats), he was profoundly motivated by the epic notions of shame and respect for public opinion *(aidōs)*. A lack of concern about "what people say," which was the essence of Critias' attack, is prominent in Archilochus and highlights the uprooting of tradition and the sense of isolated individualism characteristic of the age:

> Aisimides, no one would enjoy very many delightful things if he cared about the reproaches of the *dēmos*.
>
> (Fr. 9D)

Tyrtaeus, for whom discipline and respect for authority were paramount, urged the Spartans to obey their leaders, a notion quite similar to the Homeric conception of the ruler's position.[17] A statement by Archilochus on a public leader defies the tradition:

And now Leophilos is ruling, and Leophilos has the power; to Leophilos goes everything, and Leophilos is listened to.

(Fr. 70D)

Who Leophilos, "dear to the people," was we do not know; but he was either a real individual or a type of the popular leader. In any case, we note a lessening of respect for what is termed today public authority.[18] The same attitude of irreverence for what is conventionally great is seen in a fragment of Archilochus in which, according to Aristotle, the speaker is a carpenter:

The wealth of golden Gyges means nothing to me; I've never been envious, nor am I jealous of the works of the gods; I've no desire for a mighty tyranny — for these things are beyond my vision.

(Fr. 22D)

Gyges, the king of Lydia, was proverbial for his wealth and power; Charon, the carpenter, is the "little man" who thumbs his nose at the exalted.

Another fragment of Archilochus seems at first glance to be out of keeping with his customary tone of cynical realism:

O Zeus, father Zeus, yours is the rule of heaven, and you watch over the deeds of men both vile and lawful; and the violence *(hybris)* and justice *(dikē)* of the wild beasts is your concern, too.

(Fr. 94D)

But when we recall Hesiod's obsession with the same subject, these impassioned lines which make Zeus the arbiter of justice are not at all surprising. Cries for justice, for fair dealing, have their origin from below the ruling stratum. Archilochus was not a peasant farmer, but he was definitely alienated from the traditional ideals of the aristocratic class. The only commoner whose feelings were expressed in the *Iliad,* namely Thersites, was concerned with the same thing, the unfairness of the high-handed Agamemnon in distributing the spoils. We must hear in these appeals to a higher power for equity the voice of an emerging social consciousness raised in opposition to a ruling class, just as later the terms connoting equality become catchwords of the fledgling Greek democracies.[19]

Other evidence of Archilochus' concern for social justice is seen in the remnants of his Fables, or animal tales, in which the speakers are animals. Attempts to reconstruct these poems from the few lines we possess have been largely unsuccessful, but they appear to be concerned with social problems. The genre of the Fable is certainly "popular" in origin. The best-known of the fable writers, Aesop, is said to have been a slave who lived during the sixth century B.C. The first extant example of this folk genre is found in Hesiod's *Works and Days* where he tells the fable of the Hawk and the Nightingale, which is specifically concerned with social injustice. Archilochus' fragment on justice, quoted (opposite), is from his animal tales.[20]

Both the concern for justice and the various questionings of the heroic ideal may be seen as indications of an increasing element of social tension in the seventh century. An important clue to the form which this tension was taking is seen in a one-line fragment from Archilochus' animal tales. A fox addresses a deer:

Pass on, for you are of noble birth *(gennaios)*.

(Fr. 97)

In this line occurs the first recorded instance in Greek of a word meaning "of noble birth." In all of Homer and Hesiod neither this word nor any other words for high birth are found — surely no coincidence. The aristocratic warriors of the Homeric poems constituted a noble class of merit which was just beginning to identify itself as a social class based on claims of birth and inherited wealth; but this process had not advanced far enough for a formulation of aristocratic terminology to develop. In fact, in the Homeric epics, surprisingly little is said about noble birth, despite the interest on the part of the heroes in genealogy; conversely, there was practically no attempt to prove individual or group superiority on the basis of blood lines.[21] The superiority of the Homeric warrior-aristocrat was self-presumptive, and there were no rival claimants to challenge their natural pre-eminence. As a consequence of the emergence of the aristocratic state the lines of division had obviously deepened, so that words like *gennaios* can appear, which, if they do not betoken a completely new set of aristocratic priorities, at least indicate an explicitness not seen before.

Thus, as the claims of worth made by the other than noble segment of society increase — claims which either supersede the older aristocratic values or subsume them into the new communal ideology — signs of an aristocratic "reaction" surface. The emergence of terms of social distinction based on hereditary factors is one aspect of this reaction.

Whereas in the *Iliad* and *Odyssey* self-conscious expression of social division was absent or almost totally muted, in Hesiod there appear some indications of "class" consciousness. In an address to Perses, for example, the adjective *esthlos* is contrasted with another word, *deilos,* both of which take on social colorations different from their usual Homeric and Hesiodic usage:

> But you, Perses, listen to right *(dikē)* and do not foster violence *(hybris);* for *hybris* is bad for a *deilos* man. Even the *esthlos* cannot easily bear its burden, but is weighed down under it when he has fallen into delusion *(atē).*
>
> *(Works and Days* 213-16)

Deilos is found frequently in Homer, signifying "unlucky," "unfortunate," "miserable." In this passage it seems to have the meaning "unfortunate" in the more generalized sense of a man in unfortunate circumstances, i.e. a poor or weak man. *Esthlos* also appears to have an extended meaning here; these moralizing lines are preceded by the fable of the Hawk and the Nightingale, which was addressed to the *basileis* and which tells how the weak must submit to the strong. They, in turn, are followed by a reference to the violators of Justice, "those who devour bribes and give sentences with crooked judgments" (220–21). Logically, then, the word *esthlos* had something of a technical force, the "distinguished," "prosperous" man, an extension of the physical or ethical qualities normally contained in it. And if Hesiod is giving the "title" *esthlos* to the man who is materially successful or powerful, we must conclude that such words had, by the early seventh century, gained some popular currency as socio-economic terms.[22]

A more obvious illustration is provided by Callinus (fr. 1D), who says that the brave soldier who dies in battle is mourned by the whole people, both by the great man *(megas)* and the little man *(oligos).* In Homer the words *megas* and *oligos* could only refer to physical size or strength, never, as here, to social or economic condition. These are isolated and scrappy indications, but their force is undeniable. During the first half of the seventh century B.C. the Greek world was developing a socio-political vocabulary.

The beginning of a vocabulary of social differentiation, the signs of popular discontent with the ruling structure, the questioning of the warrior ideal, and the substitution of a communal ideal in its place, all point to an awareness of a deepening cleavage in the social structure. The most ominous sign of social division in the seventh century, how-

The Old Ideal under Challenge

ever, is the evidence of an increasing disparity in wealth. In broadest terms, the assumption of control of civic and religious institutions by the aristocratic families gave them the means to increase their holdings. These same families, it is safe to say, also participated in and were enriched by the growth of trade and commerce. Concomitantly, many of the small farmers began a slow slide to impoverishment or to dependency on their wealthy neighbors, the inevitable result of social stratification. I hasten to add that this scenario was not acted out in the same way or at the same pace everywhere in the Greek world. We know very little of the history of most Greek *poleis* in this period, and to pretend to be sure of the causes of social change would be a grave mistake. We must be careful neither to exaggerate the extent of economic incongruence (see above, pages 36-37) nor to rely on explanations of modern economic theory. For example, the amount of surplus that could be generated to support an unproductive group will have been small, while to speak of "capital" and "investment" is a modernist fallacy. Some farmers will have remained well-off; others beside the aristocracy (farmers as well as non-aristocratic entrepreneurs) enjoyed the fruits of a general increase in wealth. There were never economic "classes" in the strict Marxian sense among free citizens; and by 500 B.C. "the solid backbone of the citizenry of most Greek *poleis* consisted of small and medium farmers who cultivated their *kleroi* in ancestral fashion . . ."[23] Still, one fact of major importance is indisputable. By 700 B.C. the aristocratic landowners were *relatively* much wealthier than the rest of the farmers. Increasingly, social tension will be expressed in the form of economic inequality; "rich" and "poor" become semantic categories for the first time.

On the other hand, the increase in power and wealth of the aristocracy did not take place in a vacuum. As we have seen, counterforces were operating. After 650 B.C. the "knightly" warrior, the individual fighter of great prowess, no longer held center stage, because of the changes in military tactics. The emerging civic consciousness, closely connected to the new military formation, also had its effect; the free peasantry was not about to become an oppressed class at the same time it was fighting the polis' battles. The old tribal egalitarianism both reinforced and was reinforced in turn by these factors. Aristocrats, who were no less bound by the organic unity of the polis, could not, however much they may have wished, distance themselves too far above their fellow *politai;* a frequent counterdose to aristocratic exploitation was tyranny, itself a demonstration of the people's ultimate power.

Very few states, in fact, were able completely to restrict civic participation to a narrow group of hereditary aristocrats; some broadening of the base of government occurred in most *poleis* in the course of the seventh and sixth centuries. Nevertheless, even in the most advanced democratic *poleis*, where civic offices were eventually opened to the whole of the citizenry, political leadership continued to be dominated by aristocrats or by the wealthiest citizens. Indeed, in a good many states, a small group, relatively much wealthier, retained control of the political machinery throughout the classical period — and beyond. But no matter how oligarchical the government of his polis may have been, the free citizen was never less than that; no *politēs* was ever a member of a downtrodden mass.

Some of the shifts in attitudes caused by these social variables have already been mentioned. Certain key aspects of the old aristocratic ideal, which was founded in the natural superiority of the tribal warrior-leader, were being challenged or transvalued at the very time aristocrats were attempting to establish their superiority in a self-conscious way. One very important new element is already evident: a consciously expressed feeling among the nobles that their superiority was based on birth. Another change in the aristocratic ideal surfaces at this time; the emergence of an emphasis on a particular style of life. The Homeric poems, for all their concentration on wealth and display, show that the warrior-élite enjoyed a material standard distinguishable from that of their lesser neighbors only in degree, a fact that is confirmed by the archaeological record of the tenth and ninth centuries. Basically they were prosperous landowners who lived a better, but not essentially different life, than the smaller farmers. Homeric heroes were not above performing the simplest of manual labor, and their interests (aside from battlecraft and related activities, where the gulf was wide) were pretty much those of the society as a whole. Beginning in the eighth, and increasingly in the course of the seventh century, however, a greater emphasis on a specifically aristocratic style of life becomes evident. On the finest pottery (the kind meant for consumption by wealthy buyers) motifs depicting the gods and heroes of Greek legends are increasingly popular. By the last decade of the seventh century, when the black-figure technique of vase painting was beginning to prevail, heroic motifs dominate, and scenes depicting contemporary aristocratic life appear with greater frequency, especially the youthful warrior with his horses and (now obsolete) chariot. Through the sixth century these themes are continued; depicted are heroic legends, aristocrats in fine clothing, scenes of revelling, athletic contests, youths riding or leading horses, hunting or arming scenes.[24] Speaking of this early period, the fifth-century historian, Thucydides, tells us:

> The Athenians were the first to give up the habit of carrying weapons and to adopt a way of living that was more relaxed and more luxurious. In fact the elder men of the rich families who had these luxurious tastes only recently gave up wearing linen under-garments and tying their hair behind their heads in a knot fastened with a clasp of golden grasshoppers: the same fashions spread to their kinsmen in Ionia, and lasted there among the old men for some time.
> (Thuc. 1.6.3)[25]

These developments in the life-style of the upper class — in dress, ornamentation, hair styling, and customs — give the clear impression of overt manifestations of class consciousness. One of the "new" attitudes provides an excellent illustration. In the Homeric epics there are only the barest hints of male homosexuality;[26] Hesiod never alludes to boy-love, and Archilochus, who lived in a warrior-society, appears not to have had any male lovers. But increasingly in the aristocratic literature of the seventh and sixth centuries pederasty plays a prominent role, and the importance placed on homosexual attachments becomes a distinguishing characteristic of the aristocratic culture.[27]

Another indication of change from the older ideal is a trend towards a certain "softness" noted in the literature of the archaic period. In general this takes the form of a shift from primary emphasis on martial qualities to a mode of life that celebrated style and manners. The rejection by Archilochus of the dandified general (fr. 60D) had implied a type of aristocratic officer who consciously strove to *look* the part: tall, posturing, long-haired, carefully shaved. Xenophanes, an Ionian philosopher who wrote during the last half of the sixth century, criticizes the upper class of his native city of Colophon:

> Having learned useless luxuries from the Lydians, while they were still free from hateful tyranny, they would go into the place of assembly wearing robes of all-purple — a thousand of them, no less — boastful, glorying in their well-dressed long hair, drenched with the perfume of elaborate scents.
> (Fr. 3D)[28]

Another poet, earlier than Xenophanes, has this to say about the wealthy citizens of the island of Samos:

> And so they would go, their locks carefully combed, into Hera's precinct, covered in their splendid cloaks, sweeping the ground with their snow-white robes, with golden grasshoppers adorning their topknots. And their long-flowing hair, bound in golden ties, would swing in the breeze, and around their arms were fancy bracelets.
>
> (Asius fr. 13 Kinkel)

These are lines written in criticism, but they serve as reflection of a newer, more pronounced, emphasis by the upper class on a style of living which separated them much more sharply from their less privileged fellow citizens. In the poetry of Mimnermus, an Ionian from Colophon, who wrote in the last third of the seventh century, a preoccupation with love and youth and the horrors of old age is strikingly evident:

> But what life, what joy is there without golden Aphrodite? Let me die when these no longer matter — secret love and its honey-sweet gifts and bed — these are the flowers of youth, alluring to men and women alike. But when grievous old age comes, that makes a man both foul and ugly, then evil cares wear out his heart, and he no longer joys in looking at the sun's rays, but is hateful to boys, dishonored by women. God has made old age a wearisome thing.
>
> (Fr. 1D)

Archilochus had written about love, to be sure, and phrases like "secret love," and "honey-sweet gifts," were not original with Mimnermus.[29] What is different in these lines above is that Mimnermus makes love and youth the focal point of existence, and old age its greatest evil. We must caution against placing undue emphasis on one man's hedonistic philosophy; nevertheless these ideas, expressed by an aristocratic poet, are at the furthest remove possible from either the heroic values or the claims of community on a man's energies.

It is important to note Mimnermus' different usage of certain key words. He says that old age makes a man both foul *(aischros)* and ugly *(kakos)*. These words, which in Homer (or in Tyrtaeus, for that matter) would refer to cowardly behavior, are given an aesthetic reference.[30] Similar is the use of the word "dishonored" *(atimastos)*, another powerful term. Honor *(timē)* is always used to indicate peer evaluation within the context of success or failure; here dishonor is the consequence of growing old, and the context is a private relationship.[31] We can compare a two-line fragment of Mimnermus which conveys much the same message:

Though he was surprisingly fair, when youth has gone by, not even a father is loved or honored *(timios)* by his sons.

(Fr. 3D)

In another poem (fr. 5D) the brief period of youthful bloom *(hēbē)* is called "honored" *(timēessa)*, while old age is "painful and misshapen *(amorphon)* . . . hateful and without honor *(atimon)*" and makes a man "unknown" *(agnōstos)*. Not only is the traditional vocabulary of merit given new applications, even the standard observations on human life have been altered to reflect a more restricted vision. In fr. 2D the Homeric image of the transitory nature of life — the race of men is like the seasonal changes (*Iliad* 6. 146-49) — is narrowed to mean the brevity of youth. It is in this poem that we read the startlingly pessimistic sentiment:

> But when this time of spring has passed it is better to die straight off than live (lines 9-10).[32]

In these poems the worth of a man is expressed in terms of externals — youth and beauty; there is no feeling either for the old standard of success or the newer standard of service. Mimnermus was no mere voluptuary, of course; other fragments are of a martial and patriotic nature,[33] but it is true, nevertheless, that his later reputation in antiquity was as a love poet, and that this is a new direction in Greek values.

Another Ionian poet, Anacreon of Teos, writing about a century later, devoted himself almost entirely to erotic and convivial themes. Here the "softness" is in full flower, and Anacreon abandons the hardy virility of the traditional aristocratic ethos for the pleasures of wine, song, and love. In style, as well as in choice of subject, Anacreon's verses have a langorous, almost passive, quality. In a short poem, imitative in form of Archilochus' biting satire on Leophilos, but totally different in theme, he says:

> Kleoboulos is the one I love, Kleoboulos I go mad for,
> Kleoboulos I keep looking at.
>
> (Fr. 359 Page)[34]

A sense of how much the old values had yielded to new ones is evident in an anecdote told about Anacreon. When asked why he wrote hymns, not to the gods but to boys, Anacreon is said to have replied: "Because they are our gods." In a prayer that offended the religious sensibilities of a late philosopher he invokes Dionysus:

> I beseech you, come kindly to me, heeding a prayer that will find favor, and be a good counsellor to Kleoboulos, that he, O Dionysus, may accept my love.
>
> (Fr. 357.6-11 Page)

Many other examples of Anacreon's charmingly lighthearted view of life and love could be quoted, but this poem, to a reluctant girl, may be taken as typical:

> Thracian filly, why do you look askance at me and run away from me, and think that I am not at all wise? Please know that I could put a bridle on you quite well, and holding the reins could ride you around the race-course. But now you graze in the meadows, frisking and playing, for you do not have a skilled horseman to mount you.
>
> (Fr. 417 Page)

Anacreon's delicate approach to passion may be taken as typical of the aristocratic concentration on style and manner.[35] More basically, perhaps, there is an impulse toward restraint, a feeling that passions should be controlled:

> I love, and then again, I do not love, I am mad, and not mad.
>
> (Fr. 428 Page)

This is, in fact, "court" poetry. Anacreon spent considerable time as the guest of Polycrates, the tyrant of Samos (who reigned *ca.* 535-523 B.C.); on Polycrates' death, the tyrant of Athens sent for him. Surrounded by the elegant young aristocrats of the tyrants' circles he wrote endlessly of love and the pleasures of a leisured class, grace and charm *(charis)* the hallmark of his poetry:

> For boys would love me for my songs, since I sing charming things, and charming things are what I know how to say.
>
> (Fr. 402c Page)

In one poem real and undisguisedly deep feeling is apparent:

> My temples are already gray, my head is white, graceful youth is no longer by me, and my teeth are old. There is no longer much time left of sweet life. For this I weep often, fearing Tartarus, for the pit of Hades is terrible, and the road down to it is hard; and further, once a man has descended there is no way back again.
>
> (Fr. 395 Page)

The Old Ideal under Challenge 57

We are reminded immediately of Mimnermus and his hatred of old age. Anacreon sees in the symptoms of his body's decay the portent of eternal death; for him, as for Mimnermus, the fleeting of "graceful youth" and its eternal beauty is the real evil of life. In his almost single-mindeddevotion to love and beauty, good company and good manners, in his concentration on luxury and his avoidance of the serious in favor of light and inconsequential topics, delivered in a tone of slightly mocking irony and detachment, Anacreon stands as a living symbol of the genteel elegance affected by aristocrats (young and old) in the waning years of the Archaic Age.[36]

A slightly younger contemporary of Anacreon, Ibycus, wrote on the same subjects. A native of Rhegium in Italy, and an aristocrat, Ibycus also was at the court of Polycrates. He was, we can gather from the few extant fragments, a remarkably gifted poet, full of sensuous imagery and a keen observer of nature. Naturally, love was his main concern; in fact, Cicero calls him more amorous even than Anacreon, whose (the latter's) poetry Cicero characterized as *tota amatoria*. In one poem of Ibycus, Love comes like the Northwind from Thrace, and with "parching madness, dark and fearless, shakes me to the bottom of my heart with his might" (fr. 286 Page). In another poem on the onslaught of love he compares himself to an old champion race horse who unwillingly draws his chariot to the contest (fr. 287 Page). The characteristic fear of death is expressed in this fragment: "It is not possible to find a medicine for life for those who are dead" (fr. 313 Page).

The veneration of youth and beauty, and the celebration of love and wine and pleasure, so strikingly characteristic of aristocratic archaic poetry, had become, by the middle of the sixth century, important components of the aristocratic "thought world." One cause of the emphasis on the softer aspects of life by aristocratic poets in the seventh and sixth centuries was the vacuum created by the displacement of individual success as the primary psychological requirement of the society. Many of the traditional aristocratic excellences had been taken over, altered, or made untenable by a growing "middle class," pragmatically oriented to what was of benefit to the whole community. The polis, in other words, with its much larger number of useful citizens, had co-opted many of the values of the warrior-aristocrat.

At the same time, the ancient motivation of the aristocracy — the desire for prestige and public esteem — remained unchanged. Their economic superiority gave aristocrats the means to outshine, and even to dazzle, their less fortunate contemporaries. The museums of the

Western world today are full of the products of this urge: tripods and cauldrons, sometimes massive, statues, armor, stelae — almost all of them public dedications, intended to impress. The keeping of horses and chariots, now long outmoded as tools of battle, is simply the most obvious of the various kinds of display; and when a Greek nobleman's chariot team won a victory at one of the pan-Hellenic games, what he gained in return for expensive outlay was prestige and honor, the same *kydos* and *timē* after which the warrior-aristocrats of the Dark Age had so single-mindedly strive. It is important to stress that the relatively lavish expenditure (we must keep in mind that even the wealthiest family was rich only by Greek standards) was concentrated in buildings and objects for public display, things that all citizens could look at and admire, not on private homes and furnishings, which do not become extravagant until well into the Classical period. And that, of course, was the point. Ostentation, whether material or personal or cultural, has as its primary objective social differentiation. In a society in which the group, now institutionalized into a single organic entity, is the inescapable focus of all human activity, the means of differentiation are severely canalized. Thus the adoption of a style of life that is unmistakably "superior" assumes great importance.[37]

Greek choral lyric provides an interesting example of the connections between public display and personal or familial honor. Choral lyric was pre-eminently a phenomenon of the Archaic Age (although its greatest master, Pindar, lived until 438 B.C.). The choral ode was sung and danced by a large chorus of boys and girls (fifty is a common number) of the polis. It was thus a communal art form and an expression of the collective whole. It was also expensive, requiring elaborate costumes, payment of the poet and choirmaster and musicians. Whatever the occasion, civic, religious, or personal, the expense was borne privately. In his capacity as provider *(chorēgos)* an aristocrat both performed a public office and gained distinction in the polis for himself and his family. Choral lyric

> could only flourish where it found a well-established circle of art-loving *dilettanti* which was capable of appreciating and producing these difficult choral dances. It presupposed a society which could afford money, leisure and cultivation of the mind, and which took pleasure in elaborate and splendid performances.[38]

The aristocratic concentration on refinement and culture did not mean that the older ideal had been abandoned. One of its most eloquent spokesmen was Alcaeus, a nobleman from the island of Lesbos, who lived and wrote around 600 B.C. But even in Alcaeus, who was an aristocrat to the core, the old values are touched by the new ideas. As conscious as he was of his own class he could only view the turmoil of his native Mytilene as a citizen vitally concerned with his polis, its people and its institutions. Once, when he was in exile from Mytilene, he wrote these plaintive lines:

> I, poor wretch, live a rustic's life, yearning to hear the Assembly summoned, O Agesilaidas, and the Council; what my father and my father's father have grown old possessing, among these citizens who wrong each other, from these things I am outcast, an exile on the boundaries.
> (Fr. 130.16-24 L-P)[39]

What Alcaeus longs for most are the Council and Assembly, the living heart of the polis. In another poem, that has come down in a paraphrase by a later author, he says that "it is not stones nor timbers nor the craft of the carpenters, but, wherever there are men who know how to defend themselves, there are walls and a polis" (fr. 426 L-P). These words recall in some sense the old heroic ideal of bravery, but their main focus is the polis; Alcaeus, like Tyrtaeus, understood that the duty of fighting men is to defend the community. Another line from a much-mutilated papyrus fragment expresses the same sentiment:

> For men are the warlike tower of a polis.
> (Fr. 112.10 L-P)

The political battles of which Alcaeus speaks with so much passion were most probably not in the nature of true civil (i.e. class) war; they were partisan squabbles among the aristocratic families of Lesbos jockeying for political control.[40] On the other hand, it would be incorrect to depict the non-aristocratic population as merely passive spectators of aristocratic infighting without concern or participation. It is important to note that Alcaeus was sufficiently a man of the new polis to couch his rhetoric in terms of the larger community. Thus, in a poem directed against a former political ally, turned enemy, he says:

> Let us abate our soul-consuming discord and intestine *(emphylos)* fighting, which some Olympian has roused, bringing the *dāmos* to ruin, but to Pittacus giving glory, his heart's desire.
> (Fr. 70.10-13 L-P)

And in another poem on the same Pittacus he speaks of "rescuing the *dāmos* from distress" (fr. 129.20 L-P). Now, in both poems *dāmos*, the Aeolic form of "people," refers not to the "commons" but to the whole of the citizen body of Mytilene.[41] Indeed, in both poems Pittacus is accused of "devouring the polis," which shows that for Alcaeus polis is equivalent to *dāmos,* the human element of the state. So, this most aristocratic of men spoke, perforce, the idiom of public service, even when he meant the internal quarrels of a ruling élite.

Nevertheless, despite this wider sense of public concern, the much narrower world of the older heroic ideal had the most appeal for Alcaeus. In a long fragment the poet describes some armor, stored in his house, which he hopes will be used in the battles with his political rivals:

> The great house is agleam with bronze, and the whole roof is full-dressed with shining helmets, and from them white horsehair plumes wave down — adornments for the heads of men. Shining greaves of bronze hang round and hide the pegs — defense against the arrow's might. Corslets of new linen and hollow shields lie thrown upon the floor. By them are blades from Chalcis, and beside them many belts and tunics. These we may not forget, since first we stood to this our task.
>
> (Fr. 357 L-P)

Both the language and the spirit are heroic, but an air of unreality has been noted in the description. According to Page, Alcaeus' armory is "eccentric and relatively old-fashioned,"[42] and in this romantically vivid depiction of the armor of the single champion (there is no mention of the hoplite spear) we may perhaps detect an evocative, reminiscent, feeling, as if the poet himself suspected that the day for such bravura had passed. Could it be that even for an Alcaeus the Homeric warrior ideal had become a relic, an echo?[43] Another of his poems curiously mixes the old epic attitudes with a sense of insouciance regarding heroic exploits. It is addressed to his brother Antimenides, who had just returned from mercenary service with King Nebuchadrezzar of Babylon in his campaign against Jerusalem.

> From the ends of the earth you are come, with your sword-hilt of ivory bound with gold . . . Fighting beside the Babylonians you accomplished a great feat, and delivered them from distress, killing a warrior who lacked only one palm's breadth of five royal cubits.
>
> (Fr. 350 L-P)

The old Ideal under Challenge

Alcaeus' obvious delight in describing his brother's weapon and the height of the giant (eight feet, four inches) reflect a Homeric interest in the manly achievements of the individual warrior, but there is also no denying here what Bowra calls a "touch of gaiety in the treatment of war."[44] We are not surprised, then, that Alcaeus himself communicates in a poem to a friend how in a battle with the Athenians he had thrown away his arms and escaped whole (fr. 428 L-P). This Archilochean gesture (above, page 45) shows that the rigid heroic code of honor, even for Alcaeus, had lost much of its force; the glory of combat no longer commanded the same single-minded devotion from the aristocrat that it had earlier. True passion is reserved for politics (or for love).

A much clearer index of the evolving aristocratic ideal is seen in his characterization of his political enemy, Pittacus. We know little about Pittacus; he was, perhaps, the son of a Thracian nobleman who had attained a position of importance in Mytilene. At one time, in Alcaeus' youth, Pittacus joined the faction to which Alcaeus' family belonged, to drive out the reigning tyrant, Melanchros. Later, the alliance broke up and Pittacus associated himself with another tyrant, Myrsilus, to rule in Mytilene. When Myrsilus died Alcaeus recorded his savage jubilation at the event:

> Now must a man get drunk, and drink with might and main, for Myrsilus is dead . . .
>
> (Fr. 332 L-P)

Sometime after this, apparently, Pittacus was elected by the people of Mytilene to be *aisymnētēs*, or governor, for ten years, while Alcaeus ate out his heart in bitter exile. Pittacus' "betrayal" of the faction and the oaths of alliance he had sworn, plus his obvious popular appeal enraged Alcaeus. It is significant that in his denunciation of Pittacus the poet could think of no worse epithet than "base-born."

> The base-born *(kakopatridēs)* Pittacus they have set up as tyrant of that polis, spiritless and ill-starred; all together they shout his praises.
>
> (Fr. 348 L-P)[45]

Some lines in another fragment also appear to be a gibe at Pittacus' low birth:

> Have you, the son of such a woman, the reputation that free men, born of *esthloi* parents have . . . ?
>
> (Fr. 72.11-13 L-P)

These fragments have occasioned much controversy over whether Pittacus actually was a "commoner" or not. All the facts at our disposal (there are not many), however, show that Pittacus belonged to the best Mytilenian society into which he was accepted at the highest level.[46]

Clearly, the reason Alcaeus called Pittacus (and his other opponents) *kakopatridēs* was that by this time noble birth had become one of the most important manifestations of membership in the aristocracy. By impugning Pittacus' ancestry Alcaeus, so to speak, drummed him out of the nobility. *Kakopatris* was not the only name that Alcaeus called Pittacus. We are told that he described him as "splay-foot," "cracked-foot," "braggart," "pot-belly," "midnight glutton," and "unkempt." Other references apparently allude to Pittacus' (and his father's) heavy and intemperate drinking.[47] If our assessment of Alcaeus as one who clung tenaciously to an older conception of the good man is correct, then it is easy to see why Pittacus would be for him the antithesis of the ideal. Pittacus' foreign birth may have been the nominal basis for his being termed *kakopatridēs*, but this allegation (like the derogatory references to his appearance and habits) was after the fact. One charge levelled against Pittacus by Alcaeus, repeated several times, was that he was an oath-breaker and betrayer of comrades, a cardinal offense in the scheme of Homeric values.[48] Pittacus' real sin, accordingly, was the abandonment of the code: rejecting the narrow group, courting popular favor, and, as *aisymnētēs* (which for Alcaeus meant *tyrannos*), instituting measures that had anti-aristocratic overtones.[49]

The fact that Alcaeus chose to castigate his enemies in this particular way is significant evidence for the evolution of the aristocratic self-image. High birth and identification with a particular style of life had become more and more the indispensable proofs of an upper-class gentleman; even the inference that these were lacking was sufficient to raise serious doubts about one's position (and worth) in the society. From later sources we know that during the archaic period descriptive epithets for social groups were employed which had similar implications. In various parts of Greece, aristocrats styled themselves *eupatridai* (sons of noble fathers), *hippobotai* (horse rearers), *hippeis* (knights), *gēomoroi* (landowners), reflecting their pride of family, wealth, the aristocratic passion for horseflesh, while the lower classes were called "the naked," "club bearers," "dusty feet."[50]

The "proper" things – dress, ornamentation, hair style, the cultivation of the skills of hunting and riding, and athletics, playing a "gentleman's" musical instrument, the ability to compose spontaneously at drinking parties, knowing when to be moderate in drink and speech and (equally important) when to carouse and speak intemperately, had all become, by the beginning of the sixth century B.C., integral to the aristocratic pattern of behavior. We have already seen these ideas reflected in the poems of Mimnermus and Anacreon, full of the praises of wine and song, flowers and youths. Alcaeus is no exception, for he did not confine his lively spirit merely to political invective. A significant portion of the fragments that remain are devoted to the pleasures of drinking and friendship, and in later antiquity he had a reputation as an author of ardent love poems to boys.[51] Alcaeus, in short, may be taken as representative of the Greek aristocrat of the mid-Archaic Age: a combination of the older heroic ideal of glory and honor and the newer notions of partisan politics, pride of blood, class consciousness — all blended with a sense of nostalgic loss, bewilderment at social changes, retreat into transient pleasures. Hubert Martin's assessment is apt:

> The extant fragments lead us to conclude that Alcaeus never extended his moral vision beyond a world of masculine camaraderie and partisan politics, a world of loyalty to faction and sympotic fellowship. Yet within the narrow confines of Alcaeus' poetic cosmos, wine is a lofty and beneficent sign, conferring whatever joy and comfort this world has to offer.[52]

Still, the aristocratic concentration on pleasure was not unalloyed. Correctness of style, even here, was the moderating "form" that gave restraint and decorum to what otherwise might have degenerated into unseemly licence. Just as Alcaeus lashed out at the immoderateness of Pittacus' personal habits, so Anacreon cautions:

> But come, let us no longer pursue this Scythian kind of drinking, with din and uproar over the wine, but drink in moderation between beautiful hymns.
>
> (Fr. 356(b) Page)[53]

On the other hand, the inability of the lower classes to carry these things off well is lampooned by Anacreon:

> Once he wore a shabby tunic and a wasp-like headdress, and wooden dice in his ears, and about his ribs a bare ox-hide (the unwashed covering of a miserable shield), and mixed with bread-sellers and easy

> whores, and made a fraudulent living – the low Artemon. Often his neck was in the pillory or stretched on the wheel. Often his back was scourged with the leather whip, and his hair and beard pulled out. But now he goes around in a carriage, the son of Cyce, wearing golden earrings, and carries an ivory parasol, just like a woman.
> (Fr. 388 Page)[54]

We do not know who this Artemon was; clearly he is an example of rags-to-riches success, but for the aristocratic Anacreon he was a vulgar nobody, who, when he became prosperous, still could not disguise his low origins. In another fragment Anacreon appears to be satirizing the pretensions of a common man:

> I asked the perfume-maker Strattis if he would wear his hair long.
> (Fr. 387 Page)[55]

As a contrast to these attitudes we have some remarkable fragments of a man who was surely one of the strangest products of the lyric age of individualism. Hipponax of Ephesus, was, so far as is known, a man of good birth who had fallen on hard times. Exiled from his native city in the middle of the sixth century B.C., and penniless, he wrote bitingly satiric verses, the effect of which appears quite opposite to the aristocratic gentility of the day. While others concentrated on propriety, manners and beauty, Hipponax wrote scurrilous and obscene lampoons of his enemies and parodied his poverty, seeming almost to glory in his own abjectness:

> Hermes, dear Hermes, son of Maia, lord of Cyllene, I pray you, for I am quite chilly, give a cloak to Hipponax, and a shirt, and sandals, and winter shoes, and sixty staters of gold hidden inside the house.
> (Fr. 24a D)

In another fragment he insults the god of wealth:

> Ploutos never came to my house – for he's quite blind – and said to me, 'Hipponax, I'm giving you thirty minas of silver, and lots else besides.' For he's foolish in the head.
> (Fr. 29D)

Other lines of Hipponax, with their savage realism and abundant use of lower class slang, gave a glimpse of the life or the ordinary man and are dramatic evidence that in archaic literature there existed a kind of counter-tradition to the courtly postures of aristocratic poets like Mimnermus, Anacreon and Ibycus.[56]

Attitudes like those of Hipponax not only underscore the differences in outlook between the upper and lower classes, they also point to an increasing sense of worth on the part of the "little man," the small farmer and the medium tradesman/artisan, who had begun to formulate a social philosophy and who had found articulate spokesmen for his values.[57] As aristocrats place greater emphasis on external polish and at the same time betray a tendency towards a certain soft escapism, those who wrote in a non-aristocratic context reflect a common-sense ideal that stresses the real and the useful, and increasingly mistrusts pomp, luxury and mere appearance. Even in the sparse fragments of the lyric poets enough of this practical philosophy has come down to us to be easily identifiable. The process began early and continued through the archaic period. In the seventh century Archilochus, Tyrtaeus and Callinus had criticized aristocratic values or had recast them by stressing what was of benefit to the whole community. The sixth-century poet Xenophanes (*fl. ca.* 530 B.C.) found fault with the useless display, luxury and arrogance of the noblemen in his city, even implying that these things led to the conquest of Colophon.[58] In another poem, similar to one by Tyrtaeus, Xenophanes lists the various skills of athletes — ability in the foot race, the pentathlon, boxing, the pancratium,* chariot racing — and the glory that these win. He complains that the honors would be undeserved, for his own "wisdom" (as a poet and thinker) is superior. He concludes:

> For neither if there were a good boxer among the people, or one good at the pentathlon or in wrestling, or even in swiftness of foot (and this is the most honored of all the deeds of strength in the contests), would the polis be in better order *(eunomia)*. Small joy would it be for the polis if an athlete won by Pisa's banks, for these things do not fatten the treasury of the polis.
>
> (Fr. 2.15-22D)

By criticizing the skill of the athlete (who, at this time, would usually be a nobleman) Xenophanes attacks one of the bases of the aristocratic ideal, in both its old and new forms: its emphasis on physical prowess and individual prestige. For him the real test of worth is usefulness to the polis. Alcaeus' poetry was full of the bitter quarrels for power in

---
*An athletic contest involving both boxing and wrestling.

his native city; such divisiveness is rejected by Xenophanes in a poem on the proper behavior at banquets:

> Praise the man who, when he drinks, displays good things *(esthla)*, how he has memory, and strives after *aretē*. Do not speak of the battles of Titans or Giants or Centaurs, phantasies of old, or of violent discord *(stasis)* for there is nothing useful in these things. What is good is always to give respect to the gods.
>
> (Fr. 1.19-24D)

Again, the touchstone of value is the notion of what is useful. The word Xenophanes uses, *chrēstos*, almost always means "useful to the community," and in rejecting not only modern political strife *(stasis)* but even the mythological tales of violent intestine discord (motifs that recur again and again on the fine vases of the period), Xenophanes puts the highest premium on civic order and harmony.[59]

Xenophanes was a philosopher, and most of his poems have universal, cosmic implications; accordingly, his criticisms of aristocratic values appear somewhat detached and intellectual. A contemporary, another Ionian, Phocylides of Miletus, has a more homely touch. In the few fragments of his that have survived the common-sense views of the "ordinary" Greek of the mid-sixth century B.C. are more readily seen. His maxims, delivered in a plain unadorned style, reflect a point of view markedly different from the values expressed by the aristocratic poets of his day. For example, wealth and luxurious living, matters of great importance to the nobles of the archaic period, are reduced to the simplest level by Phocylides:

> If you desire wealth then farm a fertile piece of land; for a farm, they say, is the horn of Amaltheia.
>
> (Fr. 7D)

By equating wealth with a decent plot of farmland, Phocylides echoes faithfully the uncomplicated economic concerns of peasants since time immemorial. Equally instructive is an exchange of views, also from the mid-sixth century, which serves to underline this basic difference in outlook. An aristocratic drinking song, attributed to a certain Pythermus, contained this line:

> Except for gold, all the rest is nothing.
>
> (Fr. 910 Page)

The Old Ideal under Challenge

This was answered by some lines ascribed either to Ananius or to Hipponax:

> If someone shut up a lot of gold in a house, and a few figs, and two or three men, he'd soon know how much better figs are than gold.
>
> (Ananius fr. 2D)

Aretē (skill and its attendant accomplishments) was a constant preoccupation of the nobility of the Archaic Age; it is given a wholly different priority in this peasant precept by Phocylides:

> Seek a livelihood; and when you have a living, *aretē*.
>
> (Fr. 9D)

Since the heroic age "What people say" had been a motivating factor both for aristocrats concerned with their personal glory, and for those whose chief concern was the whole community. Phocylides naturally expresses this idea in communal terms:

> And this from Phocylides. Friend must consider with friend what citizens *(politai)* whisper around.
>
> (Fr. 5D)

This contrasts with the somewhat waspish disclaimer of the aristocratic Anacreon:

> I am not now firm-set nor easy-going with the townsmen
>
> (fr. 371 Page),

to which we may compare a similar thought by Mimnermus:

> Pleasure your own heart; for of the critical *politai* one will speak you evil, another good.
>
> (Fr. 7D)

Aristocratic concern with external appearance is criticized in these lines by Phocylides:

> Many men give the appearance of soundness, by behaving with propriety; but they are really lightweights.
>
> (Fr. 11D)

Phocylides was the first poet we know of who directly attacked the notion of high birth as a sufficient index of real worth:

> And this from Phocylides. What good is noble birth *(genos eugenes)* for those who lack grace in words and counsel?
>
> (Fr. 3D)

The ordinary man sets his sights piously low, eschewing pretence and pride in favor of stability, whether it is his polis —

> And this from Phocylides. A small polis, dwelling orderly on a height is greater than foolish Ninevah
>
> (fr. 4D)

or his own place in the polis:

> Much advantage to those who are the middle; I want to be middle in the polis.
>
> (Fr. 12D)

One striking statement preserved in Phocylides is dramatic evidence that for some Greeks a revaluation of the traditional conception of *aretē* had taken place. Since Hesiod, non-aristocratic writers had placed great emphasis on justice; in a remarkable fragment Phocylides equates the abstract idea of justice *(dikaiosynē)* with *aretē:*

> In *dikaiosynē* is summed up all *aretē*.
>
> (Fr. 10D)[60]

The new spirit of independence and sense of worth of the non-noble citizen is reflected in an unexpected source. Solon, famed as the great lawgiver of Athens, and an aristocrat, was elected chief magistrate *(archōn)* in 594 B.C. with apparently extraordinary powers to effect political and economic reforms. It is not possible to discuss in detail Solon's far-reaching legislative measures, designed to head off political and economic disaster, but a brief outline of conditions there will help to illuminate the statesman's words. When Solon became archon the wealthy upper class not only controlled political and religious offices but was also exploiting its natural economic advantages. Many of the small farmers had mortgaged their lands to their prosperous neighbors; because of debt some were reduced to a condition of dependency, having to pay a portion of their annual produce to the mortgage holders;

The Old Ideal under Challenge 69

and some, having offered their own persons as surety for debt, and being unable to pay, had even been sold as slaves. Chief among Solon's economic measures was the cancelling of debts owed on land and persons and the forbidding of future debt-slavery by making it unlawful to contract debts on the security of one's person. He thus saved the free peasant population of Attica from possible economic ruin at the hands of the noble landowners. He also made important constitutional changes, creating four new "classes" of citizenship based on annual wealth instead of birth, strengthening the citizen assembly, and instituting a strong popular court.

Because we are better informed about Athens than about any other Greek polis, it is well to pause briefly here and compare the historical background of the situation at Athens with what has been said in general about institutional development in Greece — always keeping in mind, of course, that all *poleis* evolved in response to their own particular socioeconomical circumstances and at their own pace. The territory of Attica, which comprised the polis of Athens, was very large by Greek standards (1000 square miles), consisting of three plains divided by high hills and containing a number of separate settlements. In the Dark Age these communities were ruled by tribal chiefs *(basileis)*. According to later Athenian tradition, one ranking chief, Theseus, effected a "combining" *(synoikismos)* of the separate towns and villages into a single state, with the largest town, Athens, as its center. For the classical Athenians this unification took place at a very early date (Theseus, whose very existence is problematical, would have lived before the Trojan War), but modern opinion holds that, while *synoikismos* may have begun relatively early, it was a gradual process that occurred mostly during the eighth century and was not totally completed until after 700 B.C. Unification will have been the work of strong chiefs attempting to mold a centralized chiefdom. Following the pattern observed elsewhere, the ranking lineage (the Medontidai) supplied the dominant chief, until at some time (about 750) his power was eroded by competing chiefs who instituted other offices — *archōn* (leader), *polemarchos* (war-leader)—which incorporated the political and military functions of the *basileus,* who retained only minimal authority, mainly religious. The stages in the change from a "centralized" chiefdom (never firmly established, as we have seen) to a system of collegial authority distributed among heads of lineages are obscure to us. Scholars disagree over the details and the chronology, but the general outlines are plain enough. By about 700 B.C. the Attic communities had been formed into a single state, "the Athenians," controlled by powerful local descent groups by means of annually elected magistrates and other aristocratic bodies, such as the Council of the Areopagus. In Athens, as in other aristocratic Greek states, the ruling families competed among themselves, each family group, with its local dependents, trying to solidify and increase its circle of power and influence. In the process the *eupatridai* ("descendants of noble fathers") exploited their position to the economic and political disadvantage of the common citizens. One result of this infighting was the attempt by one or another of the aristocrats to usurp authority as a *tyrannos* with the support of the discontented farmers. In 632 Cylon, a wealthy eupatrid, whose prestige was high because of a recent Olympic victory and whose power base had been enlarged by marriage to the daughter of Theagenes, the new tyrant of nearby Megara, attempted such a coup, aided by his kinsmen, his followers, and men supplied by his father-in-law. It failed, presumably because of insufficient support from the people, whose grievances had not reached the point of active withdrawal of allegiance from their local leaders. The continuing economic and political distress caused by the incessant feuding and competition for prestige among the nobility, together with a growing consciousness of unity, the result of the polis form itself and the hoplite "reform," gave rise to calls for relief measures. One such step was the reduction to writing and public posting in 621 B.C. of at least some parts of unwritten custom/law, hitherto arbitrarily enforced and unevenly interpreted by heads of kinship groups. The "law code" of Draco had the effect of concentrating the process of justice in the state itself to some extent, thereby partly diminishing the exclusive and hereditary exercise of legal authority by local aristocrats. Lawgivers like Draco were a phenomenon of the seventh century in a number of Greek states; their reforms were regarded as a democratizing influence by the later Greeks, and most modern opinion agrees.

By 600 B.C. in Athens the economic woes of the small farmers reached the point where they would either have degenerated into a position of total dependency on the wealthy landowners or have resorted to civil war. The worsening social crisis, which brought forth the call for redistribution of the land in Attica, inspired the extraordinary spate of relieving legislation by Athens' second great lawgiver. It remains only to add that while Solon's reforms did avert the bloody *stasis* he warned about and did save the free peasantry (who also formed the bulk of the hoplite force), the root causes of the economic inequality were not extirpated. Athens later experienced her own tyranny when Pisistratus, a prominent eupatrid, after two abortive attempts succeeded in establishing himself as tyrant in 546, with broad-based popular support. Such were the prelude and aftermath to Solon's appearance in history, a scenario which, in this general form, was common to many Greek states of the Archaic Age.

Although he styled himself a mediator between the two opposing groups in the state, it is quite clear that Solon's sympathy was with the non-noble element in Athenian society.[61] In his poems many of the now familiar themes of a tradition hostile to aristocracy are evident. Especially prominent is his characterization of the nobles as greedy and unjust. In a long philosophical poem Solon states the principle that while wealth is good it must be gained righteously. Wealth that the gods give will last, but,

> that which men seek through violence *(hybris)* comes not orderly, but persuaded against its will by unjust *(adika)* deeds it comes, and ruin is quickly mixed in.
>
> (Fr. 1.11-13D)[62]

He returns to this topic later in the same poem:

> But of wealth no limit is set that men can see; for those of us now who have the greatest means are doubly eager; for who could satisfy all?
>
> (Fr. 1.71-73D)

In another fragment, composed before he completed his reforms, Solon severely lectures the powerful:

> The townsmen themselves, persuaded by wealth, wish to destroy a mighty polis through their foolishness. The mind of the leaders of the *dēmos* is *adikos*, and many woes are at hand for them to suffer because of their great *hybris*. For they do not know how to keep from excess, nor to conduct in decency and in peace the present pleasures of their feasts . . . and they grow rich, persuaded by *adika* deeds . . .
>
> (Fr. 3.5-11D)

He goes on in the poem to accuse the nobles of public and private plundering, and of disregard for *Dikē*. These things cause "an inescapable wound to the whole polis" which will soon fall into an evil servitude; civil discord and war will result. He makes references to the aristocratic political "clubs" which he calls "dear to the unjust." He finally makes an appeal to "good order" *(eunomia)* which checks excess and *hybris,* straightens crooked judgments, tames arrogant deeds, stops faction and strife (12-39). Solon cautions the wealthy in lines that remind us of Phocylides' wish to be midmost *(mesos)* in the polis:

> You who have pushed into an excess of many good things, calm the strong heart in your breasts, and put your high thoughts in bounds *(metrioi).* For we shall never yield, nor will all be good for you.
>
> (Fr. 4.5-8)

The catalogue of aristocratic faults is impressive: greed, injustice, violence, excess, love of luxury, factionalism, arrogance. The ills these produce are stated in terms of the harm to the whole community. Solon in his poems reflects faithfully the major elements of the common man's view of the aristocracy.

Solon himself was enough of an aristocrat to employ aristocratic terminology; nobles are *agathoi* or *esthloi,* non-nobles are *kakoi.*[63] In other respects, too, he was representative of his class. Two fragments survive which are typical of his milieu:

> Until in the lovely flowering of youth he love a boy *(paidophileō),* desiring thighs and sweet mouth.
>
> (Fr. 12D)

And,

> The works of the Cyprus-born are dear to me, and of Dionysis and of the Muses; these make good cheer for men.
>
> (Fr. 20D)

No less aristocratic is this thought:

> Happy the man who has dear children, single-hooved horses, hunting dogs and a guest-friend from a foreign land.
>
> (Fr. 13D)

Despite these aristocratic sentiments Solon's outlook differed greatly from that of his contemporaries. Mimnermus had written

> Without disease and grievous cares, I hope that the fate of death may find me at sixty years.
>
> (Fr. 6D)

This typical piece of pessimism was corrected by Solon in a fragment containing the line,

> May the fate of death find me at eighty years

and which ends,

> I grow old ever learning many things.[64]
>
> (Fr. 22D)

Not only in his major legislative and economic reforms, which diminished the power and influence of the old nobility and increased that of the *dēmos,* but also in his minor measures Solon evidenced concern about unbridled aristocratic influence. Like those of Pittacus and other lawgivers and tyrants, they were aimed at curbing aristocratic excess. Later commentators mention his laws against overly lavish funeral expenses, regulation of the prizes and emoluments given to victors in the games and his distrust of the high honors accorded athletes.[65] Modern historians, echoing the ancient controversy, still argue whether Solon was really a "democrat" or an "oligarch." Aside from the fact that these terms (and hence the concepts) did not yet exist in Greece, what is known of Solon's life and career shows plainly that he was an aristocrat, brought up in the old traditions, who recognized that these values would have to yield to new currents of social changes. As a statesman he knew that the good of the *total* community was the truly important concern; thus equally abhorrent to him were civil discord *(stasis),* rule by one man, the nobility's greed for wealth and power, and the *dēmos'* attempts to seize power themselves. He was, in this respect, a mediator:

> I stood, casting a strong shield over both sides, and I allowed neither to win unjustly.
>
> (Fr. 5.5-6D)

And,

> I took my stand between them, like a boundary stone in the midst of no man's land.
>
> (Fr. 25.8-9D)

But, instinctively perhaps, his greatest sympathy was with the common man. Once, in a complete reversal of the usual aristocratic terminology, he calls the poor *agathoi* and the rich *kakoi:*

For many *kakoi* are rich, and *agathoi* poor; but we will not exchange with them *aretē* for wealth . . .

(Fr. 4.9-11D)

This is a very strong statement. Not only does Solon identify himself with the *agathoi* poor, he places wealth in direct opposition to *aretē*. According to the old epic-aristocratic system of values wealth was an essential ingredient of *aretē*, but by now this latter concept had been modified to the extent that wealth could be depicted as an impediment to it.[66]

◊

The evidence discussed in this chapter shows a pattern of attitudes that was evolving steadily and in a particular direction. At the beginning of the seventh century aristocratic groups enjoyed political, social and economic advantages that gave them great power in the developing Greek states. But the urge for domination, inherent in the traditional agonal code of superiority, led to factionalism among aristocratic families; their struggles for prestige among themselves resulted in economic oppression of the people as the nobles competed for the small surpluses of production that would solidify and enlarge their power base. Although the economic expansion of the seventh and sixth centuries did increase the available resources and raise the general level of prosperity, the steadily growing wealth of aristocratic families merely accelerated their need for more; increasingly aristocrats were perceived as greedy and unjust, provoking discontent and giving rise to anti-aristocratic reaction. At the same time, the polis, which by its very nature emphasized the unity and solidarity of its citizen body, provided a counterforce against rampant individualism and the social disorder that resulted from the centrifugal effect of aristocratic factionalism. Also, the new prosperity was shared to some extent both by the small group of non-aristocratic artisans and traders and by the moderately prosperous middling farmers, who still had little share in the governance of the state. The hoplite "revolution" was intimately connected with these factors. On the one hand it made the small and middling farmer the bulwark of the polis' security and diminished the traditional role of the warrior-élite; on the other hand, it fueled the feeling of worth and importance of the ordinary spearman in the ranks. Economic distress among the free peasantry threatened their ability to participate in the phalanx, thus posing a danger to the polis at the very time that warfare between city-states began to increase. These interacting forces led to the phenomenon of tyrants, lawgivers and elected semi-tyrants (such as Pittacus and Solon) who promoted the welfare of the majority against the privilege of the dominant class. During the sixth century, as a result of the manifold social pressures unleashed by the transition from tribe to polis, "the upper classes tended to lose part of their political and economic preeminence."[67] Many of these same forces insured the persistence of the ancient egalitarianism, despite the aristocracy's attempt to establish itself as a true ruling class of birth and wealth. As Polanyi perceptively noted, "The *demos* was heir to the tribal tradition of equality. The dichotomy between the *demos* and the oligarchs was fundamentally a continuance of the archaic distinction between the tribe and the manorial households that grew up outside the tribal confines."[68]

By the middle of the sixth century B.C. the old aristocratic certitudes no longer had their previous force; many of the stoutly held tenets of the traditional value system had come under fire, had been taken over (appropriately transvalued) by the mass of citizens, or had been subsumed into a communal ideal which could be claimed by all free citizens. The aristocratic class, its prestige lessened, had reacted by altering its frame of values in an attempt to prove its superiority and maintain its position of natural leadership. One way was to place greater emphasis on qualities that the lower class could not claim, such as noble birth, or to adopt a style of life that stressed external elegance and good breeding along with conspicuous display. Reaction was inevitable; upper-class claims to superiority were criticized and challenged, largely on the basis that they were not functionally useful to the polis.

The net effect of the social tensions generated, the claims and the counterclaims, was that the aristocratic élite was forced to turn increasingly inward, striving to fashion an image that could not easily be emulated or challenged. The directional thrust of the changing aristocratic ideal was into the areas of intellectual, moral and aesthetic excellence; and from the middle of the sixth century B.C. on, aristocratic spokesmen incorporated these ideas into their pattern of values, even as they continued to emphasize their claims to eminence based on birth, style of life, and, of course, value to the polis.

Ω

CHAPTER THREE
The Crisis of Identity: Theognis and Pindar

THE FORFEITURE of their claim to an unchallenged, "natural" superiority had produced a kind of "crisis of identity" among aristocrats by about the middle of the sixth century B.C. To meet the challenge of diminished political and economic hegemony and to counter the rise of an alternative pattern of values which subsumed or appropriated the traditional claims of aristocratic worth or downgraded them, and which favored cooperative and egalitarian behavior over the competitive and exclusivistic, aristocrats concentrated on formulating a conception of nobility that would be immune to discredit—or imitation. This they achieved by stressing qualities of the inner spirit: superior sensibility and sensitivity, wisdom, grace, and, ultimately, "moral" goodness.

We are fortunate to have a relatively large body of evidence in the poems of Theognis and Pindar. Theognis of Megara was an aristocrat (*fl. ca.* 540 B.C.), under whose name has come down a collection of almost 1400 lines of elegiac poetry known as the *Theognidea*. Not all of these are by Theognis himself; some are evidently later additions, while others are found in the writings of various lyric-age poets such as Mimnermus, Tyrtaeus and Solon. Nevertheless, the prevailing opinion is that the majority of verses in the first book (lines 1-1230) are from the period of Theognis' own lifetime, or earlier, and that few of the lines are later than the first quarter of the fifth century.[1] Also, despite a few contradictory passages, the "tone" of the *Theognidea* is uniformly aristocratic, and it is a safe assertion that the poems faithfully reflect aristocratic views current in Greece from the middle of the sixth century B.C. down to the beginning of the fifth century.

A brief survey of Theognis' usage of the words for "good" and "bad" will demonstrate not only his totally aristocratic thought structure but also the new directions in the aristocratic self-conception. The terms *agathos-esthlos* and their opposites, *kakos-deilos,* occur in the

Theognidea with greater statistical frequency than in any other archaic author.[2] Often *agathoi-esthloi* are used by Theognis to mean the "nobles," and *kakoi-deiloi* to signify "commoners," as automatic designators of social class; there are frequent occasions, however, when the terms appear to have a strictly moral frame of reference (that is, with no overt sociopolitical implications) or where the line between moral and class usage is unclear. The reason for this semantic blurring, obvious even on a casual reading of the *Theognidea,* has already been implied. To aristocrats of the sixth century a distinction between *agathos*-"aristocrat" (defined in terms of bloodlines, wealth and position) and *agathos*- "good man" (defined in terms of correct behavior) no longer existed. In addition, as symbols of moral worth, the merit-demerit words came more and more to express qualities of internal goodness rather than external characteristics conducive to success or failure. The Theognidean *agathos* exhibited a set of excellences which were traits of character, but which also were confined to men who, by birth and breeding, belonged to a specific social group. The morally good man, in other words, was the aristocrat, and only the aristocrat could be a morally good man.[3] This shift in aristocratic usage is no less significant a clue to changing social attitudes than the one occasioned by the egalitarian spirit of the seventh and sixth centuries which had altered the epic conception of the *agathos* by narrowing its application to steadfastness in the ranks and usefulness to the community.

In the *Theognidea* there is evidence of the tensions caused by non-noble reaction to aristocratic control of the epithets *agathos* and *esthlos*. In some revealing lines the poet talks about those who once wore their ragged goatskins to pieces and "pastured" like deer outside the city—men who knew neither "justice" nor "laws." Now, he says, addressing his friend, Cyrnus,

> these are *agathoi,* son of Polypaus, and those who were *esthloi* before are now *deiloi*
>
> (53-60).

The same thought, expanded, appears in lines 1109-12:

> Cyrnus, those who were *agathoi* once are now *kakoi;* and those who were *kakoi* before are now *agathoi*. Who could bear seeing this, the *agathoi* in lesser honor and the *kakiones* getting *timē*?

The meaning of the complaint is crystal clear. Theognis wants desperately to keep the old designations of class. He does, in fact, but he is forced to admit that those whom he considered naturally inferior had laid claim to the epithets of worth—and had made them stick. Men, who because of their background, were naturally *kakoi*—"base," "worthless"—had become *agathoi/esthloi,* "worthy"; that is, they were calling themselves *agathoi* and were considered so in the community, because they were doing what *agathoi* do: voting, gaining wealth, holding some offices, fighting in the phalanx. These lines show that by the middle of the sixth century B.C. the attempt on the part of the nobility to maintain *agathos* and *esthlos* as exclusive descriptive epithets for the upper class had failed.

There are further revealing signs in Theognis' usage of these terms. We have seen that from the earliest times *agathos* (and, to a lesser degree, *esthlos*) was primarily a predicate of physical excellence, more specifically as this excellence pertained to warcraft. In the intervening period such words had tended to lose their basically physical connotation, to be sure, but it is somewhat startling to realize that in the whole of the *Theognidea,* where the words *agathos* and *esthlos* occur so frequently, and where the sentiment is uniformly aristocratic, the old sense of "brave" is simply not found. As we see it in the Theognidean corpus the ideal of the aristocratic gentleman gives little importance to the old qualities of physical courage or to skill in war. Theognis' retreat from the traditional preoccupation with war and its glory is indicative of the inward-turning character of the evolving aristocratic ideal. The utterly unwarlike wish:

> May peace and wealth embrace the polis, so that I might revel with others—I do not love evil war. And do not listen hard to the loudly-shouting herald—for we are not fighting for our own native land
> (885-88)

is merely underscored by the disclaimer:

> But it would be a disgraceful thing *(aischron)* not to mount swift-footed steeds and look tearful war in the face.
> (889-90).

The fact that *agathos-esthlos* never occur with the meaning "brave" in the *Theognidea* is perhaps the logical culmination of the "softening" observed in near contemporaries, like Anacreon.[4] A drinking song, attributed to Anacreon, opens:

> Him I do not love who, drinking wine over a full bowl, speaks of strife and tearful war; but rather one who, mixing the glorious

gifts of the Muses and of Aphrodite, remembers our lovely feasting.

(Fr. 96D)

Other mentions by Anacreon of war have a melancholy and reluctant tone. Once he refers to someone who "fell in love with the bloody spear-point" (fr. 382 Page). In another he says: "He that wishes to fight, let him fight, for he may" (fr. 429 Page.)[5]

When we inquire more deeply into Theognis' conception of the "good" man we find further confirmation of the new dimension in aristocratic thought. In Theognis the claim of pre-eminence on the basis of noble birth appears more explicit than in previous authors. In lines 183-192 he complains to his companion Cyrnus that although men desire their stock animals to be "well-born" *(eugeneis)*, an *esthlos* man will, for the sake of money, marry "the *kakē* daughter of a *kakos* man." The result, he says, is that "wealth has corrupted race." The same note is sounded in the following lines (193-96), where a man knowingly marries a *kakopatris*, "persuaded by wealth." In other passages the doctrine that good and bad qualities are determined by birth, a concept destined to be a favorite one of aristocrats, is, for the first time in Greek literature, plainly spelled out:

> It is easier to beget and to rear a man than to put good wits in him. No one yet has devised a way to make a fool *(aphrōn)* into a man of good sense *(sōphrōn)* or an *esthlos* from a *kakos* . . . but by teaching never will you make the *kakos* man an *agathos*
>
> (429-38).[6]

Theognis' attitudes towards wealth also reveal a shift in the aristocratic value system. At first glance the many references to wealth in the *Theognidea* seem confused and contradictory. Some of them are the traditional gnomic commonplaces that had become part and parcel of early Greek ethical thought, such as the prescription that wealth was a good thing to have, but only if it was acquired honorably, or the observation that poverty is evil. But alongside these typical statements are others which show that different ideas concerning wealth were becoming part of the aristocratic scheme. Historically, of course, wealth was a distinguishing mark of the nobleman. In Homer, for example, there was no hint that wealth was not an automatic sign of merit; it was good, it was necessary, and it was an obvious by-product of the martial skill of the Homeric *agathos;* and, in general, throughout most of the archaic

The Crisis of Identity: Theognis and Pindar

period wealth was considered to be a positive good and poverty an unmitigated evil (along with the strictures noted above). All the evidence, moreover, indicates that down to about 600 B.C. nobility of birth and the possession of wealth were inseparably linked. The few statements in the literature that can be construed as negative attitudes towards wealth come from those who represent a non-aristocrat viewpoint. Most noteworthy are the disclaimer of Charon the "carpenter" in Archilochus, who says that he cares not for the wealth of golden Gyges, and statements of Solon, who not only makes a dramatic distinction between wealth and *aretē*, but also makes it clear that aristocrats were synonymous with the wealthy. There is a two-line fragment of Alcaeus that does, however, seem to contradict the view that only aristocrats had wealth. The aristocratic Alcaeus, purporting to quote a certain Spartan named Aristodamos, says:

> **Money makes the man; no poor man *(penichros)* is good *(eslos)* or honored *(timios)*.**
>
> (Fr. 360 L-P; cf. fr. 364)

This seems to be a complaint of sorts, in which Alcaeus states that without wealth a man had little social and political status, which in turn would appear to imply that there were in Lesbos non-nobles who had money and nobles who were impoverished and who had lost some of their social standing. If this is so, we may suspect that by around 600 B.C. the complacent truism that wealth was the obvious companion of the man of good birth and that poverty was the natural state of the non-noble had begun to lose its force. The corrective that must immediately be applied is that Alcaeus' isolated statement can in no way be construed as evidence of a dramatic or universal shift in the socioeconomic *status quo*. For an aristocrat like Alcaeus even a few examples of non-nobles rising in wealth to challenge the aristocratic assumption would be provocation enough to take up his pen.

The main, and only reasonable, conclusion to be drawn is that at this point in the archaic period (around the early 500's) wealth was ceasing to be an exclusive attribute of those who claimed eminence in the community. We must also understand clearly what the distinction between "wealth" and "poverty" actually meant to the ancient Greeks. It has already been noted that the gap between the wealthiest and poorest citizen was not absolutely great. And, for the Greeks of the Archaic and Classical periods a wealthy man *(plousios)* was one who could live comfortably, independently, and with leisure on his "income." A poor man *(penēs)* was constrained to toil for his livelihood. A *penēs* was not a pauper; he was typically a small farmer, tradesman or artisan (who might even have a slave or two) whose time was spent in physical work.[7] The new opportunities and the general increase in prosperity that attended the economic expansion of the seventh and sixth centuries will have seen the rise of men, not members of the landowning nobility, to the category of the "wealthy," as the Greeks understood it. This (never very large) group is sometimes referred to by modern historians as "nouveaux riches," but that term, with its misleading historical connotations, exaggerates the rather modest, if crucial, rise in absolute economic status that so troubled aristocrats like Theognis.[8] So, the apparently untypical attitudes towards wealth in the *Theognidea* became easier to understand. We have already noted a negative tone in Theognis' statements on wealth. He complains that the lure of wealth will cause a "mixing up" of the race when *agathos* and *kakos* marry (183-92) and he realizes that the threat of poverty will force an *agathos* to marry a *kakopatris* (193-96). It is not surprising, then, to find that very seldom in the *Theognidea* does wealth emerge as an unmixed good. To be sure he feels that it is fitting for the *agathos* to be rich and the *kakos* to be poor:

> For in truth, it is right that the *agathoi* have wealth, while poverty is proper for a *kakos* man to bear
>
> (525-26).[9]

Also, Theognis never admits that poverty is anything but a total evil. This is a conventional Greek attitude, of course; nowhere in the literature of this period can we find even a hint that poverty should be regarded as something else than catastrophic.[10] Nevertheless, a Hipponax could at least mock his own poverty, while in the *Theognidea* it is painted in the most lurid terms:

> Poverty depresses an *agathos* man more than all else, even more than gray old age, Cyrnus, and disease
>
> (173-74)

and a man should do anything to avoid it (175-80). Even death, he tells Cyrnus, is preferable for a poor man than to live "worn away by harsh poverty" (181-82). The passages on poverty in the collection have an especially bitter ring that seems to go beyond the standard commonplaces. We may conclude that for someone like Theognis the prospect of being poor was doubly unbearable, because it represented for him a perversion of the natural order. In a revealing personal passage he says:

> If I had wealth, Simonides, equal to my character *(ēthē)* I would not be distressed being with the *agathoi.* But now it passes by me, whom it knew, and I am speechless from want . . . The Cargo-carriers *(phortēgoi)* are in command, and the *kakoi* are above the *agathoi*
> (667-79).

His chagrin at this state of affairs is expressed in these lines:

> Many ignorant men have wealth; but those who seek the beautiful *(ta kala)* are worn away by harsh poverty
> (683-84).

Other testimony in Theognis helps to sharpen the picture of frustrated and impotent anger. Whereas for a peasant like Hesiod wealth was acquired by hard, manual labor, Theognis concludes that wealth is bestowed by chance or by the gods—and it is given to the *kakoi* often:

> Fate *(daimōn)* gives wealth even to the man who is completely worthless *(pankakos),* but to few men is given the measure of *aretē*
> (149-50).

The theme of a capricious fate rewarding those who are his moral inferiors is sounded again and again in Theognis; these pathetic lines sum up his attitude:

> O Wealth, fairest and most desirable of all the gods, with your help even one who is *kakos* becomes an *anēr esthlos*
> (1117-18).[11]

In many of the passages on wealth there is a strong moral note; poverty *forces* men to do things that are ethically wrong. Just as we have seen it compelling an *agathos* to marry a base-born woman for the sake of gain, so "harsh poverty"

> teaches me, against my will, by force, many shameless things *(aischra)* although I understand what is good *(esthla)* and noble *(kala)* among men
> (651-52).[12]

Out of the mélange of statements on wealth in the aristocratic corpus we know as the *Theognidea* a fairly coherent thematic line emerges—not so much a *new* attitude *vis à vis* earlier authors but an exaggeration and a shifting of attitude: the dangers of greed, which is often associated with the *kakoi*;[13] poverty leads to a moral dissolution; wealth has nothing to do with merit, but without it one is nothing; wealth can transform a *kakos* into an *agathos*. Most tellingly, the overwhelming impression of the passages on wealth and poverty is that those who have it are the *kakoi* and that those who are poor are the *agathoi*. An illustration of Theognis' tendency to connect wealth with the *kakoi*, and to see social and economic changes as proof of the moral inferiority of the lower classes is provided by a comparison with Solon. Solon, among whose concerns was the greed of the aristocrats, also cautions the *dēmos* against the desire for undue wealth. In one fragment he warns them in general terms:

> For surfeit *(koros)* breeds insolence *(hybris)* when great prosperity attends . . .
>
> (Fr. 5.9D)

In Theognis one word is changed to give the line a definite class bias:

> For *koros* breeds *hybris* when prosperity attends a *kakos* . . .
>
> (154).

The implications of this altered perspective as it reflects on a changing social and economic climate are great, if difficult to ascertain; but one thing is quite certain – the simple possession of wealth could no longer be regarded as proof of social superiority, and accordingly, could not figure decisively in the new aristocratic ideal.[14]

The reason for the strongly ethical tone of Theognis' statements on wealth emerges when we consider that Theognis is searching for qualities that make the *agathoi* an exclusive group – qualities that had not already been usurped by people lower on the social scale. Since superior military value or wealth no longer sharply distinguished the nobles from the non-nobles, and because the one certain mark of exclusiveness, birth, was being tainted by intermarriage, a more inwardly-directed set of values had to be paraded forth; and even, paradoxically, a sort of conscious reversal of the older standards. Thus the possession and acquisition of wealth, once an external sign of aristocratic *aretē*, can now be contraposed to *aretē*. In a rather odd passage, reminiscent of Tyrtaeus' fr. 9, but in a perverse sense, he says:

> To the mass *(plēthos)* of men this has become the single *aretē*, to be rich
>
> (699-700).

He then enumerates other *aretai:* wisdom, cunning, knowledge, rhetorical ability, swiftness of foot, saying that these are nothing compared to wealth. He ends (717-18):

> But all men must commit this maxim to memory: In every situation wealth has the most power.

Tyrtaeus, he implies, recognized manly courage as the "single *aretē*," but this age has as its "sole virtue" the acquisition of wealth. Such a strongly negative attitude points to a radical reshaping of aristocratic priorities.[15]

Some time has been spent examining Theognis' attitudes about wealth because the downgrading of wealth as a differentiating social criterion is a startling reversal of traditional aristocratic values. The divorce of wealth from birth was, without doubt, the most damaging blow to aristocratic pretensions to superiority. Inseparable for generations, their combined force as controlling social mechanisms was unassailable. When acquisition of some wealth apart from noble birth became possible, and when occasionally people of good family made marital alliances with non-aristocrats for economic advantage, a powerful psychological edge was lost. I hasten to add that the combination remained generally effective throughout Greek history simply because families of prominent lineage continued, as a rule, to be the largest landholders. Simonides of Ceos (*ca.* 556-468 B.C.), when asked who the well-born *(eugeneis)* were, is said to have replied, "those who are rich *(plousiòi)* of old"; and in the fourth century Aristotle could still describe aristocratic governments as those that chose officials not only according to wealth *(ploutindēn)* but also according to excellence of birth *(aristindēn).* Nevertheless, once the twin supports of the traditional power structure became separable, each lost something of its aura. Thus, by about 410 B.C. Euripides could generalize that wealth *(chrēmata)* was the most honored thing and confers the most power *(dynamis),* while a poor man of noble birth *(penēs eugenēs anēr)* was of no account *(ouden).*[16]

Theognis' statements on politics are as revealing as his attitudes towards wealth and birth. Political power (or its erosion) is no less a matter of perception than a tangible reality. Like the possession of wealth, political leadership had traditionally been the preserve of aristocrats.

During most of the archaic period in Greece politics were dominated by men of noble families; in almost all the Greek states magisterial offices were in fact, if not in theory, held exclusively by those in the upper class. We should expect political prominence to play an important and self-evident role in the aristocratic ideal, but, interestingly, the *Theognidea* is ambiguous about this. At times the corpus appears to presuppose that the *agathoi* wield political power. Cyrnus is advised not to associate with the *kakoi*, but to eat, drink and sit with the *agathoi*, and to please them "whose power *(dynamis)* is great" (31-34; cf. 411-12). Theognis understands the use of power in the hands of a strong man:

> Step on the empty-headed *dēmos;* strike them with a goad that's sharp, and place a heavy yoke on them

because nowhere else is there a

> *dēmos* that loves a despot so
>
> (847-50).

Elsewhere he reflects the typical attitudes of an aristocratic statesman:

> I shall put in order my native land, my shining polis, turning neither to the *dēmos* nor heeding unjust men
>
> (947-48).

These lines, whether by the "real" Theognis or not, express the perfectly predictable aristocratic outlook of men who felt they had a natural right to rule. They are, however, the only passages in the *Theognidea* which indicate that the *agathoi* possessed political power.[17] All other politically oriented passages seem to imply that the lower class also wielded political power:

> And now the evils of the *agathoi* have become good for the *kakoi;* and they rule with perverse laws
>
> (289-90).

The complaint that "the cargo-carriers are in command, and the *kakoi* are above the *agathoi*" (679) has already been quoted.[18] Theognis is no less bitter at what appears to him to be a loss of power and prestige among members of his class. Lines 233-34,

> An *esthlos* man, Cyrnus, who is a citadel and a tower to an empty-headed *dēmos*, receives a tiny portion of honor *(timē)*,

find other echoes: "Reputation *(doxa)* often attends the fool, and one who is *kakos* gets *timē*" (665-66); "the *agathoi* are more dishonored, the *kakiones* get *timē*" (1111-12). Related to this sense of impotence and symptomatic of the inward-turning trend in aristocratic values is the almost total absence in the *Theognidea* of appeal to patriotism and duty to the polis.[19]

The evidence of the Theognid poems makes one conclusion inevitable: the traditional assertions of superiority made by the upper class had become less effective, because by the last half of the sixth century B.C. non-aristocrats had, with some success, appropriated all or most of the indicators of civic excellence. Accordingly, we look for the ideal of the *anēr agathos* of Theognis and other aristocrats of the period to be expressed in terms of inner worth; his virtues will be "quiet" ones, and the focus will be increasingly ethical-moral.

In the ideal of the good man as seen in the *Theognidea* a prominent place is given to friendship and its attendant virtues, loyalty and trustworthiness. These notions have a strong social flavor; an *agathos* is a true friend and worthy of trust, a *kakos* cannot be trusted. Corollary to this is the constant advice to associate only with *agathoi* and to shun the *kakoi*, since the former are beneficial, the latter are harmful. The "good" are the repositories of all sound advice and are therefore the teachers from whom one should learn. These ideas give a kind of didactic organization to the collection. At the outset we hear (27-28):

> Because I am well-disposed towards you, I shall give you the same advice, Cyrnus, that I learned from the *agathoi* while still a child,

and,

> ... do not associate with *kakoi andres* but always hold close to the *agathoi*
>
> (31-32).[20]

To love one's friends and hate one's enemies had been a norm of Greek ethical thought from earliest times (e.g. *Odyssey* 6.184; Solon 1.5-6D, etc.). This standard is amply reflected in the *Theognidea* (e.g. 337-38, 561-62, 1087-90). But for Theognis friendship has a *moral* dimension unparalleled in earlier writings. He complains that he cannot find anyone who is as faithful a comrade *(pistos hetairos)* and free of trickery *(dolos)* as himself (415-16). He boasts that he never betrayed a friend who was a *pistos hetairos* – adding significantly that there is nothing slavish *(doulion)* in his soul (529-30). Betrayal by friends, he tells Cyrnus, is almost as dreadful as death (811-12). Lines 87-92 may be taken as a summary statement of Theognis' insistence on honesty and loyalty as preconditions for friendship:

> Do not love me with words (and yet keep your mind and heart otherwise) if you are my friend and your mind within is *pistos*. But be a friend with a pure mind, or reject me and hate me in open quarrel. Whoever has a split mind, with one tongue, Cyrnus, is a dangerous companion (better as an enemy than as a friend).[21]

Such fear and distrust is a change from an earlier ideal of friendship which simply assumed that friends were loyal. We must not be overly surprised, then, if Theognis advises his heart to show a "shifting nature towards all friends," and, like the octopus, who can change his shape at will, to adapt one's feelings to suit (213-17; cf. 73-76). The use of cunning and guile towards enemies (as in 363-64) is one thing, but to adopt such a stance with friends is a sign that the moral universe of aristocrats was in disarray. The factionalism and consequent shifting of loyalties among the upper class had blurred the sharp outlines of an older, simpler ideal. Loyalty is now contingent on political conditions:

> In times of harsh discord *(dichostasiē)*, Cyrnus, a faithful *(pistos)* man is worthy of being valued equally with gold and silver. Few comrades will you find, son of Polypaus, who remain *pistoi* in difficult circumstances
>
> (77-80; cf. 209-10).

The atmosphere is heavy with distrust:

> If someone praises you as long as he sees you, and behind your back employs an evil tongue, such a comrade *(hetairos)* is no very good friend ...
>
> (93-95).
>
> No one wants to be a friend when evil comes to a man, Cyrnus, not even if he is born of the same womb
>
> (299-300; cf. 575-76).

True moral probity transcends the "party-principle" basis of judging friends and enemies.

> I shall blame no enemy when he is acting as a good man *(esthlos)*,
> nor shall I praise a friend if he is acting basely *(deilos)*
>
> (1079-80; cf. 323-28).

Clearly, Theognis seeks to define the true friend in terms of inner values. Such a standard is difficult to attain; for those outside the narrow circle of the *agathoi* it is impossible:

> Let no one of men persuade you to be friends with a *kakos* man, Cyrnus; what advantage is it to have a base man *(deilos anēr)* as a friend? He would not save you from hard trouble and ruin, nor would he wish to share with you any good thing he had
>
> (101-104).[22]

Intimately connected to this is a consequent spiritualizing of the homosexual relationship, which implied in the strongest terms that true, morally-defined, friendship of this sort was beyond the ken of nonnobles. When Theognis gives to his friend Cyrnus proper advice and counsel calculated to make Cyrnus a better man (as befits the role of the older and wiser partner in an erotic relationship) he is again equating the standards of a social class with the norms of correct ethical behavior.

Most of the advice to Cyrnus, however, concerns matters of manners and style: how to conduct oneself in company, how to behave towards friends and elders or in particular situations, etc.[23] These maxims show how important external life-style had become; and the fact that they have a somewhat stronger ethical tone in the *Theognidea* merely underscores the centrality of proper "form" to the new ideal.

Another quality, closely tied to Theognis' notion of the trustworthy friend, and one that represents a further shift in the aristocratic ethic, is the ability to "endure," which, for Theognis, means the proper attitude in all sets of circumstances. There are, he tells Cyrnus, few "trusty companions"

> of the sort, who, being of the same mind as you, would endure to share equally in your good fortune or bad
>
> (79-81).

But an *agathos* man

> endures whether he is set in good fortune or bad
>
> (319-20).

The mind of the *deilos* man cannot adapt itself to good or bad fortune, but "the *agathos* must resolve to bear this or that" (397-98). This theme is sounded again and again:

> the *esthlos* endures when he suffers misfortune . . . while the *deilos* does not know how to keep heart and be patient either in good fortune or bad
>
> (441-44).[24]

The notion of endurance *(tlēmosynē)* is found in earlier Greek thought, but there it is a much more positive, action-oriented doctrine (e.g. Odysseus. Archilochus in a poem on *tlēmosynē* (fr. 7D) calls it "tough" *(kraterē)* and advises his friend to "endure, putting away womanish grief" (cf. fr. 67aD). In Theognis' ethical scheme, on the other hand, endurance occupies a central position, it is closely connected with social class, applies equally in good or bad circumstances, and, most importantly, it is a passive, even negative quality.[25]

Other internal values are present in the ideal of the *agathos* in Theognis. The virtue of *sōphrosynē*, "prudence," "moderation," that was to play so great a role in later Greek ethical thought has a prominent place in the Theognidean ideal. In the fifth century *sōphrōn* and *sōphrosynē* become normative terms, used by the upper class to describe themselves and what they considered one of their essential characteristics; and it is interesting that Theognis is the first of our sources to provide *sōphrosynē* with a political context.[26] For Theognis, as we have already seen in some lines quoted above (429-38), *sōphrōn*, "sound-minded," is often opposed to words like "foolish," "witless" (e.g. 453-54, 483, 497-98), traits which Theognis regarded as natural to the aristocrat and the lower-class man respectively. Theognis saw these qualities in the context of class conflict. Discussing swift and unexpected changes of fortune, he says that the poor man can suddenly become rich, the rich man can lose all,

> The *sōphrōn* can err and good fame *(doxa)* can come to the fool *(aphrōn)*, and even one who is *kakos* can get *timē*
>
> (661-66).

In another striking example of the new "social" valuation placed by aristocrats on *sōphrosynē* Theognis complains that the goddesses Pistis (Good Faith), Sophrosyne, the Charites (Graces) have abandoned earth for Olympus, so that no longer are "just *(dikaioi)* oaths in good faith *(pistoi)* among men," nor do men recognize "laws and reverence."

Sōphrosynē joins the familiar qualities of *pistis* and *charis* (conservators of the old standards) now threatened by "the crooked speech of *adikoi* men" (1135-50).[27]

The essentially cautious quality of moderation, upon which Theognis seized so eagerly as a distinguishing mark of the good man, finds further expression in the notion of the "mean." Before Theognis references to the "middle" are found in a non-aristocratic context; traditionally the aristocratic maxim had been "always to excel."[28] Now we read:

> Do not be overgrieved *(mēden agan aschalle)* when the citizens are in disorder, Cyrnus, but walk the middle path as I do
>
> (219-20),

and, also to Cyrnus:

> Cautious like me, walk the middle way
>
> (331).

This idea of the mean is ethical as well as political; here he connects it with *aretē:*

> Be not overeager *(mēden agan speudein);* the mean is best in everything. In this way, Cyrnus, you will have *aretē* — which is a hard thing to get
>
> (335-36).

Of course, like *sōphrosynē*, the mean is the property of the *agathoi*. The *kakoi*, he says, are unrestrained,

> but the *agathoi* know how to keep the mean in everything
>
> (614; cf. 366).

In one couplet he connects the notions of the mean and of endurance as characteristics of the *agathos:*

> Do not be sick at heart too much *(mēden agan asō)* in hardship, nor rejoice too much in good fortune, for it is the mark of an *anēr agathos* to bear all things
>
> (657-58; cf. 591-94).

The thematic line of caution and moderation which is prominent in the Theognis-collection puts us immediately in mind of the "soft" escapism—the concentration on style and manner, love and conviviality, a retreat from the martial spirit, a sense of detachment—that was noted in the poetry of Anacreon, Ibycus and others, writing around and after 550 B.C. There is scarcely a mention of the traditional values of achievement and valor in the *Theognidea*. Only once are the highly charged words *aretē* and *kleos* used in the Homeric (or Tyrtaean) sense of "valor," "courage," and the "glory" which *aretē* confers:

> The great glory *(mega kleos)* of courage *(aretē)* will never perish; for a spearman saves both his land and his town
>
> (867-68).

Another time *kleos* is won by poetry (245). Otherwise the *esthlos anēr* wins very little honor *(timē,* line 234), while the fool can win fame *(doxa)* and the *kakos* can win *timē* (665-66).

Another area of distinction separating the *agathos* and the *kakos* is superior mental ability and judgment. We have seen that Theognis considered the *agathoi* to be the model of proper teaching; consequently, good judgment *(gnōmē)* and other intellectual qualities are given great importance in the Theognidean scheme of values:

> A man has in himself nothing better than *gnōmē* nor more painful than its lack *(agnōmosynē)*
>
> (895-96).
>
> *Gnōmē*, Cyrnus, is the best thing the gods give to mortals. *Gnōmē* embraces the bounds of everything
>
> (1171-72).
>
> A better companion than any man, Cyrnus, seems to be one who has *gnōme* and power
>
> (411-12).

Intelligence, of course, is something found in *agathoi*, not in other men, and is conjoined to other marks of the upper-class character:

> It is well to be summoned to feast and to sit beside an *esthlos* man who understands all wisdom *(sophiē)*
>
> (563-64).
>
> *Gnōmē* and a sense of right *(aidōs)* belong to the *agathoi*, and to tell the truth, these are few among many
>
> (635-36).

The Crisis of Identity: Theognis and Pindar

Most noteworthy is Theognis' linking of *gnōmē, sōphrosynē* and endurance, which the *kakoi* do not possess:

> Cyrnus, an *agathos* man has *gnōmē* which remains constant, and he endures, whether in good fortune or bad; but if a god gives a living and wealth to a *kakos* man in his witlessness *(aphrainōn)* he cannot restrain his badness
>
> (319-22).

Since these qualities, like good birth, are inborn, they cannot be acquired, and so are the exclusive property of the aristocrat:

> Mind and tongue are good, but they are inborn *(pephyken)* in few men who have stewardship over both of them
>
> (1185-86).

> It is easier to beget and to rear a man than to put good wits *(phrenai esthlai)* in him. No one has yet devised a way to make an *aphrōn* into a *sōphrōn* or an *esthlos* from a *kakos*
>
> (429-31).

> The *deiloi* are emptier in their minds through their badness (*kakotēs*), but the deeds of the *agathoi* are always more straightforward
>
> (1025-26).

These ideas are easily extended into the political realm; twice he calls the *demōs* "empty-headed."[29]

Naturally Theognis claims the virtue of justice for the *agathos*. Poets had been urging their listeners to be just since the days of Hesiod, but Theognis denies this quality to the non-nobles, making the adjectives for "just" and "unjust" *(dikaios-adikos)* almost synonymous with *agathos* and *kakos:*

> It is proper for the *kakos* man to think ill of justice
>
> (279).

Elsewhere he says that under the rule of the *kakoi*

> Shame *(aidōs)* is destroyed; shamelessness and violence *(hybris)* have conquered *dikē* and rule throughout the land
>
> (291-92).[30]

Lines 147-48 of the collection repeat a maxim of Phocylides:

> In justice *(dikaiosynē)* is summed up all *aretē,*

adding,

> and every man is *agathos*, Cyrnus, if he is *dikaios*.

The distich has engendered a great deal of discussion; scholars have disputed its genuineness, appropriateness to the *Theognidea* and meaning. Jaeger's explanation that even if Theognis took over this thought "from a commoner like Phocylides, he could not help adopting it as the motto of his own party," is convincing.[31] For Theognis and for those who thought like him during this period, *agathos* still meant a member of the old nobility of wealth, birth (and success), but as these factors became less persuasive *agathos* had come also to mean someone who incorporated in himself higher qualities of mind and spirit. Thus the equating of *agathos* and *dikaios*, or, more precisely, the statement that a man who is *dikaios* must also be *agathos*, given the inability of non-aristocrats to possess these inner qualities, is perfectly in accord with Theognis' changed ideal of the good man. The degree of divergence from the older conception of the aristocrat is summed up in the lines which follow (149-50), where the poet says that the god gives wealth even to the thoroughly bad man *(pankakos)* but

> to few men *(oligoi)* comes the measure *(moira)* of *aretē*.

And it is in the somewhat spiritualized conceptualization of *aretē*, most powerful of words available to the Greeks to express human worth, that Theognis best reveals the change in aristocratic attitudes. No longer in the easily apprehended realm of manly valor, *aretē* must still be the exclusive property of men like himself. It can be equated with the abstract notion of justice (confined to the *agathoi*), or, similarly, may be expressed as neither doing nor suffering "shameful deeds" *(erga aischra*, 1177-78; cf. 29-30). Although wealth can come to the "totally *kakos* man," and to the "mass of men" being rich is the "only *aretē*" (699-700), true *aretē* is for the few *(oligoi*, 150). "Concern yourself with *aretē*," he advises,

> and let the right *(ta dikaia)* be dear to you. Do not let shameful gain *(kerdos aischron)* overcome you
>
> > (465-66).

The happy *(olbios)* man, honored by all, is one who combines *aretē* and beauty *(kallos)*; this, too, is granted only to the few *(pauroi*, 933-35).

Aretē is joined to wisdom *(sophiē)* as his highest goal (789-90); the way to *aretē* is through moderation (335-46).[32]

The collection known as the *Theognidea* has revealed an evolving conception of the *agathos,* whose positive attributes are mainly moral and intellectual. The *agathos* is a trusty friend, he endures, he has *sōphrosynē* and superior wisdom, he is just. These "quiet" virtues are more distinctly underscored by the omission of the traditional excellences of the *agathos.* Physical prowess (in battle or in athletics), wealth, political hegemony, public achievement and recognition are hardly evident. Those against whom the *agathoi* are ranged, the *kakoi/deiloi,* are given character traits that are the opposite of the moral/aesthetic excellences of the *agathoi* — they are not trusty or loyal, they are intellectually inferior, they lack judgment, moderation and endurance; in addition they are greedy, unjust and violent.

Such an ideal can hardly be called an ideal, stated as it was in essentially defensive terms. But the *Theognidea,* full of "a bitter and brooding resentment over the course of events," reflects a period of crisis of aristocratic self-identity, a transition from an older, no longer viable set of values to a quest for newer qualities that defined the aristocrat as an innately superior being.[33]

◊

How that crisis was resolved by the noble groups in Greek society is a splendid example of dynamic change in the cultural pattern of an upper class. We are fortunate to have a large number of choral songs, composed by the Boeotian poet, Pindar, who was born in the waning days of the archaic age and who lived to see the flowering of the high classical period (518-438 B.C.). His surviving poems are mainly victory odes *(epinikia)* written in honor of the men and boys who were winners in the various contests held at the major pan-Hellenic festivals. Most of the victors were from noble families; some of them were the most powerful men in their cities.

In most respects the social attitudes of Pindar were precisely those of Theognis; the major difference is that the *Theognidea* presents a picture of an aristocracy striving to maintain its superiority in the face of challenge, and the tone is often bitter and defeatist. Pindar celebrates his aristocrats in their moments of triumph; his odes reflect a serene confidence in the values of the upper class. Soured at what he felt to be a loss of prestige and authority among the "good," Theognis concentrated on inner values. These internal qualities are present in Pindar's poetry too, but mostly he dwelled on the successes and achievements of the nobility. In fact, it is the combination of internal qualities of character and visible, external success that is the hallmark of Pindar's conception of aristocratic excellence. This conception, which represents a different (and somewhat later) stage of the developing aristocratic self-portrait, can perhaps be best understood by comparing the outlooks of each poet.

As we might expect, Pindar's employment of the words *agathos/esthlos* is very similar to the usage found in the *Theognidea*. For Pindar, as for Theognis, *agathos* was a class word; and when Pindar uses the expression *agathos anēr*, "good man," he means aristocrat. Accordingly, the *agathoi-esthloi* form a group set apart and above the rest of the citizenry; more specifically, this group is the fittest to rule, as Pindar says in his first ode (498 B.C.):[34]

> In the hands of the *agathoi* lies the noble governance of cities, passed from father to son.
>
> *(Pyth.* 10.71-72)

The *agathoi* are also wiser. In a poem written for the tyrant of Syracuse he informs his patron that the gods give "two woes for every good," and then continues:

> Fools cannot bear this with grace, but *agathoi* can, turning the bright side out.
>
> *(Pyth.* 3.82-83)

In his usage of these words Pindar is remarkably consistent with the outlook of Theognis, and we can safely assume that the two poets expressed attitudes which were held in common by most Greek aristocrats.[35] Theognis, however, was obsessed by the opposite of the *agathoi/esthloi*, those he called *kakoi* and *deiloi*. *Deilos* is not found at all in the poems of Pindar and *kakos* is never used of persons.[36] One of the noteworthy aspects of Pindar's depiction of aristocrats is an almost total lack of overt class tension – he expresses the superiority of the *agathoi* as a group simply by excluding the *kakoi* from consideration. When he does approach social questions he finds other ways to describe those who cannot compare with his noble victors. In *Pythian* 11 he says:

> For prosperity gets an envy that matches it, but he who breathes along the ground grumbles invisible.
>
> (Lines 29-30)

He means that the successful achiever is envied, but it is better to be great and envied than to be obscure. In another ode Pindar says that deceit and envy press down upon what is brilliant and raise up

> a rotten glory of the invisible.
>
> (*Nem.* 8.32-34)

Those who do not count, that is, those who are not aristocratic victors are dismissed as "invisible."[37] Pindar's avoidance of class terminology is also evidenced by the absence of "technical" terms, like *eugenēs*, that denote noble birth; he is content to bestow on his aristocrats the simple epithet "good."

This brief sketch of Pindar's word usage amply demonstrates his aristocratic bias, but the positive quality of the Pindaric ideal is better seen by a more detailed examination of his attitudes towards some of the problems that had concerned other thinkers of the archaic period. For example, despite the lack of a technical vocabulary of birth, the belief that excellence depends on birth is stronger in Pindar than in any other poet of the archaic period. A comparison with Theognis in this respect reveals the essential difference in their outlooks. Theognis had made noble birth one of the prerequisites of the "good" man, but in a somewhat defensive or negative manner, lamenting that the purer stock of the *agathoi* was adulterated by intermarriage. In Pindar the notion of noble birth becomes a more elevated concept. For him all excellence is inborn, innate; there is a direct line of spiritual descent from the gods through the legendary heroes of the past to the aristocratic victor, which is literal proof that only by "inborn nature" *(phyā)* can a man be said to possess any excellence. In other words, Pindar does not defend the idea that superior qualities are transmitted by birth, he simply *assumes* it. Theognis, we recall, had maintained that no one can make a man good or wise by teaching (429-38); in Pindar this doctrine is expressed with loftier conviction:

> what is given by nature *(phyā)* is best.
>
> (*Ol.* 9.100)

He follows this by saying that many men strive to win fame by means of "learned skills," but this is "apart from god" and should be quelled in silence (lines 100-04). The same ideas are found in *Olympian* 2:

> The wise man knows many things by nature *(phyā)*, but those who are taught are boisterous and noisy
>
> (lines 86-87)

and in *Nemean* 3:

> A man is a man of weight who has inborn *(syngenēs)* glory, but a man who must be taught is an obscure man.
>
> (Lines 40-41)

Pindar sounds the theme of innate excellence again and again — not merely the pale notion of aristocratic superiority based on high birth, but an almost mystical conviction that the glory of the victor in his brief moment of triumph is the result of qualities inherited from legendary heroes through generations.[38] From a social point of view this conception may be regarded as the supreme rationale for superiority of birth. With absolute confidence Pindar makes a leap backwards in time, linking victors, heroes and gods in the expression of a single, spiritualized ideal.

This important and central conviction was present to the poet's mind in his earliest ode:

> Happy is Lacedaemon; blessed is Thessaly; and in both rules a race descended from one father, Heracles best in battle.
>
> (*Pyth.* 10.1-3)

And in one of his latest odes, *Nemean* 11, the honoree is glorified as being descended on his mother's side from the hero Melanippus, and on his father's side from the hero Pisander, a companion of Orestes (lines 33ff.). In *Nemean* 3 he connects Zeus, the sons of Aeacus, the victor and his country:

> Thereon is fixed the far-shining brilliance of the Aeacids, O Zeus: for their blood is yours, and the contest is yours, which my song casts at, sounding the country's joy with the voice of youths.
>
> (Lines 64-66)

When we turn to Pindar's treatment of the victory itself, we see that, like his conception of *phyā*, it has become a sign of something far greater than physical excellence and the achievement it wins. Through his victory the honoree demonstrates his ability and courage; but, in addition, the deed itself is proof of his kinship with the ancient heroes of legend. The exploits of the heroes of old are symbolically reenacted in the trials and eventual triumphs of the contestants in the games. It is difficult for us today to imagine the potency of that symbol as a means of expressing the *absolute* difference between those who thought of themselves as "the good" and the rest of society, no matter how much the social realities of the "age of revolution" had blurred class distinctions or how much those below the narrow stratum of the élite had achieved a measure of success on their own. It is no exaggeration, I think, to call Pindar's harmonious grouping of all the "positive-functioned traits" of Hellenic culture in his poetic celebrations of contest victors a triumph of propaganda. The result of this brilliant focussing was an exclusivism of the purest sort. It is no wonder that Pindar was welcome in every corner of the Greek world or that the demand for his odes remained constantly high for over fifty years.

Pindar's poems are difficult and obscure; they defy rational analysis, leaping from one topic to another, in a series of abrupt stops and starts, a complex jumble of colorful images, myths, obscure allusions, ethical commonplaces, all expressed in richly ornate language and complicated rhythms. The effect on the listener of the odes is impressionistic, not logical; yet the confusion of image, ancient myth and present occasion have a single unifying core — the symbol of victory itself — which stands for the entire spectrum of aristocratic values. Pindar's non-diachronic technique of melding myth and history, the actions of gods and legendary heroes, the achievements of the victor's family and of the victor himself, conveys an effect of timelessness, as if all the concrete examples were simultaneous proofs of the validity of the underlying social values.

Those values, presented as universally agreed-upon statements of truth, are, of course, predominantly the values of the topmost group. The great athletic festivals themselves were the institutionalized expressions of the pursuits of aristocrats — controlled by the wealthy and reflecting their style of life. They were, first of all, religious celebrations. Dominance of religious cults and offices, temples, shrines, and dedications by aristocrats identified them as the legitimate transmitters and interpreters of religious norms; and those norms coincided, naturally, with the values of the Greek élite. Pindar's odes served to make the identification even more explicit. The games were also musical festivals, reflecting, again, the refined aesthetic sensibilities of the narrow group: recitations of Homer, choral lyric and dance — not the music of the "people." Participation in the games was the almost exclusive domain of the upper class. Not only were the contestants men and boys whose families could afford the considerable expense in time and wealth for training, but even the spectators needed wealth and leisure to travel the long distances to the games. The major festivals, as Andrewes says, can justifiably be called "an international aristocratic world," in which nobles from all parts of the Greek world received mutual reinforcement of their values, and reflected outward to the non-noble majority the seeming permanence of their cultural assumptions.[39]

If we want a visual counterpart to the odes of Pindar as witness to the expression of exclusivistic class superiority, then, out of all the surviving dedicatory monuments, we need only look at the magnificent bronze charioteer of Delphi, commemorating the chariot victory of the brother of the tyrant of Syracuse in the 470's. Serene, aloof, supremely self-confident, the driver parades his horses before the assembled throng, reminding us, by the way, that the horse and chariot, functionally useless, was the ideal symbol of the wealth, luxury, pride and ostentatious display of the Greek aristocracy.

Not the least of Pindar's achievements was his ability to evoke a simple and direct line of descent from mythical hero to modern patron, as if there had been no intervening questioning of the primacy of the particular *aretē* of physical prowess. From the time of Archilochus there had been a line of thought which seriously challenged this simplistic notion. Like Tyrtaeus before him, Xenophanes had questioned the relationship of the Olympic victor to the good of the community; the polis, he had said, is not in a greater state of Eunomia for this (fr. 2.19D).[40] One of Solon's chief concerns had been that the rich and powerful nobles were going their own selfish ways, and were not concerned with "our city" and its well-being. Theognis, who had drawn away from the old aristocratic ideal, spoke hardly at all of physical skill or individual glory; at the same time he neglected the city-state ethos of service to the community. In his representation of the aristocrat, however, Pindar combines all these elements; by means of the single symbol of victory in the games he links the heroic past with the present, the individual interest of his noble victors to the prosperity and glory of their *poleis*.

Thus, in *Olympian* 4.11-12 the victor is "eager to win glory for Camarina." Another victor is "an ornament to Athens" (*Nemean* 2.8). In *Nemean* 3 Aristocleides of Aegina has brought this island into glorious praise.

(Line 68)

The youthful Strepsiades is praised for his victory in the Isthmian games, and the poet commends his strength, beauty and courage. By his victory he has shared his glory with his uncle, Strepsiades, who died in battle. Pindar then says that whoever defends his fatherland provides

> the greatest glory to the race of his townsmen, both in life and in death.
>
> (*Isth.* 7.29-30)

In Pindar we observe no trace of the conflict between individual achievement, so prized by the nobles, and service to the community, the constant theme of those not committed to the aristocratic tradition. Rather, as one critic notes,

> The tales of the gods, the myths of the heroes, the achievement of the victor, the greatness of his city — Pindar ties them all together and makes the union a triumph of aristocratic achievement.[41]

Nevertheless, in one important area there is a decided similarity of attitude between the two poets. During the crucial period between 500 and 480, when all Greece was threatened by the Persian Empire and the spirit of Greek patriotism was running high, Pindar reveals a reluctance to celebrate Hellenic resistance to the invader, exhibiting instead what Ehrenberg calls a "neutralism, a form of pacifism which was practically defeatism or at least blindness."[42]

Other differences appear when we compare Pindar's attitudes toward wealth with those of Theognis and Solon, both of whom (but for different reasons) were fearful of its effects. Theognis, especially, had seen in the desire for wealth and its levelling tendencies a danger to his own class. Pindar displays none of this fear. Some wealth was a necessary precondition for participation in athletic contests, and substantial wealth was needed for horse and mule racing. Pindar did not have any poor clients; his own fee, the cost of a chorus and the attendant victory celebration were heavy expenses. Therefore it is only natural that Pindar would praise the wealth of his patrons, who were among the richest men of their states. Even so, Pindar's attitude is substantively different from that of Theognis. For Pindar wealth is a sign and a proof of the nobility of the victors, and possession of wealth is companion to their merit. Thus, he says that the race of Iamids has been famous in Hellas, and

> prosperity *(olbos)* followed together, and by prizing achievements *(aretai)* they have passed along a road conspicuous.

Numerous passages reflect the high premium Pindar places on wealth. In *Nemean* 9.46-47 wealth is regarded as one of the ultimate prizes:

> For if a man win conspicuous glory together with many possessions there is no other height for a man to touch with his feet.

Hiero and his brothers won honor *(timā)* from the hands of the gods

> such as no one of the Greeks has culled, a lordly crown of wealth.
> (*Pyth.* 1.48-50)

In the same ode (line 46) Pindar prays for prosperity *(olbos)* for Hiero which is seen to consist of two things: "a giving of wealth" and "forgetfulness of pain." Elsewhere the ultimate in human felicity is represented as a combination of wealth, beauty and might in the games (*Nem.* 11. 13-14). Success and praise are considered the "two flowers of life" along with *olbos* (*Isth.* 5.13-14). In *Nemean* 5.19 Pindar says that wealth *(olbos)*, might of hands, and mail-clad war are subjects for his verses. Even in his own case Pindar connects wealth with fame:

> If God were to give me luxurious wealth I have hope to gain lofty fame in the future.
> (*Pyth.* 3.110-11)

The admonition that only wealth with "virtue" is acceptable, a recurring theme since Hesiod, is a commonplace in Pindar also; but even with this stricture the possession of wealth emerges as something glorious. In *Olympian* 2 he states:

> wealth *(ploutos)* adorned with virtues *(aretai)* brings opportunity for this and that, providing a deep concern for achievement, is a shining star, the truest light for a man.
> (Lines 53-56)

The Crisis of Identity: Theognis and Pindar

Pythian 5 opens with a similar thought:

> Wide is the might of wealth *(ploutos)* given of fate, when some mortal man brings it home mingled with unspotted virtue *(aretā)* a ministrant providing many friends.
>
> (Lines 1-4)

The accent in these passages is clearly more on the goodness of wealth than on the warming that it must be coupled with *aretē*.

Theognis' deep suspicion of wealth and the possible evils which attend it is only palely mirrored in Pindar. In *Isthmian* 3.1-3 he says that if a man has good fortune

> either with games that bring good fame or by the might of wealth *(ploutos)*, and checks odious surfeit *(koros)* in his heart, he is worthy to be mingled in the praise of townsmen.

Here wealth is linked to victory in the games as a high aspiration, and the admonition to "repress *koros*," while meant to be heeded carefully, is not a dire warning but a caution not to allow success to go to one's head. Similar is his praise of the victor Xenocrates in *Pythian* 6, who

> tends his wealth with judgment, nor plucks his youth with injustice or arrogance but culls wisdom in the haunts of the Pierides.
>
> (Lines 47-49)

In like manner, the youthful Aristomenes in *Pythian* 8, exalted by his victory:

> has a care which is mightier than wealth.
>
> (Line 92)[43]

The idea of friendship was important in the Theognidean image of the good man; Pindar, too, values friendship highly and includes many examples of it in his odes.[44] The combined evidence of the two poets shows how important was the notion of the faithful and trustworthy friend in the evolution of the aristocratic ideal. This fits well the picture of an aristocratic circle drawing ever inward and increasingly conscious of the mutual ties that bound nobles even from different cities in a common interest. There is one significant difference, however, between the two. There is not in Pindar, as there is in Theognis, the same moralizing about friendship and the agonizing over the faithless friend. Theognis' attitude may well reflect factional differences among the nobles of sixth-century Megara, just as many of the poems of the aristocratic Alcaeus mirrored the internal squabblings of the Lesbian nobility. There is little trace of this in Pindar; he emphasizes instead the positive aspects of friendship; and this perhaps reflects a more pan-Hellenic conception of aristocratic friendship and a more universal appreciation of the bonds between nobles throughout the Greek world. A passionate interest in local problems gives way in Pindar to the realization that aristocrats in Sicily share the same outlook as those in Africa and Asia. With friendship, as with other aspects of the evolving ideal, Pindar seems to have a sense of the essential unity of the aristocratic ethos.

Theognis' *agathos* was superior ethically and intellectually. These qualities also have an important place in Pindar's ideal, and one of the prominent terms of approbation in Pindar is *sophos*, "wise." Often *sophos* in Pindar refers to the poet, but others are also *sophoi* in this sense. Thus the Aeginetans are

> wise stewards of the Muses and of athletic contests.
> (Fr. 1.6 Bowra)

A victor's fellow-townsmen are called "wise," i.e. skilled in song *(Pyth.* 4.295).

However, the adjective is not confined to describing skill in poetry and song. Apollo, Jason and the Muses are called "wise." The seven sons of Helios have "wisest understanding" (*Ol.* 7.71-72); and a client, Xenocrates, is called "wise," that is, understanding (*Isth.* 2.12). Further, the quality of being *sophos* is a gift from the gods, and it is by *phyā*, not by learning, that a man is *sophos*.[45] The high praise inherent in the word is indicated by its being associated with other terms of merit; for example, *Olympian* 9.27-28:

> ... men become *agathoi* and *sophoi* by the gods ...

In *Olympian* 14.7, *sophos* is coupled with "beautiful" and "famous"; these qualities proceed from the Muses. Elsewhere Pindar says that thanks to the gods men are *sophoi*, physically capable and eloquent (*Pythian* 1.42).[46]

In view of these passages, it is not surprising that the *sophoi* are sometimes treated as an exclusive group who alone understand his meaning. In *Pythian* 9.77-78 "a few things among many, deftly adorned" appeal to the *sophoi* in poetry. Twice the *sophoi* are directly equated with the nobles. In a victory ode for Arcesilas of Cyrene, Pindar says:

> The *sophoi* bear more gracefully the power given them by the gods
> (*Pyth.* 5.12-13)

and in *Pythian* 2.87-88, the *sophoi* are the rulers of the city as opposed to the "noisy host."[47]

Thus, Pindar, like Theognis, makes wisdom an important attribute of the *agathos*, but he does this less contentiously and more confidently than Theognis. The latter neglected physical prowess in favor of mental qualities, but Pindar displays no sense of tension between physical and mental *aretai*. Physical and intellectual ability, recognition among one's peers and in the polis are all combined harmoniously in Pindar — the noble victor has all these qualities equally.

Pindar's confidence in the inherent superiority of the *agathos* is seen very clearly when we compare the ideas of patience and endurance in Theognis and Pindar. In the *Theognidea* the virtue of "endurance" emerges as something rather passive and withdrawn. Pindar, on the contrary, always expresses this notion in the context of confidence. The verb which means "endure" *(tolmān)* is not, in Pindar, simply a passive ability to hold out, but is a much more positive quality of "courage" and "daring" (always in a good sense) directed toward achieving an end (which is always victory or triumph). Thus, in *Olympian* 9.82 the poet prays for *tolmā* and *dynamis* (power). The victor wins the "greatest of prizes" with *tolmā* and "might" (*Pyth.* 10.24). Melissus of Thebes is

> like in soul to the boldness *(tolmā)* of loud-roaring, wild lions.
> (*Isth.* 4.45-46)[48]

The quality of moderation (*sōphrosynē*, etc.), so prevalent in Theognis, has a correspondingly high place in the Pindaric value scheme. Conservative Thebes is praised for having "prudent law and order" (*sōphrōn eunomia, Paean* 1.10). In this, as in other "sensitive" areas, Pindar differs essentially from Theognis. North points out that although Pindar uses *sōphrōn* only five times, and the noun *sōphrosynē* never specifically occurs, four of the five instances of *sōphrōn* are in political contexts; and interwoven throughout the poems are many examples of *sōphrosynē* and praise of the "mean" which are connected with his aristocratic victors and their families.[49] What Theognis felt constrained to emphasize, Pindar, in his confident manner, need only allude to.

As we might expect, Pindar placed great emphasis on manner and style. Those whom he celebrated knew how to conduct themselves correctly on social occasions, saying and doing the "proper" thing. His victors and their circle enjoyed the good things in life: feasting, singing, dancing. As aristocrats they appreciated the fine points of horsemanship and understood the intricacies of athletic training, for they had the leisure and means for these upper-class pursuits. They alone were able to understand the importance of song and to appreciate their poet (hence *they* were the "wise"). They cultivated luxury without excess; above all, they were imbued with a sense of grace and charm and beauty. For Pindar the maintenance of a splendid appearance, whether in one's own person and accoutrements, in the grand pomp of the games, in the rich costumes of the choral dancers, in the lavish hospitality of patrons, or in the flashing brilliance of the odes themselves, was evidence not only of wealth and cultured leisure, but also of nobility and character. Hardly any ode is lacking in praise of a combination of these interests and attributes, and it would be tedious to enumerate the passages. But one aspect of Pindar's ideal should be discussed in some detail, since it illustrates the major position that the notion of physical beauty had come to hold in the aristocratic self-conception.

Throughout Greek aristocratic culture, as we have seen, external appearance was of considerable importance. Often the notion of physical beauty *(kallos)* was connected with *aretē*. As early as Homer the adjective for beautiful *(kalos)* was frequently combined with other words denoting size, stature or skill. The noun *kallos* is found in similar combinations. Beauty was an important aspect of the Homeric ideal and a desirable attribute of the heroic warrior (and of his women), and its possession contributed to a person's *aretē*. In the Hesiodic poems, on the other hand, physical beauty was in no way connected with human worth.[50] During the course of the archaic period the ideal of personal physical beauty came more and more to be associated with the aristocratic groups, and played an increasingly important part in the cultural pattern of the upper classes in Greece. The emphasis on beauty is, of course, connected with the general rise of aristocratic refinement during the archaic period. We recall Thucydides' statement that the nobility in Athens had only recently left off wearing linen chitons and fastening their long hair with golden "grasshoppers." Long hair and luxurious dress as marks of the well-born are abundantly illustrated on

Attic vase paintings of the period, many of which contain variations of the erotic inscription *ho pais kalos* (beautiful youth). The period of greatest popularity of this formula appears to have been from the middle of the sixth century B.C. through the last quarter of the fifth, and the majority of identifiable *paides* were from the highest echelon of Athenian society.[51] In the *Theognidea* the motif of *pais kalos* figures prominently, and there is even an explicit linking of *kallos* and *aretē:*

> Upon few of mankind do *aretē* and *kallos* attend; happy the man who has a share of both
>
> (933-34).[52]

The aristocratic preoccupation with physical beauty is further illustrated in drinking songs that have survived. For example, in a sixth-century song "to be *kalos* in body" is rated as the second "best" next to good health.

But it is in Pindar most of all that beauty is made an integral part of aristocratic *aretē*. Thus in *Olympian* 8 a winner in the wrestling contest is said to have been "*kalos* to look upon, not betraying his beauty" in victorious competition (lines 19-20). Similarly, the victor of *Isthmian* 7 is "wondrous in strength and shapely to see; and he carries *aretā* that does not shame his nature" (line 22). This intimate connection between deeds and beauty is seen at *Olympian* 9.94, where the victor is "in his youthful prime, and *kalos*, having achieved the fairest deeds *(kallista)*." In his invocation to the Graces in *Olympian* 14 Pindar links beauty, wisdom and fame together, saying that it is due them if any man is *sophos* or *kalos*, or famous (lines 5-7). This nexus is proclaimed most emphatically in *Nemean* 3.19-20: where "the son of Aristophanes, being *kalos* and doing deeds that fit his beauty, has attained to the heights of manliness . . ."[53]

We may now examine more closely the few passages in which Pindar expresses his social and political views more directly. We have seen that Pindar considered the *agathoi* a separate group, superior to the rest of the population. On the other hand, there is little indication of a group opposed to the *agathoi;* Pindar does not speak of the *kakoi-deiloi*. there is some evidence that he considered the non-aristocrats as *aphantoi*, "invisible," but the number of such allusions is small. Just as there are no mentions of the "lower classes," so there is no mention of lower-class life, the life of toil for one's bread. The one exception, as Fränkel points out, has a "contemptuous" tone. In *Isthmian* 1.47-51 he compares "every man" *(pas tis)* who "strains, defending his belly *(gastēr)* from weary hunger," to the victor in the games or in war whose prize of "graceful fame" *(kydos habron)* and praise from citizens and strangers is the loftiest gain *(kerdos hypsiston)*.[54] In such subtle ways Pindar does display political attitudes that are typically aristocratic. Another is his distrust of "mass opinion." In *Nemean* 7 he speaks of Homer's "falsehood," "winged skill" and wisdom *(sophia)*, which

> deceives, leading astray with tales.

He says further:

> the greatest mass of men *(homilos ho pleistos)* has a heart which is blind.
> (Lines 22-24)

Another passage which reveals something of his political and social attitudes is found in *Pythian* 2:

> But in every form of state the man of straight speech excels – in a tyranny, or when the noisy host, or when the wise watch over the polis.
> (Lines 86-88)

In enumerating all the possible forms of government, rule by one man, rule of the many, and rule of the few, Pindar reveals that he considered oligarchical rule the best, for he calls them *"hoi sophoi,"* a term of high approbation. Democracy is characterized as the "noisy host" *(ho labros stratos)*, and this descriptive phrase fits in with his suspicions about "mass opinion."

The instances in which Pindar comes closest to making a definite political commitment appear in *Pythian* 10.71-72 (above, page 96), where he upholds the principle that rule of the hereditary *agathoi* is best, and in *Pythian* 11.52-53:

> I have found that of the orders in the polis the middle *(ta mesa)* flowers in the longest prosperity, and I condemn the lot of tyrannies.

Some have seen in Pindar's praise of the "middle estates" a leaning toward government by the middle class. But, like all aristocrats, Pindar most hated and distrusted control by one man. For him the "middle" was the mean between a tyrant's rule and the rule of the many—namely rule by a small group of aristocrats, those whom he would characterize as the "good" or the "wise." In Pindar's conception of political schemes this would represent the same ideal of moderation as Theognis' "middle." We must remember that for an aristocrat the political extremes were democracy and rule by a single powerful figure, and that power in the hands of the wise and cultured few was the ideal constitution. Although aristocratic hegemony was in decline in many parts of Greece, it was possible for Pindar to "ignore" this ugly fact because his main contact was with the conservators of the old way of life, the Sicilian tyrants, the lords of Thessaly, the king of Cyrene, the landowners of Thebes, or with men in other states who were rich and powerful even if they no longer controlled absolutely. Pindar's easy confidence in the superiority of the social group which he celebrated on a pan-Hellenic level enabled him to be detached from the localized class tensions which obsessed Theognis.[55] And yet, the very lack of vehemence in Pindar's poetry paradoxically foreshadows the beginnings of a new political attitude, in which the archaic age's feeling of loyalty to one's community (by all the groups within the community) yields to a class loyalty which transcends the bounds of the individual polis. In its developed form this is to become a destructive force in the various Greek states, when ". . . common sentiment between the upper classes of different cities had an influence which tended to outweigh the common sentiment shared by all classes in their joint citizenship of a single *polis.*"[56]

◊

We may say in summary that Pindar's ideal was a positive and confident definition of the "good man" as opposed to a negative and defeatist definition. Theognis had retreated from an external conception of the *agathos* to a different one, based on superior intellectual, ethical and aesthetic qualities. Pindar incorporated these inner qualities into his standard of aristocratic excellence; but, in addition, he gave new vigor to the old Homeric notions of valor, skill and personal glory, ignoring the seventh- and sixth-century controversy over the validity of these *aretai*. He also included in his ideal the most forceful of the archaic concepts, that of service and usefulness to the polis (although he was careful not to *define* the *agathos* as the "useful" man).

Pindar was able to accomplish this because he chose as his unifying symbol victory in the national games, which allowed him, first of all, to concentrate on a small group of men who had the wealth and the inclination to compete. Thus he could ignore all the rest except as applauding spectators, whom he could, therefore, treat with dignity as "townsmen" or citizens," and only occasionally as the "noisy host." Second, by means of this unifying theme, Pindar was able to posit a direct relationship among god, hero, victor, family and city. The *agathos* is superior because he is a descendant of the ancient heroes; he proves this superiority in the *deed* by being victorious. The victory not only proves superiority, but, according to Pindar, the victory is due to *innate* superiority. In other words, there is an unbreakable circularity of cause and effect. The glory of the victor becomes the glory of his family, which becomes the glory of the collective aristocracy, whose inherited pattern of values makes possible the achievement of individual victory in the first place. Finally, by linking the valor and skill necessary to win in competition with the valor and skill necessary in war, and by combining the victor, the ancient hero and the city, Pindar could make the victor the benefactor of his city in peace, as the hero had been its champion in war. All this is done with careful avoidance of overt involvement in political or social questions.

The ultimate unity of Pindaric thought is a unity of all value. Every element in his poetry is directed towards that which, in his conceptual framework, is good, noble, glorious, pure, pious; all else is excluded from mention. To partake of any aspect of the good is to partake of the whole, for the good is an indissoluble unity. *Aretē* (achievement, manly worth) can be expressed or acquired in a number of ways, but it cannot be divided, because any separate manifestation of *aretē* (skill, courage, daring, endurance, beauty, wealth, power, civic contribution) is living proof of a single mode of transcendent excellence that was available only to those who incorporated in themselves its separate (but inseparable) components.[57]

In some ways, of course, Pindar's scheme was as self-deceiving as was that of Theognis. The latter retreated from the harsh realities of aristocratic decline into a world of inner excellence; and to some extent this is what Pindar did also. Pindar chose to ignore the political and social changes by creating a world of aristocratic splendor which placed the nobles on an Olympian plane, apart and above the rest of mortals. He found his chief inspiration in the epic virtues which had long since ceased to be of practical importance. That he was able to do this attests to the continuing attractiveness of those ancient ideals. Also, we must not forget that he was most welcome in those places where the aristocratic outlook still had some real force. Despite this, it must be recognized, as one scholar says, that the heroics of Pindar no longer enjoyed a suitable milieu. The practical ideals for which the poet stood were no longer practicable, and we recognize his protest in the spiritualization of those virtues which had originally been so eminently practical and concrete.[58]

Pindar's creation was a *tour de force,* essentially a conscious idealization of the aristocrat, compounded partly of the antique and outmoded notions of epic *aretē* and partly of inner-directed attitudes like those of Theognis which stressed ethical and intellectual superiority. In his choral odes "the archaic ideal was expressed in impeccable purity," while Pindar "remained untouched by the revolution in ideas that was going on around him. As one born out of due time, he lived on into an age that became more and more alien to him."[59]

Ω

CHAPTER FOUR

The Aristocratic Ideal in the Classical Period

THE POEMS of Theognis and Pindar are a coherent formulation of aristocratic values during the last half of the sixth and the early years of the fifth centuries B.C. A brief consideration of other evidence available to us will provide some supplementary detail, and may serve to illustrate more precisely the form that the aristocratic ideal was to have in the Classical Period.

Simonides of Ceos (556-468 B.C.) provides an interesting contrast in values. A generation older than Pindar and a sometimes bitter rival of his in the composition of victory songs, Simonides had the reputation in later antiquity of a wise and philosophical poet. The few remains of his epinicians (in the development of which he was an important figure), while they lack the craggy grandeur of Pindar, show grace and originality. But it was as a writer of dithyrambs and epigrams that he was chiefly famed. Later generations hailed him as the laureate of the wars between the Greeks and the Persians; the poems and epigrams he wrote about this great struggle display a consciousness of pan-Hellenic unity and a remarkable affection for democratic Athens and her leaders who formulated policy during the war years. As a consequence his outlook is rather different from the defensive aristocratic posture of Theognis and the almost mystical ideal of Pindar. In his usage of the key terms of merit and demerit, for example, Simonides betrays none of the bias of the other two; he was not anti-democratic and therefore felt no need to equate *agathos/esthlos* and *kakos* with social classes. He shared with Theognis and Pindar the late archaic inclination for ethical/intellectual speculation, and in his poems there is great emphasis on internal moral qualities. In fact, he appears to have approached a conception of individual "goodness" which was more "progressive" than that of other poets of the period. But, unlike Theognis and Pindar, he did not make the possession of internal morality the exclusive preserve of aristocrats. Concerned to define true individual worth, Simonides sees goodness as existing in *intent* to act properly rather than in external success or in the mere appearance. For this reason the possibility of goodness is available to all men, not merely to a class. This philosophy is expressed in a famous poem addressed to a Thessalian dynast, Scopas.[1] Having said that the "all-blameless man" cannot exist he goes on:

> But I praise and love all, whosoever does nothing shameful *(aischron)* of his own free will.
>
> (fr. 4.19-21D)

Among the many noteworthy elements of this poem two stand out. First, is the universality of application. Simonides speaks of "every man" (10) and "as many of us who enjoy the fruits of the spacious earth" (16-17). Second, he sets his sights low. Perfection is not possible, intent not to commit *aischron* is sufficient for praise. He ends the poem with these lines (28-29):

> Everything is noble *(kala)* in which no evil *(aischra)* is mixed.[2]

The essential difference in his outlook is also vividly demonstrated in the poems that celebrate the collective triumph of the Greeks over the barbarians. A famous eulogy commemorating those who fell at Thermopylae evidences a spirit that is not found in Theognis and Pindar but which is reminiscent of the communal ideal of Tyrtaeus and Callinus:

> Of those who died at Thermopylae full of glory *(eukleēs)* is their fortune, and noble their fate. For a tomb they have an altar, for lamentation remembrance, for pity praise. Such a funeral neither decay nor time, the all-conqueror, shall dim. This shrine of *agathoi* men has gotten for its guardian the goodly fame *(eudoxia)* of Hellas. Leonidas, king of Sparta, is witness, who has left behind a fair ornament of *aretā* and everlasting glory *(kleos)*.
>
> (Fr. 5D)

What we have here resembles the Tyrtaean concepts of the *agathos* and *aretē*. There is, however, an important development of the older ideal — the service praised is not on behalf of a single state, but for Hellas, and the glory which the men are awarded comes from all of Greece. The piece is full of words and images of glory and fame which are almost totally lacking in the Theognidean corpus — not the traditional competitive, agonistic fame, but rather a collective fame won in a cooperative exercise. Ehrenberg calls this the "new patriotism" celebrating a "new consciousness" of the Greeks.[3] Such a patriotism is not found in Pindar, whose own pan-Hellenism was directed to the common bonds that yoked the aristocratic class in various parts of the Greek world. Although Pindar was at the height of his literary career during the period of the Persian wars his attitude is ambivalent; it is the older Simonides who captures the new spirit of collective exuberance and pride — and Pindar's "pacifism" in the wars of independence seems to have been shared by other aristocrats. The reason for Pindar's almost total silence about the most perilous and exciting events the Greek world had experienced in centuries is simple to understand. A number of Greek states not only did not join in the struggle against the Persians but even aided them against other Greeks. Among these were Pindar's first patrons, the dynasts of Thessaly, Macedon, and his own polis, Thebes, which actually fought on the Persian side at the battle of Plataea in 479. In fact, many aristocrats, their loyalties directed to their own "trans-national" class, resentful of their declining hegemony and fearful of the unstable fledgling democracies, favored the autocratic rule of Median princes and satraps. A new verb, "to Medize" *(mēdizō)* came into the language to describe states and individuals who sided with Persia. Apollo's oracle at Delphi leaned towards mighty Persia, advising the Greeks to surrender. These anti-war lines occur in the *Theognidea:*

> But let Apollo keep straight our tongue and mind, and may lyre and pipe sound a holy song. And conciliating the gods with libations, let us drink, saying graceful things to one another, and not fear war with the Persians. Let it be so. And it were better to spend our lives with cheerful heart in merry feasting far from cares . . .
>
> (759-67).[4]

Simonides was not a democratic partisan; neither was he concerned to represent the attitudes of the "common man." Like Pindar and the other aristocratic poets he felt at home in the tyrants' courts; the victors whom he praised were the same nobles who provided Pindar's inspiration. But he was not a spokesman for the aristocracy. In his old age he was stirred by the events that were happening in Greece and his poetry reflects his sense of admiration for what men — all men — could accomplish with good will and determination. His poems are full of the dominant theme of archaic Greece's great preoccupation, service to the commonality. He was in tune with the times and understood that the men who beat back the Persian threat had rendered spiritually obsolete the older heroic conception. The victories which caught the aging poet's imagination were the sum of the collective efforts of many "unheroic" men. Even in the poem to Scopas, which has been interpreted by many as containing a strictly moral definition of the *agathos*, he appears to be content with the average citizen of good intent:

> Nor am I a fault-finder . . . sufficient for me is the man who is not *kakos*, nor too helpless, but knows at least the justice *(dikā)* which aids the polis, a sound man. Him I will not blame.
> (Fr. 4.22-27D)[5]

Implicit in Simonides' version of the morally acceptable man is an awareness of his civic responsibility. Elsewhere he says that "the polis teaches a man" (fr. 53D). The same notion that the individual's worth is intimately connected with the community is apparent in another fragment:

> No one has gotten *aretā* without the gods, neither polis nor mortal man.
> (Fr. 10.1-2D)

For Simonides individual and polis are an inseparable unit.

It has often been said that despite the difference in their ages (forty years) Simonides seems more "modern" than Pindar. The reason is that Pindar looked backwards, seeking the inspiration for his aristocratic ideal mainly in the old epic values, blending these with qualities of brilliance and achievement that were unique to men of noble blood. Simonides found his inspiration in the deeds of the hoplites of Thermopylae, Marathon and Plataea and the rowers of Salamis. Aristocratic apologists concentrated on what was exclusive to their class, Simonides found merit in the qualities and potential for good that were common to all men.[6]

Bacchylides of Ceos, Simonides' nephew, was born about the same time as Pindar; like Simonides, he was a rival of Pindar in the writing of victory songs. Although he lacked the breadth of intellect and moral insight of his uncle, their sociopolitical views appear similar in most respects. The spectrum of Bacchylides' ethical and social attitudes reflects the standards of the late archaic period. These lines, from a dithyramb, may be taken as typical:

> But it is possible for all men to attain to straightforward Dika, the attendant of holy Eunomia and wise Themis. And happy they whose

> children have made her a dweller in the home. But unabashed Hybris, flourishing on shifty gain and unrestricted foolishness *(aphrosynē)*, who quickly gives a man wealth and power that belong to someone else, sends him down to deep destruction ...
>
> (Fr. 15.53-61 Snell)[7]

All men can attain to justice; *hybris,* greed, unrighteous power, lead to destruction. This kind of universalized philosophy for "Everyman" is found in a victory ode:

> To have a happy destiny from the gods is best for men, but Chance, coming with heavy weight, crushes the *esthlos,* and, bringing prosperity, makes the *kakos* eminent. Different are the forms of *timā* and myriad the *aretai* of men, but one stands out from all: whosoever guides what lays at hand with a mind that is just.
>
> (Ode XIV. 1-11 Snell)[8]

Esthlos and *kakos* here have no social class significance, but neither do they have a deeper moral force. Rather we should understand them as meaning "capable," "of worth" and the opposite. What is of great interest in these lines is that by now the notion that the best *aretē* is justice has become something of a commonplace in ethical thought, and can be considered valid on a universal scale. In almost every respect the system of ethical values that Bacchylides expounds is sufficiently generalized to be applied to the whole of Greek society, noble and non-noble alike; and even when he honors aristocratic victors he does not claim any exclusive excellence for aristocrats. In an ode celebrating an Athenian youth's win in the foot race at the Isthmian games he lists the various ways one can gain "conspicuous fame" *(doxa).* A man may be "wise" *(sophos)* or "have obtained *timā* from the Graces" or be versed in divination. In terms of the ideal expressed by Pindar and Theognis these particular skills and attributes would be the province of aristocratic gentlemen. He then goes on to say that some men pursue wealth, others expend their spirits in farming or herding. Here activities that cannot be considered exclusively aristocratic are listed. All this is prelude to the thought that we do not know what the future will bring. The next lines are:

> The finest thing of all is to be an *esthlos* man envied by many. I know also the great power of wealth, which makes the useless man *(achreios)* useful *(chrēstos).*
>
> (Ode X.47-51)

As in Ode XIV, just quoted, *esthlos anēr* does not signify "aristocrat," but has the general meaning of "worthy" or "estimable" because of achievement. In other words, although life is unsure, the moment of triumph in which one is called *esthlos* is fate's fairest gift. And this is naturally expressed in terms of approbation (or, in an agonistic situation, "envy") by society at large. Bacchylides' statement that money has the power to make a useless man seem useful is not an attack on wealth or the wealthy, but merely the recognition of the fact that wealth without achievement can make a man honored in the community.[9] Implicitly he rejects this narrowest conception of excellence in favor of a broader vision of *aretē*.[10] A similar pattern of thought is found in another victory song (Ode I.159-84):

> I say, and I shall say, that it is *aretā* which has the greatest glory *(kydos)*. Wealth attends even the *deiloi* of men ...

Bacchylides then praises piety, good health and moderate means; if a man has these,

> He rivals the most important of men *(prōtois)*. Delight follows every human life (apart from disease and helpless poverty) ...

Then follow some familiar gnomes: that abundance is no guarantee of pleasure, mortal hopes are transitory; a man who is stirred by empty cares

> gets honor *(timā)* for only as long as he lives; but *aretā*, toilsome as it is, when completed rightly, leaves a man an envied monument of glory *(eukleia)*.

As Lesky says, this is "very every day philosophy that he imparts ...," and it might be said, perhaps, that the same sentiments are found in Theognis and Pindar. Nevertheless, in "this inherited cloak of philosophy that he never makes his own," there is lacking the persistent sense of social exclusiveness found in the aristocratic apologists.[11] Just as Simonides allowed to every man the possibility of moral worth, Bacchylides conceives general excellence to be something attainable by all, and not a quality belonging exclusively to a particular class. It has been recently demonstrated that while Pindar, in his epinicians, "insists relentlessly on the genealogical principle," Bacchylides exhibits an "overwhelming difference" in his treatment of the same theme, referring only rarely to birth and descent.[12]

It is because Simonides and Bacchylides were not spokesmen for a class, even though they wrote poetry commissioned by aristocrats, that their evidence is such a valuable counterbalance. They are further proof that at the end of the archaic period the aristocratic pretensions to superiority on the basis of higher ethical and moral standards of behavior were not universally accepted. By allowing such standards to be the property of all men of proper intent (Simonides) or by presenting them as a kind of common coin (Bacchylides) they implicitly negate the exclusivism of those who insisted that only by birth and breeding could a man legitimately aspire to moral and intellectual excellence.

There has survived another body of poetry quite different in form from the epinicians of Pindar and the elegiacs of Theognis, but which echoes faithfully the social attitudes observed in their writings. This collection of about thirty short poems has come down under the title of *scolia,* or "drinking songs," mostly Athenian and composed during the last part of the sixth and the first part of the fifth centuries B.C.[13] Sung at informal gatherings of nobles, and embracing a number of subjects, their tone and content express the sentiments of their anonymous composers. They show that most of the tenets of the aristocratic ideal that had evolved during the preceding centuries continued to flourish into the fifth century, largely unchanged, but, by this time, somewhat stylized.

The aristocratic insistence on reserving the epithet *agathos* as an exclusive self-designation persists in the *scolia.* A couplet commemorating an early opponent of the Pisistratids goes:

> If it is proper to pour wine for *agathoi* men, pour a drink for Cedon, attendant, do not forget.
>
> (Fr. 906 Page)

Here the aristocratic Cedon is directly equated with "good men." Another *scolion* laments the loss of members of the Alcmeonid clan in a battle against the tyrants on Mount Leipsydrion in Attica:

> Alas, Leipsydrion, betrayer of comrades. What sort of men have you destroyed, *agathoi* at fighting and *eupatridai,* who showed at that time from what fathers they were sprung.
>
> (Fr. 907 Page)

The nobles "good at fighting" are given the by now familiar aristocratic epithet "sons of noble fathers." The primary emphasis of the quatrain is on the noble ancestry of the men, which is seen as the basis of their bravery. An early love song, not in the collection of *scolia*, but surely of aristocratic origin, combines the themes of homosexuality, noble lineage, proper style and bravery:

> O youths, who have the Graces *(Charites)* and are of *esthloi* fathers, do not begrudge to share your youth with *agathoi*. For in the *poleis* of the Chalcidians Love, the looser of limbs, flourishes along with manliness *(andreia)* . . .
>
> (Fr. 873 Page)

The aristocratic obsession with friendship and loyalty is the subject of several songs:

> Would that it were possible to open each man's chest, just as he really was, and look at his mind and close it up again, and think he was a friend with guileless heart.
>
> (Fr. 889 Page)

> Whoever does not betray a friend has, to my mind, great *timē* among both mortals and the gods.[14]
>
> (Fr. 908 Page)

The second poem, by making faithfulness in friendship a source of glory, shows not only the great importance attached to the virtue of personal loyalty in the aristocratic scheme, but also to what degree the ideal had turned from the standard of external success as the basis of *timē*, to internal considerations. The social aspect of the aristocratic concept of friendship is seen in the following couplet:

> Having learned the tale of Admetus, comrade, love the *agathoi*, but keep away from the *deiloi*, knowing that in the *deiloi* there is little *charis*.
>
> (Fr. 897 Page)

As in Theognis, *agathoi/deiloi* are used as social catchwords, right knowledge is made the province of *agathoi* and proper style is denied to the *deiloi*. The correct mode of behavior expected of an aristocratic friend is given in two lines that might have come from the pens of Alcaeus, Anacreon or Theognis:

> Drink with me, be young with me, love with me, be crowned with me. Be mad with me when I am mad, restrained *(sōphronein)* when I am restrained.[15]
>
> (Fr. 902 Page)

Succinctly listed in another *scolion* are the qualities of life that commended themselves most to young nobles of this time:

> The best thing for a mortal man is to have good health, second to be born *kalos* in body, third to be wealthy without deceit, and the fourth to be young with friends.
>
> (Fr. 890 Page)

The high priority placed on personal beauty in the ideal had by this time become a convention, as, in fact, had the rest of the qualities mentioned in the song. An earlier age would have rated all these things highly, of course, but the omission of personal glory achieved by some great effort or by service to the polis reveals the inward and non-assertive character of the evolving aristocratic ideal. The slight and the frivolous are often the main subjects of interest:

> Would that I were a pretty *(kalē)* lyre made of ivory and *kaloi paides* take me to the dance of Dionysos
>
> (fr. 900 Page),

eclipsing the older calls to glory and achievement.[16] With very few exceptions the collection is devoid of martial themes or exhortations to political activity. At a time when great events were stirring the hearts of men throughout the Greek world and patriotic pride was especially high in Athens the *scolia* concentrated on the good life—song, boys, feasting—all implying the superiority of the values professed by the aristocrats. If these *scolia* are typical of aristocratic songs of the late 500's and the early 400's then they provide a perfect illustration of the psychological outlook of the aristocratic class. When noble youths raised their cups and sang,

> A mortal man does not need to have much, but to make love and eat — but you are too sparing
>
> (fr. 913 Page),

the impression given is of an outlook far removed from the practical cares and anxieties of their peasant countrymen and from the ideal of glory (personal or communal) that we think of as being so integral to Hellenic culture.

A much different point of view is found in a *scolion* attributed to a Cretan aristocrat named Hybrias. Like the others quoted above its date is uncertain, perhaps late sixth century. In conservative, oligarchical Crete, untouched by new currents of social change, aristocratic superiority is a matter of blunt fact:

> My great wealth is my spear, my sword and my fine shield, my skin's defence. With this I plow, with this I reap, with this I tread the sweet wine from the vines, with this I am called master *(despotās)* of the "serfs" *(mnoia)*. They who dare not have spear and sword and fine shield, skin's defence, all fall at my knees, bow down and call me *despotās* and great *basileus*.
>
> (Fr. 909 Page)

Opponents of the Athenian democracy were later to term the intense interest in civic affairs by the rank and file *polypragmosynē* (meddlesomeness) and their own withdrawal into the "quiet" life *apragmosynē* (retirement from public affairs). The aristocratic tendency to retreat, already evident in the late archaic period, was to become more pronounced as the fifth century progressed. The upper class defiantly adopted it as a symbol of their superiority, while non-aristocrats branded it as anti-social. In the famous Funeral Oration, reportedly delivered by Pericles shortly after the outbreak of the Peloponnesian War, Thucydides has the Athenian statesman give the classic democratic rebuttal to this attitude:

> Here each individual is interested not only in his own affairs but in the affairs of the state as well: even those who are mostly occupied with their own business are extremely well-informed on general politics — this is a peculiarity of ours: we do not say that a man who takes no interest in politics is a man who minds his own business *(apragmōn)*, we say that he is useless *(achreios)*.[17]

The fifth century was, as we have intimated, a period of crisis for the aristocracy. During the course of the century, in many of the *poleis* of the Greek world, especially in Athens, the largest and the most powerful, the balance of political power had shifted to the *dēmos*. Space and the nature of our study permit only a brief account of political and constitutional developments. We may begin by stating some general considerations. First, "We do not know when or in which states or by what stages the demos as a whole first gained the constitutional power of decision in a Greek city."[18] The process varied in time and in degree from state to state; broadly speaking, however, the evolution took place during the turbulent sixth century, in face of the deep resentment and active resistance of the dominant élite of birth and wealth. By 500 B.C. "rule by hereditary aristocracies had become rare in the Greek world,"[19]

The Aristocratic Ideal in the Classical Period 123

having been replaced by governments with a broader base of participation – typically ones in which the *whole* of the citizenry, the *dēmos* (freeborn, adult males with kin-group membership), enjoyed equal protection under law and formed a sovereign assembly whose decision on communal matters was final. Second, "citizen" *(politēs)* was "defined" along a narrower or broader spectrum of property ownership. In some *poleis* (like Athens) even those with no land had citizen rights, while in others ownership of land was prerequisite even for assembly membership. The same criterion of property ownership dictated the extent of wider civic participation – as in the holding of political and judicial offices and in military status – so that during the fifth century power could be said to be in the hands of "the few" or "the many." Thus, both explicitly and implicitly "rule by the few" *(oligarchia)* and "rule by the *dēmos*" *(dēmokratia)* stated, politically, the range of economic control in a polis. In a "broad-based" oligarchy, for example, the whole of the hoplite class (defined in terms of landholding) will have been full citizens; other polities would extend to the left or right of this centrist pattern. Third, in all *poleis,* oligarchic or democratic, despite the loosening of its exclusive hold on the machinery of government, the ancient aristocracy maintained its unique position of leadership, providing the bulk of prominent politicians and exerting a constant (if uneven) pull towards more oligarchical rule. Although Athens exemplifies the movement towards the extreme form of democracy, she can serve as a model of the constitutional evolution of most Greek states during this period.

As we saw (above, pp. 68-69), the reforms of Solon did not solve Athens' political and economic problems. The difficulties of the poor remained, and infighting among aristocratic factions continued; the result was a period of civic disorder, culminating in the emergence of a *tyrannos,* Pisistratus, in 546 B.C. Although he was an aristocrat (a kinsman of Solon, in fact) Pisistratus' rule favored the *dēmos,* which had supported him, and tended to neutralize the powerful aristocratic houses: by centralizing the powers of government, giving loans to small farmers, initiating large public works, strengthening the state cult of Athena (over local, hence aristocratic, hero cults), enlarging the Panathenaic festival, and increasing the scope of Athens' interests abroad. He was succeeded at his death by his sons, one of whom was assassinated by a pair of aristocratic lovers, and the other exiled when rival aristocrats, led by the Alcmeonid Cleisthenes, called in the Apartans (always eager to bring down tyrants) who ended the dynasty in 510.

After two years of renewed aristocratic quarreling Cleisthenes and his faction won out over his conservative opponent Isagoras, by offering to the people a revolutionary political program which transformed Athens into a democratic state.

Space allows only the briefest sketch of Cleisthenes' complex legislation, by which, as Herodotus says, "he took the *dēmos* into partnership" (5.66). The essential step was the replacement of the four ancient Ionian tribes by ten new and totally artificial "tribes," into which citizens from the whole of Attica were redistributed in such a way that each tribe contained a geographical cross-section of the population. Thus at one stroke the old allegiances to region and to the aristocratic lineages which held local political power were broken up. The ten tribes also mustered as hoplite regiments and formed the framework of a new democratic council *(boulē)* of 500 members (50 from each tribe) selected annually by lot. The basic building blocks of the new tribes were the 170 or so existing "demes" (villages or urban neighborhoods) which had their own governmental apparatus. By making the deme the focus of a citizen's daily life (one's deme became part of one's name) Cleisthenes preserved the vitality of the local tribal principle, at the same time reducing the extent of control of powerful local families. Henceforth the Athenian's political activity centered on his residential "home rule" deme and the central state, freed from dependency on coalitions of regional "big men."

Of the many striking features of this remarkable restructuring of an ancient government, the most striking is that it was a deliberate act, by one of the most powerful aristocrats, consciously intended to give power to the majority and take it away from the old ruling families. The event is proof of the increased power of the non-aristocratic majority. After 508 B.C. the would-be leader had to accommodate himself to the interests of the sovereign people. Athens' internal politics after Cleisthenes is the record of steady (if uneven) growth of democratic government, punctuated by the continued jockeying for leadership by prominent nobles, some favoring, some opposing, the rapid rate of democratization, but all constrained to woo the *dēmos*. Those politicians with oligarchical tendencies inclined towards Sparta and were reluctant witnesses to the widening rift between the two powers, which solidified after the Persian Wars. Democratic leaders pushed for Athenian expansion and were committed to an Athenian "empire" overseas, made possible by a strong navy, manned by rowers who were from the lowest socioeconomic stratum. By the late 460's the "radical" democrats had prevailed; under Ephialtes, and later Pericles, sweeping popular reforms were enacted which further reduced the authority of the old aristocratic institutions and placed their powers firmly in the hands of the majority. Both in Athens and elsewhere by the middle of the fifth century there had evolved a consciously expressed democratic ideology, based on the fundamental premise that every citizen, regardless of status, was equally useful to the community. As the old, exclusive organs of government, by which a few could make policy binding on the many, were dissolved or rendered impotent, and as decision-making at every level and on every matter became the prerogative of the entire citizenry, an aggressive spirit of total equality surfaced.

The most eloquent exposition of the Athenian democratic system is preserved in Pericles' Funeral Oration of 431 B.C.

> Our constitution *(politeia)* is called a *dēmokratia* because power is in the hands not of a minority *(oligoi)* but of the whole people *(pleiones)*. When it is a question of settling private disputes, everyone is equal before the law; when it is a question of putting one person before another in positions of public responsibility, what counts is not membershp in a particular class *(meros)*, but the actual ability *(aretē)* which the man possesses. No one, so long as he has it in him to be of service to the polis, is kept in political obscurity because of poverty . . .
>
> Our love of what is beautiful does not lead to extravagance; our love of the things of the mind does not make us soft. We regard wealth as something to be properly used, rather than as something to boast about. As for poverty, no one need be ashamed to admit it: the real shame is in not taking practical measures to escape from it . . . .
>
> Taking everything together then, I declare that our polis is an education *(paideusis)* to Greece, and I declare that in my opinion each single one of our citizens, in all the manifold aspects of life, is able to show himself the rightful lord and owner of his own person, and do this, moreover, with exceptional grace *(charis)* and exceptional versatility . . . .
>
> (Thucy. 2.37.1; 40.1; 41.1;
> adapted from the Warner trans.)

Even in these brief excerpts the main aspects of the democratic ideology, in contradistinction to the aristocratic ideal, are evident: positive equality (as opposed to the earlier, less inclusive, notion of equal protection under law), service to the polis as the sole basis of approbation, preference of ability over privilege, and, not insignificantly, slighting reference to aristocratic life-style. The condition of political equality inevitably fosters the idea of social equality, and the dilemma of the aristocrat in the fifth century was the maintenance of a sense of class superiority in a society which now consciously opposed manifestations of class superiority. The dilemma was heightened by the very nature of Greek ethical thought. Since the early archaic period the ultimate justification for calling oneself *agathos* had been expressed in terms of service and usefulness to the community, in accordance, naturally, with the demands of the society at any particular time. In a democracy one could be *agathos* only insofar as he fostered the interests of the *democratic* state; thus the traditional upper class indicators of exclusiveness and superiority were in jeopardy. Adkins neatly summarizes the problem which confronted the aristocrat:

> If one is a democrat in a democratic society, and finds those who are traditionally held to be the 'best' citizens — i.e. men of wealth and good family — not to one's taste, the manner in which one will redefine the term *agathos* is clear. The cry must be 'It isn't what a man is that matters, but what he does.'[20]

Accordingly, it became important in the fifth century to devise subtle means of suggesting superiority without antagonizing middle and lower class democratic sensibilities. In general, those who wanted positive recognition of their status as aristocrats managed to impress on the public consciousness the traditional claims to excellence. Some fifth-century aristocrats resolved the problem with little strain, making themselves champions of the *dēmos,* identifying themselves with the aspirations of the common people and the ideals of the democratic institutions, while all nobles in public life could exploit their ancestry and wealth by referring to the services of their forebears on behalf of the state or to their own public expenditures as trierarch or choregos.[21] The aristocratic ideal, then, lived on through the fifth century, adapted to the pressures which democracy placed on the open expression of class superiority.

Other new directions in the evolving aristocratic ideal are connected to the changes in political life. As automatic hegemony in the sphere of political activity diminished, the aristocratic tendency to claim higher intellectual and moral worth, observed in the late archaic period, becomes more pronounced, while at the same time manifestations of a distinctive life-style become even more obvious. This section will treat the main elements of the self-image of the upper class in the fifth century B.C.: subtle evocation of noble lineage and ancestral wealth, and pretensions to innate qualities of mental and moral excellence possessed only by this group. The final chapter will deal with the style of life peculiar to the noble class.

As in the previous chapters an examination of social terminology will illuminate trends in the aristocratic class' conception of itself and of the lower classes. We are immediately struck by the fact that in the course of the fifth century sociopolitical vocabulary became much richer and more varied. A larger number of such terms is found, many apparently for the first time, and these have greater social impact. They are, for example, more vividly descriptive and emotional, attesting to a deepening awareness of social and economic distinctions. Words indicating noble birth and pride of ancestry had been evident in Greek literature since the early seventh century. In the fifth century expressions of birth appear more often, with some increase in variety.[22] More significant is the appearance of a larger number of "valuative" words employed by aristocrats to describe themselves and others. Epithets like *eugeneis* and *gennaioi* had, through long usage, achieved by this time a quasi-technical status, but other terms reveal a much higher level of class consciousness. The common use, for example, of *hoi oligoi* (the few) as a self-appellation of aristocrats signals the desire for an appearance of exclusiveness. The opposite term, *hoi polloi* (the many) was almost always used disparagingly, as was very often the case with *ho ochlos* (the mob) or *to plēthos* (the mass). Other words had an even greater value significance. Fifth-century aristocrats called themselves *gnōrimoi* (well-known, notable), *epieikeis* (capable), *epiphaneis* (conspicuous), *charientes* (elegant, accomplished).[23] *Agathoi* and *esthloi* continued to be used as class terms, although by the fifth century these had become more generalized in meaning and application and hence less exclusive; the superlatives *aristoi* and *beltistoi*, which were very seldom found as social terms in the archaic period, became more favored epithets.

Most such terms of self-designation stress both the ability and the visibility of the upper class and illustrate an important dimension in aristocratic thinking during the classical period. With the triumph of "government by popular consent" in the fifth century it became even more imperative for those who wished to lead to convince the majority of their value to the community. Whereas in the earliest period aristocrats had ruled by virtue of automatic prestige, exercising a natural control over their communities, under the impact of popular challenge to this self-assumed hegemony the nobility began to insist on its pre-eminence in birth, manners and character. But during the classical period when control by popular assemblies became more widespread it was necessary to create a broader image of superiority of talent and innate ability. It was for this reason that so many of the epithets chosen by aristocrats to describe themselves during the fifth century self-consciously affirm that the upper class was "fittest" to hold positions of political and social eminence.

Other items in the arsenal of aristocratic vocabulary were designed to reinforce this impression. For example, the terms *hoi dynamenoi*, *hoi dynatoi* (the able, the powerful – sometimes found in the superlative form, *hoi cynatōtatoi*) were commonly applied to the oligarchical factions of the various Greek states to underline the capability and the political potency of the aristocratic class.

Still another group of descriptive terms proliferated in the fifth century, accenting the fact that the upper class possessed the requisite material means to allow leisure for political activity. Words describing the wealthy class during the archaic period, like *plousioi* and *olbioi*, were fairly neutral in meaning, with little inference of value judgment. Fifth-century expressions describing possession of wealth or its lack were more heavily laden with ethical implications: e.g. *hoi euporoi* (those who have the means), *hoi ta chrēmata* (or *tas ousias*) *echontes* (those who possess goods, those who possess the means). The fact that a number of valuative epithets denoting the opposite condition come into use, shows how important this aspect of the aristocratic self-conception was. Thus the neutral term *hoi penētes* (the poor) was often joined in context with the disparaging "the many," while others, like *hoi aporoi* (those without means), *hoi ouk echontes* (those who do not have) reveal a similar bias. The pejorative intent of such a clear-cut delineation of economic competence is seen in new words like *misthioi* and *misthophoroi* (wage earners), applied to the common people.

Most revealing are the words used by aristocratic writers to describe the lower class which have definite overtones of moral inferiority. Some of them survive from the archaic period – *kakoi, deiloi* – others, like *hoi cheirous* (the inferior), seldom used earlier with social significance, now become common descriptions of the lower class. A good example of this process is the frequent use of the words *ponēroi* and *mochthēroi* as synonyms for the lower class. Both words derive from roots indicating difficult labor, toil or suffering, and had a neutral sense until the fifth century, at which time they became ethical/social terms describing persons who, because they had to work hard, were politically and socially inferior, "knavish." [24]

The depth and intensity of the battle of semantics, in which old words were given social, political and moral nuances and new terms were coined which were colorfully emotive is symbolized in the fifth-century usage of *dēmos* and *kaloskagathos*. *Dēmos* was not a descriptive term; as ancient as the language itself, it had, until the end of the archaic period, little social or class significance and very little sense of a political division within the polis. But in fifth-century aristocratic usage it served as an equivalent to "the mob," "the commons," as opposed to the "better" class of people. It was also during the fifth century that adjectives and nouns were formed from the originally pallid *dēmos* – *dēmotikos, dēmokratikos, dēmokratia* – which, in the mouths of the nobles, were often used as pejorative terms. *Kaloskagathos* (beautiful and good) made its appearance only in the fifth century and shows clearly the psychological "mood" of the aristocratic class during this period, for it evoked a powerful range of responses, combining the ancient (but now disputed) aristocratic self-epithet with one that by universal consent was confined to the noble group. *Kalos* signified not only external physical beauty but also the whole range of elegance in style and appearance, fine manners and proper comportment, with overtones, in addition, of the aristocratic practice of pederasty. If we translate it as "gentleman" in the sense that it was used in England during the eighteenth and nineteenth centuries we can fairly closely approximate its meaning.[25]

The preceding sketch of sociopolitical vocabulary makes clear the main intent of the self-image projected by aristocrats in the fifth century: because of their superior natural ability and qualities of mind and spirit, together with their greater economic competence, aristocrats were more fit than others to assume leading roles in the machinery of government. A closer examination of the writings of fifth-century intellectuals will reveal these attitudes in greater detail. It must be borne in mind that the literature that has survived from this period (as from the earlier periods) is largely the expression of an intellectual and social élite, often antagonistic to the claims of the classes below them, even in a democratic state like Athens. Less has come down to us of the democratic opposition to the "propaganda" of aristocratic reactionaries. When, for example, we find those who would term themselves "the rich," referred to as "the fat" *(hoi pacheis),* we can assume that this was a popular counter-epithet meant to disparage, but too little of this kind of thing survives to indicate the extent or manner of lower class rejection of aristocratic terminology.[26] The one-sidedness of our information makes it difficult to identify fully the complete spectrum of social attitudes; nevertheless, enough has survived to demonstrate the existence of an anti-aristocratic, pro-democratic body of opinion.

The intellectual foundations of the democratic ideology were laid by certain fifth-century thinkers, known collectively as the "sophists." The so-called "sophistic movement," a free-wheeling, radical reexamination of man in relation to his environment — described by Fränkel as "the emancipation of the intellect from any and every shackle laid upon it"[27] — took place after the middle of the century in Athens, by then the acknowledged intellectual center of Greece, which magnetically drew thinkers from all over the Hellenic world. So complex a mélange of ideas as the sophistic movement is not easily summarized, especially since the sophists were individual thinkers, not a systematic school. Nevertheless, certain fundamental attitudes were shared by all the sophistic teachers, among which were a strong bias towards the practical and the possible (grounded in the realm of common-sense reality) and a thoroughgoing scepticism which negated the possibility of absolute knowledge. The most controversial result of sophistical speculation was the dichotomy they perceived between "law" or "custom" *(nomos)*, the result of pure convention, and "nature" *(physis)*, an impersonal force, the real state of things. The application of the *nomos-physis* antithesis to human society led to the bold idea that law and custom were man-made conventions relative to the natural human state. All laws and all "moral" values, including even justice, were creations of human intellect. The state itself was an invention of man, a social contract, evolved over time for mutual security, support and benefit. Such an "anthropological" view of humankind and its institutions, which sees all men as genetically similar and possessing a common set of drives, leads easily to the idea that society is necessarily a cooperative endeavor, in which everyone had an equal stake (and share). The primary objective of political organization is the cohesion and stability of the group; hence, all group members, regardless of status, are essentially equal.

These principles, arrived at by means of strict rational enquiry, naturally favored the fact of Athenian democracy, and the "liberal" teachings of the sophists were diffused into the general intellectual climate of fifth-century Athens. The "twin articles of faith" of the liberal theorists — first, that men are biologically equal and demand a relationship in law and justice that conforms to this equality, and second, that men possess a fundamental good will that would be dangerously thwarted by any principle which advocated superior force — were, as we have seen, quite antithetical to the traditional presuppositions of the upper class.[28] The reaction against such reasoning was fierce, especially because the sophistic notion that egalitarian democracy, for all its faults, was "a natural and historical condition," responded to the deep-rooted sense of egalitarianism inherited from the Greek tribal past.

Two quotations from the political theorists will give us a sense of their pro-democratic, egalitarian point of view. Democritus of Abdera (in Thrace), known not only as a scientist but as a political philosopher, was active in Athens in the second half of the fifth century. Among his political maxims this one stands out:

> Poverty under democracy is as much to be preferred to so-called prosperity under an autocracy as freedom to slavery.
>
> (B 251)

Antiphon, the fifth-century sophist, has this to say about noble birth:

> We revere and honour those born of noble fathers, but those who are not born of noble houses we neither revere nor honour. In this we are, in our relations with one another, like barbarians, since we are all by nature born the same in every way, both barbarians and Hellenes . . . .
>
> (B 44)[29]

At this point we can attempt a more developed analysis of the configuration of the aristocratic ideal in the fifth century B.C. The centrality of the notion that aristocrats were *by nature* better suited than others to lead is evident from our examination of terminology, and it is to be expected that the noble class would concentrate its greatest energy in proving this contention. Theognis, we recall, had expressed the idea as a kind of forlorn hope and Pindar had proclaimed it with myopic optimism, saying that the *agathoi* were fittest by birth to rule, and proving it by connecting the *agathoi* of his day with the ancient heroes of their *poleis*. Pindar's somewhat simplistic appeal to inborn superiority was not without force during the fifth century, and from time to time we find this idea expressed in the literature, put in the mouths of aristocratic spokesman.[30] In the *Ajax* of Sophocles, Menelaus, confronting Ajax' brother Teucer, says:

And yet, it is the mark of a *kakos* man when one who is an ordinary citizen *(dēmotēs)* thinks it right not to heed those who have been set over him.

(1071-72)

Implicit in Menelaus' statement is the value judgment that men are naturally divided into rulers or the ruled, a notion that is made explicit in 666ff., where submission to leaders *(archontes)* is analogous to natural law, as when winter yields to summer. To be sure, this sort of sentiment could be accepted by everyone since the appeal is not overtly to rule by an upper class but merely by those who have been set above. Menelaus, in fact, continues to speak in terms of the safety of the polis and the need to respect the laws. After Menelaus' speech the chorus agrees that his were "wise words" (1091-92). Still, Teucer recognizes the social implications quite clearly; he retorts that it is no wonder that a man "who was nothing in birth" would commit wrong when "those who claim to have been born *eugeneis*" err so in their speech. Teucer's point is that Menelaus was in no way the rightful lord of the Salaminians:

You came as lord of Sparta, not as ruler over us; you had no more right of rule over them than he over you.

(1102-04)

Teucer makes the clear distinction between a ruler who commands by right (i.e. by consent of the people, in democratic terms) and one who assumes it by the claim of birth or heritage (1093-1108).

This exchange is significant in that it expresses the polarization between the claims of democracy, in which all men are (at least theoretically)equal and the aristocratic conviction of a group fittest to rule by "nature."[31] An excellent example of such tension is found in an anecdote related by the historian Herodotus. He says that when the tyrant of Samos, Polycrates, died *(ca.* 522 B.C.), his apparent successor, a man named Maiandrios, assembled the citizens and proclaimed that he wished not to be tyrant but wanted to give the Samians their freedom. His democratic gesture was met by the retort of a Samian aristocrat, who immediately rose in the assembly and said: "But you are not fit *(axios)* to rule anyway, since you were badly born *(gegonōs kakōs)* and a plague," and demanded instead that Maiandrios give an accounting of public monies (3.142). The point of interest to us is not that the nobleman, Telesarchus, was not anxious to see a democracy in Samos, but that he also gave voice to his resentment that a man of low birth could presume to hold or relinquish power.

A similar attitude is found in the *Oedipus Tyrannus* of Sophocles, from a different vantage point. Although the passage in question (1062ff.) is primarily concerned with the dramatic irony of Oedipus' real parentage, the situation may be taken as sufficiently representative. Thinking that he may be the son of a slave, Oedipus is determined to discover the truth. Jocasta, fearing the real truth and trying to dissuade Oedipus from further enquiry, appears to Oedipus to be upset at his low birth. Throughout the scene the reaction of Oedipus is that regardless of his low birth, or the shame that his high-born queen may feel, he is still the same man and (by implication) worthy to rule. Here again, the polarity in fifth-century political thought is revealed. On the one hand was the jealously guarded democratic tenet that low birth was not a deterrent to high position or prestige; on the other, the aristocratic idea that low birth was an automatic disqualification.

There are instances of this aristocratic conceit in the plays of Aristophanes. In the *Knights* the ignorant Sausage Seller is being interviewed as a possible successor to the democratic politician Cleon as the leader of the Athenians. Surprised at being considered for the post he demurs that his position makes him unqualified, but Demosthenes insists that the very baseness of his life makes him the perfect replacement for Cleon. When the Sausage Seller continues to say that he is unworthy Demosthenes asks:

>   You are not of the *kaloik' agathoi* are you?
> S.S. No, by the gods, but sprung from knaves *(ponēroi)*.
> De. Oh, blessed man, the perfect background for public life!
> (*Knights* 185-87)

Here, in exaggerated form, is the aristocratic feeling that in the extreme democracy high birth was a distinct disadvantage for high position. These passages also obliquely demonstrate that during the classical period aristocrats made specific claims to public leadership on the basis of innate superiority and that this claim was resisted by the mass of public opinion. They show, in addition, that noble birth, *eugeneia*, one of the chief emblems of superiority during the archaic period, continued to hold a certain pride of place, but not the foremost by any means; public sentiment was so suspicious of it that it could function as only one of the indexes of upper-class superiority. The problem for the aristocrat was that as *eugeneia* became more important in the aristocratic self-conception it clashed head on with democratic ideas of equality. The consequence of the tension was that *within the context of democratic politics* noble birth could not be used as a primary justification of superiority, and yet it could not be omitted without abandoning a fundamental precept of the aristocratic ideal. The obvious solution to the paradox was to align *eugeneia* with other qualities, giving it an emphasis, but not an absolute one. This raises another difficulty: *eugeneia*, if coupled with other, more active qualities, will inevitably appear extraneous and accidental, hence, more vulnerable to attack. Thus the objective accident of *eugeneia* had to be made to appear an intimate part of the nexus of aristocratic personal qualities, integral to it and not an isolated phenomenon. It was this kind of necessity that motivated the coinage of a term like *kaloskagathos,* which subsumed the idea of *eugeneia.*

In contexts other than purely political the argument from birth is more frequently found. In these instances the resort to *eugeneia* is not the bald assertion of automatic superiority but a (more or less implicit) plea that good lineage makes a man a better man. It was least assailable when it was linked to the good of the polis and stated subtly, as in the *Knights* (565 ff.) where the youthful knights praise "our fathers" who made the polis great and protected her against the foe. The appeal to the great deeds of ancestors as a justification for the goodness of the present generation was a potent one, frequently resorted to by the upper class. And, in general, precisely because *eugeneia* was not advanced as a simple justification of superiority but as an index to a higher mode of ethical behavior, it was not as vulnerable to challenge. When Antigone says to Ismene, concerning Creon's order denying burial to their brother, "You will soon show whether you are *eugenēs* or the *kakē* daughter of *esthloi*" (Sophocles, *Antigone* 37-38), she is using noble birth as a criterion of moral courage. Should Ismene prove morally weak, however, she would, in essence, belie her heritage; thus *eugeneia* is not made a *guarantee* of better conduct but a *spur* to better conduct. Such an attitude is really a form of *noblesse oblige,* which could be appealed to by aristocrats with little fear that society at large would oppose or contradict, especially because its basis was the tradition of heroic behavior, long enshrined in the Greek consciousness. As Ajax says, before he commits suicide:

> But either to live nobly or to die nobly *(kalōs)* is the duty of the *eugenēs.*
>
> (*Ajax* 479-80)

A similar attitude is reflected by Philoctetes who, grateful to Neoptolemus for his kindness, praises the youth by telling him that "your nature *(physis)* is *eugenēs* as you are from *eugeneis*" (Sophocles, *Philoctetes* 874), but when he felt betrayed by Neoptolemus he reverses the praise: "Most shameful *(aischistos)* born of an *aristos* father" (1284).

The opposite claim did not find general acceptance. When Agamemnon berates Teucer in Sophocles' *Ajax* (1226 ff.) for attempting to bury the body of Ajax against his orders, he concentrates on Teucer's slave parentage and the temerity of a "nobody" in challenging the will of a king; but Teucer easily counters by citing his own courageous service at the side of Ajax:

> Such were the deeds he did, and I at his side, the slave, born of a barbarian mother.
>
> (1288-89)

· This was, nevertheless, a touchy issue for the fifth century; and even when, as here, the appeal to real excellence overrides low birth the absolutist claim that true worth was inextricably connected with noble birth still had force and had to be combatted on its own terms. Teucer continues by criticizing Agamemnon's own parentage (in semi-moral terms: Pelop's Phrygian descent, Atreus' monstrous crime, his mother's infidelity), boasting in turn of his descent from Telamon and a royal mother. He can, then, call himself "*aristos* son of two *aristoi*" (1304). Oedipus' response to Jocasta's apparent misgivings about his low birth is similar. He is determined to learn his background "even if it is paltry *(smikros)*" and even though Jocasta may "be ashamed *(aischynomai)* at my base birth *(dysgeneia)*." As "fortune's child" he is secure:

> So sprung, I would never prove to be other than I am; so shall I learn my birth.
>
> (1076-85)

Of the fifth-century dramatists Euripides was the most concerned with conflicting social attitudes, and he expresses the problems and tensions of class from many vantage points. The aristocratic doctrine that their class was morally superior by virtue of birth is stated explicitly several times in his plays. In the *Iphigeneia at Aulis,* for example, Agamemnon, faced with the terrible prospect of having to sacrifice his daughter to ensure a sailing of the Greeks for Troy, laments:

Low birth *(dysgeneia)* has such advantages—for it is easy for them to weep and to speak out everything. And one who is *gennaios* by birth has the same suffering, but dignity rules over our lives, and we are slaves to the mob *(ochlos)*.[32]

(446-50)

This is a clear statement that dignity and restraint are natural (and exclusive) attributes of the aristocratic class.

It must be noted that these passages on *eugeneia* are concerned with ethical/moral superiority; the traditional "success" standard is not in question, since by this time no one, aristocrats included, could reasonably assert that birth (or upbringing) were guarantees of success in war, business or politics; and in democratic Athens it was politically dangerous to claim *tout court* that birth or background made one fitter to direct the destiny of the state in peace or war. These passages also point up one of the thorniest social issues of the age: To what extent was the possession of the "quiet" virtues attributable to birth and upbringing alone or to qualities of character quite independent of these? The discussion thus far indicates that the aristocracy had the natural edge in the argument; those who disagreed could only claim possession. Thus the slave messenger in Euripides' *Helen* says:

For he is *kakos* who does not reverence his master's fortunes, and rejoice with him and sorrow with him in his evils. Indeed, may I, even if I was born a slave, be numbered among the noble slaves *(gennaioi douloi)*, not having the name of free, but the mind. For this is better than being one person to bear two evils – to have a *kakē* mind, and, as a slave, to do the bidding of others.[33]

(726-33)

The "noble slave" type of argument may have been an attempt to bypass the difficulties of debate on the social level and to put the question of personal excellence on a more general plane. In the *Hecuba* of Euripides the queen has just been informed of the sacrificial slaying of her daughter Polyxena by Achilles' son, Neoptolemus. Hecuba's philosophical musings deal with the relationship between natural goodness, lineage and upbringing, but in purely moral terms, skirting explicit mention of any underlying issue of social class. Hecuba says that it is strange that bad *(kakē)* soil can bear good crops and good *(chrēstē)* soil bad crops, depending on circumstances, but always among men the *ponēros* is nothing but *kakos,* and the *esthlos* is *esthlos,* nor is his nature *(physis)* destroyed by misfortune, but he is always worthy *(chrēstos).* Then is it his parentage *(hoi tekontes)* or his upbringing *(trophai)* that makes the difference? In truth, being brought up nobly *(kalōs)* gives the lesson of what is *esthlon;* and if someone has learned this well, he knows what is *aischron,* too, because he has learned according to the standard of the *kalon.*

(592-602)

This is an equally clear statement that blood does not determine good or bad behavior, but that education and training do. Neoptolemus has acted basely, Polyxena has died nobly (546-82). Neither *eugeneia* nor *dysgeneia* are at question since the bloodlines of both characters are excellent, and this gives the playwright an opportunity to set forth egalitarian social philosophy in a non-polemical context. We note, too, that the terms of merit and demerit, all of which were social catchwords in the mouths of aristocrats, have been generalized into a transcendent moral vocabulary, applicable without reference to social standing.

It is in the *Electra* of Euripides (413 B.C.) that we see the clearest exposition of the social problem. Clytaimnestra had forced her daughter Electra to marry a Mycenaean peasant, to insure that there would be no high-born heir to pose a danger to Clytaemnestra and her paramour Aegisthus. But the peasant, out of deep respect for his princess, had not consummated the marriage. The dramatic crux of the relationship between the peasant and Electra rests on the disparity of their stations and the *natural* high-souled quality of the peasant. The peasant establishes his condition in the prologue:

... sprung from Mycenaean ancestors — in this I am not ashamed. For illustrious we are in birth *(genos)* but poor in goods, whereby *eugeneia* is destroyed.

(*Electra* 35-38)

Such a description would fit (as it doubtless was intended to) the majority of the Athenian spectators, freeborn but with little wealth. The problem of the peasant husband's justification of his worth despite lack of high station would have been of great interest to the audience. The justification is given, appropriately enough, by Orestes, Electra's brother, who has just learned of the peasant's reverent and chaste care of his sister. He is ushered into the humble cottage by the peasant, who says proudly:

> For even if I was born poor, in no way will I show a nature low-born *(ēthos dysgenes)*.
>
> (*Electra* 362-63)

Orestes' statement is worthy of being quoted at some length. He begins:

> There is no sure gauge for manliness *(euandria)*; for the natures *(physeis)* of mortals have much confusion. I have seen the son of a *gennaios* father turn out to be nothing, and *chrēsta* children come from *kakoi;* starvation in the soul of a rich man, and great wisdom *(gnōmē)* in a poor body.
>
> (*Electra* 367-72)

Here Orestes contradicts the aristocratic assertion that while an evil man may come of noble parents, no good man can come of *kakoi* parents. Earlier in the play, in a dialogue between Electra and Orestes, Electra terms her peasant husband "born *sōphrōn*" (self-controlled, prudent) because he has not slept with her. Orestes replies:

> A noble man *(gennaios anēr)* you have named him; he should be rewarded.
>
> (261-62)

By having the highborn pair confer on the peasant the important qualities of *sōphrosynē* and *gnōmē* (long claimed as exclusively aristocratic traits), Euripides makes a direct attack on the aristocratic position. An even more explicit statement (clearly traceable to the "anthropological" arguments of the liberal sophists) that noble birth was an accident, and therefore no warrant for claiming exclusive excellence, is found in Euripides' *Alexandros:*

> It is an excessive statement if we praise *eugeneia* in mortals. For long ago, when first we came to be, and earth, our mother, brought mortals forth, the land impressed a like appearance on us all. We have no peculiar trait *(idion);* high birth *(to eugenes)* and low birth *(to dysgenes)* are a single stock *(gona)*; but time, through custom *(nomos)*, has made it a thing of pride.
>
> (Fr. 52.1-8 Nauck)

The preceding discussion has traced the general outlines of the ideological controversy of the second half of the fifth century. Aristocrats could not press too hard the proposition that noble birth *(eugeneia)* made them naturally fit to assume political leadership; direct appeals to *eugeneia* as authorization for political hegemony are infrequent because of the sensitivity of public opinion to bald assertions of this type. More persuasive (and therefore more frequent) is the claim to social priority based on the beneficial deeds of noble forebears. The most complex area of disputation was the extent to which birth and ancestry could be said to determine individual traits of character. The aristocratic presumption that good character was somehow the result of noble birth had a broader latitude of acceptance — such was the force of tradition, coupled to the "by nature" argument, which could be used to support aristocratic superiority as well as democratic equality. Nevertheless, aristocratic insistence that noble birth was an indispensable factor of ethical/moral worth (or its corollary, that low birth automatically precluded internal excellence) was not allowed to go unchallenged. Although it was an essential ingredient in the aristocratic self-conception, ancestry could not stand alone as the determinant of class superiority, whether in questions of political leadership or of social preeminence. Other qualities had to be joined with *eugeneia* in order to make a commanding case. The true role of *eugeneia* in aristocratic propaganda of the fifth century was the subtly stated assumption that nobility of birth was somehow the *basis* of the aristocracy's mental and moral superiority over the other groups in the democracy. *Eugeneia*, then, was fundamental and indispensable because it could appear as the wellspring of those qualities of mind and spirit that made a nobleman a superior person. Intellectual and moral proclivities are traced back to character, which, in the final analysis, is determined genetically.

◊

Keeping in mind this extremely sophisticated, almost subliminal, justification, we can now turn to the more obvious aspects of the upper-class cultural pattern which functioned to demonstrate the depth of the gulf that separated aristocrats from the other orders of Greek society. The pattern may be described as a mosaic of interconnected elements — wealth, moral/intellectual superiority, style of life, education and upbringing — the central and seminal feature of the pattern being noble birth, *eugeneia*.

In the *Electra* of Euripides it was seen that the question of wealth was intimately bound up with nobility of birth. Possession or lack of wealth was a major index of individual worth during the fifth century and was very important in the aristocratic self-image. The reasons for this are obvious; first of all, historically the upper class was composed of families rich in land, and the traditional identification of an aristocracy of birth with the large property holders held true throughout the classical period. There were impoverished nobles and wealthy non-nobles, but for the most part the old landed aristocracy, even after trade and commerce became important sources of income, remained the rich.[34] This fact took on far greater significance in democratic states where large numbers of men of little means had begun to enjoy unprecedented political power, with the result that the needs and demands of the poor were much more apparent. Additionally, for the ancient Greeks (as for many people today) the problems of wealth and poverty were regarded as moral issues as much as purely economic ones. The rich took the position that poverty was a disgraceful condition which diminished the worth of a man and even led to anti-social behavior, whereas the poor maintained that poverty strengthened the will and was an effective inducement to good.[35] In general, however, those who had money held the moral advantage. Even in Pericles' praise of the democracy the bias against poverty is evident. No one should feel shame *(aischron)* in admitting poverty, he says; the more shameful thing *(aischion)* is not to do something to escape it (Thuc. 2.40.1).

These attitudes help to explain why, in an openly partisan attack on the democracy (the so-called *Constitution of the Athenians,* attributed in antiquity to Xenophon), the author could indiscriminately link terms connoting birth, economic status, intellectual ability and moral capacity, everywhere equating the upper class with the rich and useful elements and the lower class with the poor and depraved.[36] In the aristocratic assumption of superiority the intimate connection between wealth and worth was almost axiomatic. Thus, in the *Ion* of Euripides, king Xuthus assures the young prince Ion that his fortune is secure:

> You will not be called either of the twin diseases, ill-born *(dysgenēs)* and poor *(penēs)* together, but *eugenēs* and a man of great wealth.
> (579-81)

Birth, wealth and competency to lead are all connected in a fragment from Eupolis' *Demoi* (412 B.C.?). The chorus of old citizens, complaining of the bad leadership of contemporary Athens, say that in the old days

> We had our generals *(stratēgoi)* from the greatest houses, first *(prōtoi)* in wealth and birth *(ploutos, genos)* to whom we prayed as if to gods – and indeed they were!
> (Fr. 103.4-6)

In an anti-democratic polemic delivered by the Theban herald in Euripides' *Suppliants*, the argument is that ordinary people lack the mental and moral capacity to rule themselves. Democracy is rule by the mob *(ochlos)*, which is easily twisted by unscrupulous demagogues; the *dēmos* cannot reason clearly and, therefore, cannot run the polis. Moreover,

> A peasant *(gaponos)*, a poor man *(penēs)*, even if he were not ignorant, would not be able, because of his toil, to oversee the common interest.
>
> (420-22)

The "Old Oligarch" (as the author of pseudo-Xenophon *Constitution of the Athenians* is called) directly blames the poverty of the *dēmos* for their inclination to commit shameful acts *(aischra)*, adding parenthetically that lack of money is also a reason for their ignorance (1.5). Such was the importance of wealth as an index of personal value that at times it is made to supersede even the powerful commendation of birth, as is apparent from this exchange between Jocasta and Polyneices in Euripides' *Phoenissae*:

> Jo. Did not your *eugeneia* lift you to a high station?
> Poi. To have nothing is an evil; my *genos* did not feed me.
>
> (404-405)

In the same play Polyneices makes a statement with which the majority of the audience would doubtless have agreed:

> An ancient saying, but nevertheless I will speak it — wealth is the thing most honored by men, and of things on earth has the most power. And in quest of it I come with a countless host of spearmen; for a *eugenēs* man who is *penēs* is nothing.[37]
>
> (438-42)

The question of wealth was also central to theoretical discussions of forms of government. In his defense of democracy in the *Suppliants* of Euripides Theseus speaks only of rich and poor (406-408, 433-37). The famous passage in the *Suppliants* on the classes which make up the polis is most instructive in this regard. Theseus divides the state into three groups: the rich *(hoi olbioi)*, who are "useless," and "ever greedy for more"; the poor *(hoi ouk echontes)*, full of envy and easily controlled by base leaders *(ponēroi prostatai)*; and those "in the middle" who save *poleis* and keep the order ordained by the polis (238-45). The class division is purely economic, but at the same time wealth or its lack is made a function of ethical behavior. Thucydides puts a defense of democracy in the mouth of a Sicilian demagogue *(dēmou prostatēs)*, Athenagoras (6.39), which also demonstrates how important economic status was in the Greek conception of political competency. Athenagoras begins by repeating the oligarchic credo:

> There are people who will say that *dēmokratia* is neither an intelligent nor a fair system, and that those who have the money *(hoi echontes ta chrēmata)* are also the best fitted to rule *(archein arista beltious)*....
>
> (Adapted from the Warner translation)

It is important to note the weakness of the Sicilian's rebuttal of this doctrine. The *dēmos*, he says, is the name for the *whole* people, *oligarchia* is only a portion; the rich *(hoi plousioi)* are the best guardians of wealth, the wise *(hoi xynetoi)* are best at counsel, and the many *(hoi polloi)* are the best at listening and judging. He concludes by saying that in a *dēmokratia* all the groups share equally while in an *oligarchia* the many *(hoi polloi)* are given a share of the dangers but get little or none of the benefits. Athenagoras has simply skirted the issue without really addressing himself to the aristocratic claim of superiority based on wealth.[38]

The passages we have examined show quite plainly that in the debate over economic status as a determinant of civic worth the wealthy had a definite edge. The practical Greeks never seriously questioned the advantages of wealth over poverty for individual well-being, but, more importantly, both sides were in increasing agreement that wealth was the real basis of grouping within the political structure of the state. Our fifth and fourth century sources are, in fact, virtually unanimous on two points: first, that "class struggle" was perceived in economic terms, i.e. as the contest between the propertied classes and the poor; and second, that forms of government themselves, quite aside from any ideological trappings they may have acquired, were based on wealth and its lack. Oligarchy was rule by the few wealthy, democracy by the many poor.[39] For propaganda purposes, the realization that wealth was the criterion for rule gave a clear advantage to the elitist position: oligarchs could proclaim that poverty made men inferior or valueless to the polis, at the same time listing the benefits that the rich conferred on the polis through liturgies and taxes.[40] The only effective line of argument for the poor was to accuse the wealthy of arrogance and greed, and assert that poverty actually strengthened a person's character.

◊

We have examined in some detail the importance of wealth in the aristocratic scheme of values; we have also seen that those who were distinguished by noble ancestry were permitted to claim that their lineage was, somehow, an effective inducement to a high standard of ethical behavior. When we probed more deeply into this attitude we found that aristocratic propaganda of the fifth century often went much further, maintaining not simply that noble birth required one to act in a certain way or that it created a predisposition to admirable and praiseworthy characteristics, but that moral and intellectual excellence were inborn qualities possessed only by the nobility. Naturally, if aristocrats could persuade the general populace that this was indeed true, then they possessed a valuable means of retaining the social and political deference of the lower class, even in democratic states. It is easy to understand, therefore, the intensity of the debate among thinking men of the time.

Intelligence, moral rectitude and aesthetic sensibility had become integral to the aristocratic self-conception by the end of the sixth century. During the fifth century those ideas received more systematic articulation, and an even greater intensification of the premium placed on the "quieter" aspects of human nature can be observed (a process which accelerated and reinforced the already apparent inward-turning tendencies of the upper class). By the latter part of the century the claims of mental and moral superiority were central elements in the nobility's defense of its primacy, and aristocratic self-justification increasingly and explicitly asserted that those who were not members of their class were incapable of high ethical behavior or refinement of thought and feeling.

These pretensions were closely linked to the other aristocratic claims of superiority based on noble birth, wealth, education and style of life. The obscure and fragmentary sayings of the Ionian philosopher Heraclitus (*fl. ca.* 500 B.C.) provide an early illustration of these ideas:

> For *hoi aristoi* choose one thing in place of all else, everlasting glory among mortals; but *hoi polloi* are glutted like cattle.
>
> (B 2)

> Although the logos is common, *hoi polloi* live as though they had private understanding.
>
> (B 29)
>
> One man is worth a thousand if he is *aristos*.
>
> (B 49)
>
> For what mind or understanding do they have? They believe the poets of the *dēmoi* and use as their teacher the crowd *(homilos)* not knowing that *hoi polloi* are *kakoi*, and the *agathoi* are *oligoi*.
>
> (B 104)

By the last quarter of the century we see the network of attitudes more fully worked out in the Theban herald's speech against democracy in the *Suppliants* of Euripides in which are expressed ideas that recur again and again in anti-democratic arguments: Thebes is ruled by one man, not by the fickle mob *(ochlos)*, seduced by a self-serving, glib demagogue; the *dēmos* cannot reason straight (410-18).

> It is a pestilence *(nosōdes)* to the better sort *(ameinones)* when a base man *(ponēros)* gets honor, charming the *dēmos* with his tongue, having been a nobody before.
>
> (423-25)

In the famous political debate of the Persian princes in the *Histories* of Herodotus the arguments are also moral/intellectual. Speaking in favor of oligarchy and against democracy Megabyzus calls the populace "useless," "witless," "violent," "undisciplined," "without knowledge."

> For how could it know anything when it is untaught, and perceives neither what is *kalon* nor what is fitting; and rushes headlong into affairs without thought, like a river in winter time?
>
> (Herodotus 3.81)

The oligarchs are called by Megabyzus simply *andres aristoi*, as if there could be no argument about their mental and moral superiority.[41]

The Old Oligarch also makes the moral and mental pre-eminence of the upper class the basis of his attack on the democracy. As in the passages previously cited noble birth is not directly named as a proof of aristocratic superiority. The only birth word that appears in the Old Oligarch's political broadside is *gennaios*, found but three times and given no special prominence. The author's principal argument is that the Athenian upper class enjoyed, innately and by virtue of its life-style, higher ethical and intellectual standards than the mass of citizens:

The Aristocratic Ideal in Classical Greece 145

> Throughout the world the best element *(to beltiston)* is opposed to democracy. For among the best people *(hoi beltistoi)* there is the least amount of licentiousness *(akolasia)* and injustice *(adikia)*, but a very keen sense of probity *(ta chrēsta);* among the *dēmos* there is a great deal of ignorance *(amathia)*, disorder *(ataxia)* and depravity *(ponēria)*, for poverty makes them more prone to disgraceful acts *(aischra)* — their lack of education *(apaideusia)*, too, and ignorance *(amathia)*, which in some men is due to lack of money.
>
> (Pseudo Xen. *Ath. Pol.* 1.5)

Later in the same chapter it is explained why the *dēmos* likes a knavish *(ponēros)* leader: it is because his *amathia* and *ponēria* are more profitable to them than the *aretē* and *sophia* of a worthy *(chrēstos)* man (1.7). For the Old Oligarch ignorance and moral turpitude are emblematic of the lower class, wisdom and "virtue" the hallmark of the aristocrat. It is further stated that good government *(eunomia)* is dangerous to the *dēmos* because in such a constitution laws are made by the most clever *(dexiōtatoi)*, the *chrēstoi* punish the *ponēroi*, the *chrēstoi* do the deliberating and do not allow the "madmen" to take part in Council or even to speak in assembly (1.9). The obvious implication is that the upper class possesses a moral and intellectual integrity which the lower class does not, and which it fears. An even more explicit statement of this notion occurs in 2.19 where it is said that the *dēmos* knows which of the citizens are *chrēstoi* and which are *ponēroi*, and that they prefer the *ponēroi* if such are useful to them, and hate the *chrēstoi:*

> For they do not think that the *aretē* of these [*chrēstoi*] was inborn *(pephykenai)* in them for their own [the *dēmos'*] benefit but for their harm.

Here the idea that *aretē* is an inborn quality of the aristocracy is stated as a simple article of faith. Its complement, that the *dēmos* finds this innate *aretē* inimical, means that *aretē* is by nature lacking in the lower class. Assertions of this kind permit the statement (logically absurd, but perfectly consistent with aristocratic doctrine) which follows, to the effect that whoever is not (by birth) a member of the *dēmos* and yet prefers to dwell in "a polis which is democratically rather than oligarchically ruled has prepared himself to be unjust *(adikein)*, and knows that it is easier for a *kakos* to hide in a democratically ruled polis rather than in one that is oligarchical" (2.20)

The comedies of Aristophanes abound in examples of the aristocratic assumption of mental and moral superiority. In a passage from the *Knights*, previously cited, the Sausage Seller confesses that, in addition to his low birth, he is also ignorant:

> But I don't know literature *(mousikē)*, except for my letters, and these few and badly.

Demosthenes retorts that it is a pity he knows even this much,

> For *dēmagōgia* is not for the literary man, nor for one who is *chrēstos* in his habits, but for the ignorant *(amathēs)* and the disgusting *(bdelyros)*.
>
> (188-93)

How important these criteria were is seen in the constant employment by aristocrats of epithets connoting mental and moral capacity. The upper class man is invariably *chrēstos, sōphrōn, dikaios;* others are *ponēroi, amatheis,* and so on. The nobility of birth and wealth simply assumed for its own the entire realm of positive traits of mind and spirit. This process, already advanced during the archaic period, became more widespread during the classical period, and, in addition, was extended more fully to cover all aspects of the "interior" life, private as well as public. The all-embracing quality of the aristocratic point of view is exceptionally well illustrated by a chorus in the *Frogs* of Aristophanes. There they complain that the city behaves towards the *kaloi te kagathoi* of its citizens as it does towards its ancient coinage of silver. Those perfect, most beautiful, unadulterated coins, they sing, the Athenians do not use; instead they prefer the *ponēroi* bronzes, newly minted and of *kakistos* stamping. Just so, the city prefers as its leaders those who are "bronze and strangers and outlanders, and *ponēroi* sons of *ponēroi*" (730-31), and treats with contempt those

> whom we know are *eugeneis* and *sōphrones* men, and *dikaioi* and *kaloi te kagathoi,* who were nurtured in *palaistrai* and *choroi* and *mousikē*.
>
> (727-29)

At the end, the "foolish" *(anoētoi)* citizens are urged to change their ways and to use again the *chrēstoi* (734-35). In this familiar litany of fifth-century aristocratic terminology, birth, intellectual and moral qualities, and style of life are all combined to present a composite image of aristocrats and their non-noble opponents.

Aristocratic contentions of this sort had great force and power, and democratic apologists found themselves hard-pressed to combat them. The only line of counterclaim available to the non-nobles was, in fact, simply to declare that they themselves possessed the same virtues and qualities; but almost always their arguments are accompanied by statements to the effect that despite their poverty and lack of high birth they were nevertheless good citizens and good men. So, a character in the *Diktys* of Euripides says:

> I can say little good about *eugeneia*. In my eyes the good man *(esthlos)* is *eugenēs,* and the unjust man *(ou dikaios)*, is base-born *(dysgenēs)*, even though his father be greater than Zeus.
>
> (Fr. 336 Nauck)

Peleus, in Euripides' *Andromache,* asserts that

> it is better for mortals to have a poor and useful man *(penēs chrēstos)* than a bad and rich man *(kakos kai plousios)* for marriage-kin or friend.
>
> (639-41)[42]

Otherwise, non-aristocrats had to be content with the standard complaints about the greed and arrogance of the rich and powerful. A good example of the difficulties of this counter-argument is provided by the *Ploutos,* the last of Aristophanes' comedies, produced in 388 B.C. A constant, underlying current of the play is the non-noble dilemma of having to demonstrate that the poorer class in Athens was neither morally inferior nor socially useless. The theme of the *Ploutos,* that wealth is blind and therefore honors the wrong people, is an old one in Greek thought. It had a special timeliness in the late fifth and early fourth centuries when the gulf between rich and poor was widening and when money as an index of civic usefulness had become a central issue. Those who had no wealth were constrained to defend their worth by appealing to their own transcendent qualities of goodness. Thus the old Athenian, Chremylus, laments:

> Even though I am a pious *(theosebēs)* and *dikaios* man, I have been unlucky and poor *(penēs)* . . . while others, temple breakers, politicians, informers and knaves *(ponēroi)* grew rich.
>
> (*Ploutos* 28-31)

Chremylus' plan to restore Ploutos' sight has as its purpose to make "only the *chrēstoi*, and the bright *(dexioi)* and the *sōphrones* rich" (386-88). Throughout the play it is the poor who are characterized as *dikaioi, chrēstoi, agathoi,* while the rich are called *ponēroi, atheoi.*[43] Even more striking, at one point the goddess Penia (Poverty) argues that her people are really better *(beltiones)* than Wealth's (557ff.): they are better in *gnōmē* and in appearance, have *sōphrosynē*, are orderly, while Wealth's are fat and hybristic.[44]

Two special points of interest emerge from Aristophanes' treatment of social problems in the *Ploutos*. First, those who are not members of the wealthy upper class, unable to resign themselves to a position of social inferiority, could only assert that they themselves possessed the qualities proclaimed by aristocrats as exclusively their own; second, the aristocracy of birth is not attacked directly, but unscrupulous politicians, informers, and the like. Quite clearly, even if the animus of the non-nobles was directed against the nobility for its wealth and its pretensions to a higher mode of intellectual and ethical behavior we have little evidence that anti-aristocratic sentiments were extensively exploited or that leaders of the *dēmos* were willing (or able) to initiate serious class conflict. Thucydides puts a speech in the mouth of Cleon, Pericles' successor as the leading man in Athens, which illustrates, I think, the limit to which a popular leader in the fifth century could go in publicly asserting the superiority of lower-class values. The scene is the dramatic debate in the Athenian assembly over the punishment of a recalcitrant "ally," Mytilene. He says that

> ignorance *(amathia)* combined with *sōphrosynē* is more helpful than this kind of cleverness that gets out of hand *(dexiotēs meta akolasias)*, and that as a general rule *poleis* are better governed by the man in the street *(hoi phauloteroi)* than by intellectuals *(hoi xynetōteroi)*. These are the sort of people who want to appear wiser *(sophōteroi)* than the laws . . . and who, as a result, very often bring ruin on their *poleis*. But the other kind – the people who are not so confident in their intelligence *(xynesis)* – are prepared to admit that they are less wise *(amathesteroi)* than the laws, and that they lack the ability to pull to pieces a speech made by a good speaker; they are unbiased judges, and not people taking part in some kind of competition *(agōnistai)*; so things usually go well when they are in control.
>
> (Thuc. 3.37.3-5 adapted from the Warner trans.)

We may be sure that Thucydides, who disliked Cleon intensely, intended this attack against the ruling intellectual élite to be taken as an example of the demagogue at his most demagogic (Cleon was the "most violent of the citizens," 3.36.6), but as a polemic against the upper class or as an attempt to demonstrate the superiority of the common citizen it is certainly mild. The *dēmos' amathia* is combined with *sōphrosynē*, the intellectuals' cleverness is coupled with "intemperateness," *akolasia*, the opposite of *sōphrosynē*. In praising ignorance Cleon has simply made a "virtue" out of the defect for which the *dēmos* is most commonly attacked. His essential message is that the *dēmos* is *sōphrōn*, moderate and law-abiding, the nobles are arrogant, self-serving and ruinously competitive; the *dēmos*, in other words, is the true possessor of the qualities claimed by the upper class.[45]

Even the old jurymen, die-hard democrats all, in Aristophanes' *Wasps*, are not virulent in their resentment of the rich and powerful. Their dislike is expressed in terms of apprehensions that individual members of the upper class may be aiming at a tyranny, alliance with Sparta, destruction of the democracy, exploitation of wealth for private ends, but with complete confidence that the ruling majority is in control of the situation. There is a fierce determination to preserve the rule of the *dēmos* with all its advantages to the non-rich and non-powerful of the citizens, but there are few indications of an attempt to establish a "proletarian" ethic.

It seems, in fact, that it was almost impossible for the non-nobles in Greek society to list ethically positive qualities of mind and spirit that were exclusively their own, because for so long the aristocracy, with its greater ability for self-expression, had simply claimed them as the property of their class. This attitude was both a conviction deeply held, hence implicit in all aristocratic writers, and self-consciously propagandistic, intended to persuade the *dēmos* that those born noble possessed superior mental and moral capabilities. The cumulative psychological effect of the "automatic reflex" and vigorous public propaganda must have been numbing.[46] As a consequence, any lower-class challenge to aristocratic assumptions of ethical/intellectual superiority in the fifth century was essentially negative and passive: either to insist that they too were wise, just, moderate, pious, and so on, or to assign to the upper class (or segments thereof) the same bad qualities they were accused of. The only "positive" claims to excellence in this sphere are statements like those in the *Ploutos*, that Penia strengthens character or, like Cleon in Thucydides, that *amathia* is more beneficial to the common good than *xynesis*.[47]

The most carefully worked out justification during the fifth century of the lower class' equality in goodness of mind and character is found in the *Electra* of Euripides. There Orestes, in his praise of the peasant husband of Electra, asks by what test the worth of a man *(euandria)* is determined. He considers the various criteria of birth, wealth (and poverty), and the ability to bear arms. These, he concludes, are improper and indeterminate. He continues:

> For this man is not great *(megas)* among the Argives, nor puffed up by the reputation of a noble house, but, although he is numbered among *hoi polloi*, he has been found to be *aristos*.
>
> (*Electra* 373-82)

Although the peasant fails the conventional test of the aristocratic conception he is still somehow *aristos*. The true measure of worth is given in the lines immediately following:

> Will you not cease to be foolish *(aphroneō)*, you who wander about full of empty notions — judge mortals by their intercourse *(homilia)*, and by their characters *(ēthē)* judge men *eugeneis*. For such men administer well their *poleis* and their homes; but hulks of flesh, devoid of mind are statues in the market place. Neither does the strong arm endure the spear better than the weak — this lies in one's nature *(physis)* and in his courageous spirit *(eupsychia)*.
>
> (383-90)

The passage is instructive for several reasons. First, it shows how potent still were the external valuations — birth, wealth, prowess, success — throughout the whole of the fifth century. Second, Euripides does not say that the traditional standards have no validity at all, simply that they are inadequate to explain the fact that the peasant, despite his lack of the obvious qualifications, was a truly worthy man. Third, what is put in place of the visible criteria is a series of very vague standards of measurement: *homilia* and *ēthos*, which seem here to mean correct ethical conduct in daily life and soundness of character; *physis*, which is one's inborn nature; *eupsychia*, which is the spirit of courage. Not only is the measuring device internal rather than external, but also the very qualities that prove Electra's husband to be truly "noble" (i.e. that he is *gennaios, sōphrōn, aristos* and has *euandria*) are internal and spiritual: in this particular case his self-restraint and reverence for Electra.

Arnheim's comments on *Electra* 367-85 bear some consideration here.[48] The passage is an expression of the "increasing doubts about the primacy of birth as the determining factor in human merit"; Orestes' tribute "is an eloquent assault on aristocratic notions . . . All the traditional criteria of human worth are here unceremoniously rejected . . ." Nevertheless, "what Euripides is *not* saying is that all men are equally good. The problem for him is one of criteria and measurement, and although he suggests some criteria in the last lines quoted, he clearly regards the problem as insoluble . . ." Therefore, according to Arnheim, the passage gives "an exaggeratedly radical impression of Euripides' social values." Euripides hedges somewhat here, because to claim that one who is poor and of ignoble birth is at the same time *gennaios* and *aristos* is impossible. That is why the poor peasant is given a noble pedigree and is not permitted to consummate the marriage.

> Not even Euripides can bring himself to allow a peasant to be his heroine's real husband. Euripides' ambivalent attitude is a good reflection of the dilemma confronting his age. The traditional aristocratic canons were now unacceptable, but what was there to replace them?

Arnheim is partly correct in his assessment. There is no question that Euripides and other champions of democratic equality were convinced that social and ethical goodness was possible for those who lacked noble birth. They expressed the conviction frequently, as we have seen. The problem was, as Arnheim says, one of criteria — non-aristocratic justification of social equality always came up against some version of the deeply ingrained equation of goodness with birth and wealth. The intellectual difficulty was to demonstrate that noble lineage and all that went with it were merely accidents, not fundamental determinants, a point not easy to make in a hierarchically conceived society.

Euripides presents us with another exemplar of the "naturally" good man in the *Orestes*. The scene is the Argive assembly, debating the murder by Orestes of his mother:

> Another man, standing up, spoke in opposition to this man; in outward form not handsome to look on, but a manly man *(andreios anēr)*, seldom found in town or the circle of the market place, a peasant *(autourgos)*, the sort who alone save the land, yet wise *(xynetos)* when he wanted to grapple with words, uncorrupted, a man trained in the blameless life.

The peasant speaks for the acquittal of Orestes, on the grounds that he had acted correctly according to the traditional social and religious norms,

> and to the *chrēstoi* he seemed to speak well, and no one spoke after him.
>
> (*Orestes* 917-31)

The peasant lacks the obvious qualifications by which the contemporary upper class defined a man as good — birth, good looks, social polish, wealth, education. He is, nevertheless "manly," has an untutored wisdom, is blameless in character and conduct.[49]

These examples show that the ultimate basis for non-noble justification of individual goodness had to be an appeal to *behavior,* with no reference to external or accidental factors. The *source* of this behavior was necessarily unidentifiable; the non-noble could only insist that somehow or other he possessed the qualities of mind and spirit admired by the society, either despite or because of the lack of the criteria flaunted by the upper class. The principle was stated by a messenger in the fragmentary *Melanippe* of Euripides:

> I do not know how one should inquire *(skopein)* into *eugeneia.* For I say that those who are *andreioi* and *dikaioi* by *physis* are more noble *(eugenesteroi),* even if they are slaves, than those who are empty show.
>
> (Fr. 495.40-43 Nauck)

The same idea is voiced by Electra, speaking over the corpse of Aegisthus:

> This wealth is nothing, a companion for a brief time only, for it is *physis* which is constant, not possessions *(ta chrēmata).*
>
> (*Electra* 940-41)

It is true, as North says, that "With regard to the origin of virtue, including sophrosyne, Euripides is firmly of the opinion that *physis* plays the chief role";[50] in fact, there was no other source from which to draw if one wished to make a case for lower-class excellence. Otherwise the paradoxical assertion must do, as did the messenger in the *Orestes,* who calls himself (870)

> a *penēs* man, but *gennaios* in the way I treat my friends.

But the posture, inevitably, was a defensive one. Peleus, in the *Andromache* of Euripides, defends the native intelligence of the common man against the pretensions of the mighty, who

> sitting haughty *(semnoi)* in authority, being nothing, despise the *dēmos* in the polis, who are wiser *(sophōteroi)* a thousandfold than they ...
>
> (669-701)

Even a simple emotion like parental love must be given explicit utterance, as Heracles does:

> In all respects are men alike. They love their children, both the better sort *(ameinones)* and those who are nothing. They differ in wealth — these have it, those do not — but every sort loves its children.
>
> (*Hercules Furens* 633-36)

◊

Aristocratic self-justification had turned increasingly inward since the late archaic period, but the internal excellences claimed by aristocrats rested, in the final analysis, on external conditions. An aristocrat proclaimed himself better on the grounds that his character or "nature" were better; but a superior nature was eventually (and inevitably) traced back to tangibles: noble birth, wealth, education, a particular life-style. As we saw from the passages above, the non-aristocratic claim was that much vaguer, hence, less compelling. From earliest times the Greek mind had been conditioned to adjudge merit according to the yardstick of success, achievement, appearance; and even though a long tradition of thought existed (and found eloquent expression in the fifth century) which challenged the standard of external social measurement, it was still powerful enough at the end of the fifth century to make an appeal to worth founded simply on intent or *physis* or proper behavior not universally persuasive.[51]

In short, appeals to birth, wealth and "inherited" excellence of mind and character gave aristocrats a decided advantage in their attempts to show that they were better suited to rule and to maintain themselves as leaders of the society. This need for visible demonstration of superiority accounts, I believe, for the very great emphasis placed on a style of life that appeared unmistakably the property of the noble class.

Ω

CHAPTER FIVE

Aristocratic Life-Style in the Fifth Century

LIFE-STYLE may be characterized as the visible manifestation of the cultural "personality" of an individual or group within a society. It reveals, often in small and trivial ways, the basic psychological needs of its practitioners, and is, therefore, an excellent sociometric indicator. We saw how, in response to the pressures generated by rapid and radical social change, the Greek nobility of the archaic period evolved a style of life which was distinctively "aristocratic." We might expect that in the classical period, at least in those states whose constitutions were democratic and whose sociopolitical norms were professedly egalitarian, an aristocratic life-style would be deemphasized; but quite the reverse seems to have been true. The reasons for this apparent paradox are not difficult to perceive. In societies that emphasize equality it is even more imperative for those who would be prominent to project an image of uniqueness that is unambiguous. Non-aristocrats had increasingly laid claim to or had challenged the exclusively aristocratic patents of excellence, including even the "quiet" virtues; consequently the need for visible proof of superiority was the more compelling. In addition, the traditional success standard still had much force. When a distinctive life-style can be tied to other claims of superiority, especially in a culture that was essentially competitive and where the ability to carry anything off with verve and brilliance commanded respect, it can have a powerful psychological effect.

There are dangers, too. Style of life is subject to attack by moralists when it offends the wider cultural norms, and it is susceptible to some degree of imitation. But these problems can be circumvented by careful avoidance of extremes of behavior which provoke popular censure on the one hand, and, on the other hand, by jealously limiting the possibilities of social mimicry. The greatest advantage, in fact, of the upper class life-style lay in its inimitability. Because it depends (by definition) on birth, wealth and an inherited set of attitudes, in short, on existing membership in a class, it is the ultimate and indisputable area of social differentiation. It is for this reason that fifth-century Athens, the most belligerently egalitarian, polis in the Greek world, evolved something resembling a cult of aristocratic exclusiveness that permeated every aspect of social behavior. The aristocratic style of life must have had an especially vivid impact in the compact polis, with its small number of inhabitants. Even in populous Attica, which in the mid-fifth century had perhaps 40,000 citizens (native-born, free males over eighteen), the tiny group of men of noble lineage and landed wealth will have stood out sharply against the much larger, essentially undifferentiated mass of non-aristocrats — all the more so because of their efforts to appear as a visibly distinctive minority.

In his essay on the democracy at Athens the Old Oligarch makes frequent reference to the social and political levelling which is the consequence of a democratic constitution. Anyone, he says, can hold office, and anyone who wishes can speak in assembly (1.2). In an even more pointed comment on equality he notes that it would be better if they did not allow every citizen to speak or be a member of the Council *(boulē)* equally *(ex isēs)*, but only the "cleverest" men *(dexiōtatoi)* and the *andres aristoi;* but democracy best suits and strengthens itself when the *ponēroi* are allowed to speak (1.6). As an example of the extreme lack of distinction in Athens (an excellent example, too, of cultural mimicry) the Old Oligarch points out that it is impossible to distinguish free citizens from slaves, resident aliens *(metics)* and freedmen, "for the *dēmos* is no better dressed than the slaves and the metics, and no better in appearance either" (1.10).

As we have already seen, the Old Oligarch (1.5) maintained that it was the *dēmos'* lack of education and their poverty which led them to prefer a levelling of social differentiation. Education or its lack, was, in fact, one of the essential elements adduced to make clear the distinction between aristocrats and non-aristocrats, and the Old Oligarch seizes upon this eagerly:

> The *dēmos* has broken down respect for preoccupation with gymnastics and *mousikē*, thinking this not to be *kalon*, knowing that they are not able to pursue these occupations
>
> (1.13).[1]

Our sources make it abundantly clear that education beyond the elementary stage, predominantly athletic training *(gymnastika)* and instruction in the "arts" *(mousikē)* were, practically speaking, available

Aristocratic Life-Style in the Fifth Century 157

only to young men who had leisure and money — the upper stratum — and that the possession of this kind of education identified the aristocrat.

> The noble was instructed and trained in the palaestra, in sports, dancing and music; these were the usual forms of education in earlier times. The gymnastic and musical education, with its emphasis on the 'agonal' feelings, was the inevitable accompaniment of nobility.[2]

A statement by the chorus in the *Knights* of Aristophanes shows that the wrestling-ground (or palaestra) was considered to be the special province of the upper class:

> When peace comes and we are freed from toil, do not begrudge us our long hair and our cleaning and scraping with oil.
> (579-80)

In the *Frogs* it is the *eugeneis, sōphrones, dikaioi, kaloi te kagathoi* who are "nurtured in *palaistrai, choroi* and *mousikē*" (727-29). We are immediately reminded of the Sausage Seller, who, having said that he was unworthy of high position because he knew nothing of *mousikē* and could barely write, was answered that *dēmagogia* was not "for a *mousikos* man, nor for one who was *chrēstos* in character, but for an ignorant *(amathēs)* and disgusting *(bdelyros)* man" (*Knights* 188-93).

Gymnastic training had another social effect, important to the aristocratic image. Since earliest times the spirit of competition had been ingrained in the Greek consciousness; and, traditionally, the upper class was the principal guardian of the agonal impulse.[3] Victory in the national and local games brought great glory to the winners, their families and *poleis;* and since ability to compete successfully depended on training (usually very expensive) and leisure, the upper class naturally dominated this important aspect of Greek life. In this way education could be, and was, exploited by the aristocracy to their own social advantage, simply because it was they and not the lower class who exhibited this particular *aretē*. The aura of glory won in the games was often converted into political prominence. A related advantage was that training in *gymnastika* was identified with the Dorian ideal of manliness; thus the noble youth of Athens and of other states acquired some of the exotic glamor attached to the citizens of Sparta, universally respected (if not admired) for their courage and strict discipline. As an added consequence of the prominence of physical training in higher education, the universal Greek ideal of the beautiful male body, finely exercised and cared for, became almost exclusively the property of the upper class, and was equated with moral and civic worth.[4]

"Higher" education, which was a creation of the fifth century, consisted primarily of training in public speaking, with the purpose, both avowed and implicit, of preparing young men to be political leaders. During the latter half of the fifth century the word for "speaker" *(rhētōr)* came to signify "politician." Higher education, which also included deeper study of literature, mathematics and moral philosophy, was provided by the sophists, whose brilliance and novelty made them immensely popular among the wealthy young men of Athens. The sophists, most of whom charged substantial (and sometimes enormous) fees, supplied a demand for more refined techniques of persuasion in an open and increasingly litigious society. Rhetorical education inevitably tended to widen the social gulf; the trained speaker, who of necessity belonged to the wealthy class, had a distinct practical advantage over poorer citizens in gaining public prominence and influence.

Paradoxically, for those few who enjoyed the advantage of wealth but not the old family connections, sophistic training was an entrée into power; for the first time (in Athenian history at least) a number of men who did not belong to the ancient aristocratic lineages rose to prominence in the state. Thus, from the point of view of the traditional aristocracy, sophistic teaching could be considered subversive, since the claim "to teach the art of politics and to undertake to make men good citizens" (Plato, *Protagoras* 319a) was precisely what aristocrats felt themselves exclusively fitted to do by a kind of natural instinct peculiar to their class. Despite the great variety in personality, methodology, and style, which prevents us from calling the sophistic movement a "school," all the fifth-century sophists taught rhetoric, and all shared "one epistemological standpoint . . . namely, a scepticism according to which knowledge could only be relative to the perceived subject."[5] Consequently, sophistic relativism and the *nomos/physis* argument could be employed to champion either the natural superiority of the old élite or the ideals of democratic equality. Now oligarchic and democratic leaders both had the means to express, in logically persuasive terms, competing ideologies.

The net result of the "sophistic mentality," which permeated Athenian intellectual thought in the second half of the fifth century, was a measure of moral confusion. Sophistic influence is evident in such disparate figures as Thucydides the historian, Euripides the dramatist, Critias the extreme oligarch, the medical writers. The *dēmos* itself, by

Aristocratic Life-Style in the Fifth Century 159

constant exposure in the assembly and law courts, developed a keen critical appreciation of persuasive eloquence, and in our sources is constantly faulted for its tendency to be swayed by clever orators. To some contemporary critics, like Aristophanes, the new intellectualism was a sign of decadence; in the *Clouds* and elsewhere he attacks it as being morally corrupting to both individuals and the state. The main victim, perhaps, was the traditional aristocratic certitude of the superiority of birth and wealth, but the democratic process also was affected. Democracy's vaunted lack of distinction, proclaimed by the catchwords *isēgoria* (the right of equal speech) and *parrhēsia* (freedom of speech), was theoretically true; in practice these rights were effectively exercised by a highly trained élite, whether of conservative oligarchs or of "champions of the people."

In point of fact, most of the recipients of formal higher education were young aristocrats. But the distinctive factor of their educational formation was the patterns of behavior they learned informally at home in association with their elders. This enculturation into the ways of the subgroup was primary — and exclusive. The study of poetry, music, mathematics, athletics, served to reinforce the basic values; training in rhetoric and ethical speculation fostered the persuasive expression of an ingrained system of beliefs. What finally mattered, though, was the elusive quality of "style" — the ultimate differentiation. The poorer classes were completely excluded from participation; wealthy non-nobles might attempt to imitate an aristocratic life-style, but such mimesis is rarely effective.

In Aristophanes' *Wasps*, the old juror Philokleon, prodded by his son Bdelykleon to enter high society, is given lessons to prepare him socially to take part in a symposium. The son asks if the old man knows how to tell "respectable" *(semnoi)* stories if he dines with men who are *polymatheis* and clever *(dexioi)*; Philokleon can only come up with coarse or simple barnyard tales. Bdelykleon gives as proper examples stories relating to incidents that occurred on foreign embassies (on which only the eminent were sent), or sporting tales of athletic contests, for "that is the way the *sophoi* are accustomed to converse" (1174-96). When Bdelykleon urges his father to tell the manliest *(andreiotaton)* adventure of his youth the old man can only recall the time he stole someone's vine poles. The son, exasperated, exclaims:

> You'll be the death of me! Vine poles! Tell how you hunted boar or rabbit, or ran the torch race; give us your most youthful prank.
> (1201-04)

The best that Philokleon can do is to reply with a feeble tale about the time he "hunted down" a famous Olympic runner in the law court. The lesson then turns to the proper way to behave at a symposium; the context makes it quite clear that Philokleon had never attended a drinking party. The son tries unsuccessfully to teach the father how to recline "elegantly" *(euschēmonōs):*

> Stretch out your knees, and, in a gymnastical way, ease yourself languidly on the cushions; then praise the table setting, look up at the ceiling, admire the tapestries.
>
> (1212-15)

Next follows a lesson in the singing of *scolia* (1219-49). Satisfied now with his father's progress in learning polite behavior, Bdelykleon invites him to a drinking party. The old dicast's response to the invitation typifies both the distance between the upper class, trained to "correct" behavior, and the ordinary citizen, to whom such things were foreign, and the general public's conception of aristocratic society:

> Phil. No! Drinking is bad! Wine leads to breaking down doors, beatings and blows – then a fine to pay and a hangover.
> Bd. No, not if you do it with men who are *kaloi te kagathoi*. For either they will intercede with the injured party and get you off, or you tell an urbane story, a joke from Aesop or from Sybaris that you learned at a symposium. And so, you turn the thing into a joke, and he goes off and leaves you be.
>
> (1252-61)

The result of the drinking party is predictable – Philokleon gets drunk and insults the other guests,

> making fun of them like a country boor *(agroikōs)* and telling inappropriate stories in a most ignorant way *(amathestata)*.
>
> (1320-21)[6]

As comical as these scenes are, they incisively indicate the rather deep social gulf that existed in the fifth century, directly traceable to education and to the conscious fostering of a particular manner of life. Philokleon was not from the lowest stratum of the Athenian citizen body; he was of hoplite status, an old-fashioned patriot, respectable and fairly well-off economically.

The literature of the fifth century abounds in references to aristocratic customs and manners which detail, in more specific terms, the importance of life-style to the upper class' "image" of itself as a group that was different and better. Physical appearance was an obvious, but telling, mode of differentiation. The custom of wearing the hair long, a sign of aristocratic vanity since the archaic period, continued to be in the fifth century an outward manifestation of their apartness. This somewhat obsolete fashion, along with careful attention to other aspects of personal grooming, such as frequent bathing, oiling and scraping, are treated in our sources as identifying traits of the nobility. Thus, Strepsiades contrasts the noble youth with the followers of Socrates who "never take care of their hair, nor anoint themselves with oil nor go into the bath to wash" (*Clouds* 836-37). In the *Birds* of Aristophanes a character expresses surprise to a poet (who called himself a "slave" of Homer): "What? You are a slave and you wear your hair long?" (911). The very noun *komētēs* (a man with long hair) is often used as a synonym for aristocrat.[7] Frequently there is, in this identification, a sense of class tension. The chorus of young aristocrats in *Knights* 579-80, we recall, ask the audience not to "begrudge" *(phthoneō)* their long hair and oiling and scraping. In one of the speeches of the orator Lysias a youthful aristocrat defends himself:

> And, indeed, it is according to this standard [proper conduct and bravery as a soldier] that one should judge the ambition and propriety of a citizen, and not hate a man because he wears his hair long *(komaō)*; for habits like these do harm neither to private citizens nor to the public good.... Thus it is not fair, members of the Boulē, to like or dislike someone because of his external appearance *(opsis)*; judge him by his acts instead. For many men who speak little and who dress soberly have been the cause of much evil; others, who do not care about such things, have done many good deeds for the state.
> (16.18-19)

Sometimes the verb which means "to wear the hair long" *(komaō)* is equivalent to "act grandly." Old Philokleon at the symposium berates one of the guests:

> Tell me, why do you play the nobleman *(komās)* and pretend to be elegant *(kompsos)*?
> (*Wasps* 1316-17)[8]

The verb *komaō* could have, in popular parlance, a sinister, oligarchical intonation. Herodotus, speaking of the conspiracy of the sixth-century aristocrat, Cylon of Athens, says that he "aimed his sights *(ekomēse)* at a tyranny" (5.71). In an argument with Bdelykleon the chorus of jurors in the *Wasps* says:

> So then, isn't it quite clear to the poor that tyranny is secretly creeping over us, if you, you wicked rascal and long-haired Amynias,[9] keep us from the laws which the polis has set up . . . ?
>
> (463-67)

Even minor manifestations of aristocratic vanity bear witness to an intentional fostering of a visible differentiation between the classes. In the *Ecclesiazusae* (631-33) the wearing of seal-rings distinguishes "the more elegant gents" *(hoi semnoteroi)* from the poor citizen in his cheap sandals *(embades)*,[10] and in the *Birds* the aristocratic Poseidon (patron of the *hippeis*) expresses disdain for a barbarian god because he wore his cloak on the left side instead of the right, saying:

> O democracy, to what a pass are you bringing us if the gods elect someone like this?
>
> (1570-71)

In the scene in the *Wasps* between Philokleon and Bdelykleon, preparatory to the lessons in symposium etiquette, much attention is paid to the difference between the old man's peasant clothing and the fashionable attire his son wants him to wear to the party (1131-69). Bdelykleon urges his father to throw away his short inexpensive cloak *(tribōn)* and to don the more costly, longer mantle *(chlaina)*. It is evident that the father has never worn such a garment, for he does not even recognize it for what it is—a woolen, tasseled cloak imported from Persia. The same ignorance (and disdainful reluctance) is shown when Bdelykleon tries to persuade his father to exchange his peasant sandals *(embades)* for expensive red boots *(Lakonikai)*. Thus accoutred the old man is advised to "walk like a rich man *(plousiōs)* with a dainty, pretentious swagger," and Philokleon, having practiced a bit, asks:

> O.K., now look me over and see what rich man my walk most resembles.
>
> (1168-71)

In this exchange, as in the rest of the scene, is manifested not only the obvious, external distance between the classes, consciously engendered by distinctions in clothing and manners, but also the suspicion and distrust with which the ordinary man viewed the pretensions of the upper class.

Another pervasive popular attitude during the fifth century was that aristocratic youths were addicted to luxurious and dissolute living. Even allowing for the fact that an older generation is always inclined to view the high spirits of the young (regardless of their social standing) with a critical eye, and the fact that the poor naturally resent the ability of the rich to pamper themselves, the nature of the evidence shows clearly that this kind of behavior was considered specifically class oriented, and, further, that it was an integral element of a life-style purposely designed to create an impression of class superiority. The following exchange between Aeacus and Dionysus' slave, Xanthion, occurs in the *Frogs:*

> Ae. By Zeus the savior, your master is some nobleman *(gennadas anēr).*
> Xan. How could he not be a *gennadas* when all he knows is how to drink and screw?
>
> (738-40)

In the *Wasps* it is said that drinking is "the disease of *chrēstoi andres"* (80). The popular image of the aristocrat as one who behaved in a manner divergent from the ordinary and acceptable norms of society is reinforced time and again. Demus in the *Knights* depicts them, censoriously, as beardless young dandies who hang about the perfume market engaging in pseudo-intellectual chatter which they learned in the schools of the sophists (1373-80). In a fragment of the comic poet Hermippus a character says:

> But, by Zeus, it isn't right for an *agathos* man to get drunk and take hot baths — the way you do.
>
> (Fr. 76)

A father in the *Banqueters* of Aristophanes says of his son:

> But when I sent him to school he didn't learn this; instead they taught him how to drink, sing badly, keep a Syracusan table, Sybaritic feasts, Chian wine from Lakonian cups, get drunk in a pleasant and friendly way.
>
> (Fr. 216)[11]

In addition to distinctive personal appearance and grooming, a proclivity for drinking and licentious behavior, affectations of manner and speech, there were other particular manifestations of aristocratic life-style that set them apart from the rest of the citizens. Nobles were addicted to the keeping and racing of horses, an expensive hobby far beyond the reach of the average citizen. Strepsiades, a fairly well-to-do Athenian citizen, is tormented by the expensive habits of his "socialite" son Pheidippides, lamenting that he is being eaten up

> by expenditures, feed bills and debts . . . while he, with his long hair, rides his horse and races a chariot — he even drives in his dreams!
> (*Clouds* 12-16)[16]

Strepsiades' reaction to his son's activities shows that such pursuits were understood to be a deliberate means of expressing differences of class. He styles himself a simple rustic *(agroikos)* who had married above his station. His wife, "a niece of Megacles, son of Megacles," was a "high class" *(semnē)*, "luxurious" *(tryphōsa)* member of the ultra-aristocratic clan of the Alcmeonids, and Strepsiades bitterly contrasts her refined and expensive upper-class habits with his own peasant way of life (41-55). When their son was born she wanted to give him a "horsy" name like Xanthippos, Charippos or Challippides; the father wanted to name him after the grandfather, Pheidonides ("Thriftson"). The wife would say to the young child:

> When you are grown up you'll drive your chariot to the Akropolis, like Megacles, in your fancy robe,

while Strepsiades would say:

> When you are driving the goats from the rocky hills, like your father, in your sheepskin coat.
> (69-72)

Another, and most distinctive, characteristic of the aristocratic lifestyle, was male homosexuality. Our sources leave little room for doubt that in the popular conception the practice of pederasty was the almost exclusive preserve of the upper class and one that was viewed with some disdain by non-aristocrats. This (perhaps exaggerated) general notion is summed up succinctly in a line from a lost comedy:

> There's no long-hair *(komētēs)* who hasn't been buggered.
> (*Adespota* 12-14)

Aristophanes twice describes himself as never having made advances to young boys in the palestrai,[13] and in many of the allusions of the period to the pederastic impulse there is a strong note of disapproval.

Some of the favorite butts of the comic poets were nobles notorious for their chasing of boys.[14] It is impossible to say for certain that homosexuality was a consciously expressed manifestation of the aristocratic self-image, but there was certainly a strong identification. To the comedians homosexuality and effeminacy were almost synonymous with aristocracy, and even allowing for comic exaggeration this must have been the universal public opinion. Without a doubt homosexuality fitted the pattern of upper-class values in the fifth century. It had a long association with Greek aristocratic culture, hence it was "traditional"; because it was an expensive practice it had definite overtones of conspicuous display; it was connected with the Spartan ideal of manliness (which had great appeal to the oligarchical-minded Athenian upper class), and with the aesthetic ideal of the beautiful male body and the training and refining of it.[15] And, in its idealized form, the relationship between an older, experienced man and a young man who looked up to and depended on his lover, male homosexuality gave scope to the expression of qualities to which the aristocracy had long laid claim: loyalty, fidelity, moderation, intellectual and moral superiority.

Dover's researches on Greek homosexuality confirm in detail the pattern described above. The absence of homosexual allusions in Homer, Hesiod and the seventh-century iambic and elegiac poets, and the fact that the earliest scenes of homosexual courtship on Attic vase paintings occur at the time of Solon, lead Dover to conclude that homosexuality's "social acceptance and artistic exploitation" became widespread only by the end of the seventh century B.C. By the middle of the fourth century heterosexual love dominated and "was beginning to sweep homosexuality under the carpet."[16] Thus the period of greatest outward manifestation of homosexual activity coincided with the rise of aristocratic emphasis on a particular style of life, reaching its height in the late sixth and early fifth centuries, which "witnessed a more open, headstrong, sensual glorification and gratification of homosexuality than any other period of antiquity."[17]

Also, according to Dover, the contrast between the generally favorable attitude towards male-centered eroticism in Plato and the "fundamentally heterosexual" point of view of comedy was the result of class distinctions. Among the youthful rich heterosexual satisfaction was difficult because of sexual segregation in the upper class, while the poorer classes had more opportunities for male-female contact. Dover's evidence confirms the fact that homosexuality was perceived by the general populace as the province of the upper class, with the result that

> the ordinary Athenian citizen, however ready to identify himself as a man of property with his social superiors, could also pride himself that he wasted no time on homosexual love-affairs such as occupied idle young men who had more money than was good for them.[18]

The ultimate causes for homosexuality as a positive-functioned trait, the appeal of which was largely confined to the upper stratum, are complex. Dover sees the underlying basis in the need for intense personal relationships not available in the family, eventually traceable to the political fragmentation of the Greek world, in which competitiveness and the emphasis on the male warrior inhibited the full development of marital or familial intimacy. Inasmuch as these tensions manifested themselves most among the ruling élite, and because the upper class homosexual ethos was transmitted as part of the educative process, it is proper to conclude that male homosexuality in ancient Greece functioned as an identifying (and exclusive) sign of class membership, self-consciously expressed to a significant degree.[19]

One other example will show how pervasive was the awareness of life-style among Athenians and how intimately associated with public morality it had become in the minds of the citizens. In the *Clouds* of Aristophanes (produced in 423, a year before the *Wasps*) there is a long *agōn* between "Right Argument" and "Wrong Argument," who represent, in the play, the old style of education and the new sophistic teaching. Somewhat naively, perhaps, Aristophanes fixes the blame for what he sees as a disintegration of the older, conventional values on the new education, and retrospectively views the old education *(archaia paideia)* as the key to the past greatness of Athens – a mistake not unknown in modern times. It should be added that although Socrates was the focus of Aristophanes' criticism, the figure of Socrates in the *Clouds* was more likely an agglomerate of the popular conceptions (and misconceptions) of the fifth-century sophists. Additionally, and very importantly, it is necessary to realize that the bad social effects which Aristophanes traces directly to the teaching of "Wrong Argument" is really the whole network of life-style and attitudes prevalent among young men from the best families.[20] If, then, we take this exchange as a fairly coherent depiction of the older and newer cultural patterns, keeping in mind that the practitioners of the "new" style would be youths from the upper class, we have a valuable summary of the ordinary Athenian's perceptions of the aristocratic self-image in the last quarter of the fifth century. We are told that the old upbringing, the *archaia paideia*, fostered *ta dikaia* and *sōphrosynē*. Under its stringent regimen boys did not complain; they walked through the streets of the city in an orderly *(eutaktōs)* and modest fashion, in groups, thinly clad regardless of the weather, singing the old patriotic songs, shunning the newfangled and effeminate tunes, under threats of beatings. At school they sat modestly, hiding their genitals: no boy ever oiled himself below the navel, nor whispered in a soft voice to his lover, or prostituted himself to the gaze of others. They were not allowed to be choosy about their food, nor to giggle, nor to dangle their feet (961-83). "These are the things," says Right Argument, "from which my *paideusis* nurtured the men who fought at Marathon." But now, he continues, boys go to school all wrapped up in warm cloaks and are not able to hold their shields out straight in the shield dance (985-88). He urges the youth to hate the agora and to spurn the baths, to be modest, respectful to elders and parents, to stay away from dancing girls and whores (991-99). If these things are done the young men will be physically fit and athletic, will not waste their time in idle jesting and chatter in the agora or be constantly in court on trifling matters (1002-04). Right Argument further extols the rewards of good training in the field of Akademos, comparing that to the afflictions which result from the manner of life today. If you follow my way, he says

> You will always have a firm chest, shiny skin, big shoulders, short tongue, big rump, short penis — but if you adopt today's customs, first you'll have pale skin, small shoulders, thin chest, big tongue, small rump, big penis — and a long decree.
> (1011-1019)

Wrong Argument's prescription for education, according to Aristophanes, is nothing more than a life-style of pleasure and licence:

> Boys, women, cottabus, feasting, drinking, laughing. Is life worth living if you don't have these?
> (1073-74)

These, then, are alternative life-styles presented to the young socialite Pheidippides. Wrong Argument triumphs in the *agōn* and the youth becomes an adherent of his teaching.

◊

By the middle of the fifth century Athens and Sparta had become locked into a fateful power struggle which, for much of the rest of the century, took the form of open warfare between the two powers and their allies and dependent states. In Athens itself the "democrats" (the vast majority of the citizens and their leaders, mostly the non-rich, non-noble elements) were deeply suspicious of the "oligarchs," that minority of the civic body largely identifiable as the wealthy upper class. Increasingly disaffected by the democratic constitution, the oligarchs set themselves in conscious opposition to the democracy and twice, towards the end of the century (in 411 and 404), succeeded briefly in overthrowing the democracy and in establishing minority rule at Athens. As we have seen, the sympathies of the upper-class oligarchs were often with the enemy itself, manifested by expressed admiration for and aping of Spartan customs and manners. Not unnaturally this "laconizing" was frequently interpreted by the lower class as part of an attempt to subvert the democracy, hence the often stated feeling that those who adopted Spartan mannerisms were inimical to the state. Homosexuality, for example, was viewed as a Spartan practice, which helps to account for popular reaction against it. Even the rather innocent practice of Athenian upper-class youth to dress and style themselves in Spartan fashion was given a sinister connotation. Thus the chorus of old jurors in the *Wasps* call young Bdelykleon

> hater of the *dēmos* and a lover of monarchy, an associate of Brasidas, a wearer of woolen fringes and a cultivator of an uncut beard.
> (474-75)[21]

For the same reasons the aristocratic phenomenon of the drinking club *(hetairia)* was viewed with alarm. Ostensibly organized for purely social purposes, these gatherings of the well-born and wealthy were sometimes occasions for oligarchical plottings against the democracy. Thucydides relates how the *hetairiai* at Athens were the focal point of the plots to overthrow the democracy in 411.[22] In the *Knights* Cleon calls the chorus of young Knights *synōmotai* ("conspirators") and frequently this word is used as a synonym for club members.[23]

Apart from the literary illustrations of the aristocratic self-image in the fifth century B.C. there is one historical figure whose life is a paradigm of the characteristics which have been discussed in this chapter — Alcibiades, son of Clinias, distinguished by his wealth and noble lineage. It is not possible here to detail the career of this spoiled darling of the Athenian people, who was alternately seen as the hero and the villain of his polis. Of interest to us is the style and manner of his life which was consciously cultivated to set him apart, distinct and unique, from his fellow citizens. As the most prominent young politician in Athens at the time of the ill-starred Sicilian adventure (415 B.C.) Alcibiades was considered the natural "leader" of the youthful aristocrats and was viewed with a mixture of admiration for his dashing personal qualities and suspicion of his unconventional life-style. Even the sober Thucydides seizes upon these aspects of his personality as being the most characteristic. Nicias, a conservative, older, general, speaking in opposition to the expedition to Sicily, accused Alcibiades of wishing to be a commander in order to further his own personal ambition. Alcibiades is too young to command, the assembly was told; he wishes "to be admired for his keeping of horses *(hippotrophia)*, and, because of the expense, hopes to profit from his command." Nicias ends his attack by counselling the Athenians not to allow Alcibiades to gain distinction at the polis' risk, but consider that "people like him harm the common interest *(ta dēmosia adikein)* and squander their own private fortune" (Thuc. 6.12.2). Thucydides himself gives the same assessment of Alcibiades' motivations, saying that he was eager to command in order to increase his wealth and fame *(doxa):*

> For he was held in esteem *(axiōma)* by the townspeople, and his enthusiasm for horse-breeding and other extravagances went beyond what his fortune could supply. This, in fact, later on had much to do with the downfall of the city of Athens. For *hoi polloi* became frightened at the quality in him which was beyond the normal and showed itself both in the lawlessness of his private life and habits and in the spirit in which he acted on all occasions. They thought he was aiming at a tyranny, and so they turned against him. Although in a public capacity his conduct of the war was excellent, his way of life made him objectionable to everyone as a person; thus they entrusted their affairs to other hands, and before long ruined the city.
>
> (6.15.3-4; adapted from the Warner translation)

Alcibiades' speech in reply to Nicias' criticism is a masterful defense of the style of life he typified. The very things he was accused of, he says, bring *doxa* to his ancestors *(progonoi)* and to himself and profit to the fatherland — namely the entering of an unprecedented seven chariots in the Olympic Games, which won first, second and fourth prizes. He realizes that this kind of display and other liturgies arouse envy, but:

> Indeed, this is no useless foolishness *(achrēstos anoia)*, when a man spends his own money not only to benefit himself but his polis as well. And it is not *adikon* for a man who has a high opinion of himself not to be put on a level *(isos einai)* with everyone else.
>
> (6.16.3-4; adapted from the Warner translation)

It would be difficult to find more convincing evidence than the (not unfriendly) treatment by Thucydides for our contention that the aristocratic style of life was deliberately cultivated to bestow on that group an aura of superiority, the ultimate purpose of which was political and social hegemony. In addition, this kind of behavior explains the alternate effect of respect and distrust aroused in the mass of the citizens by the man for whom, in exile, the polis

> yearns for and hates and wants to have.
>
> (*Frogs* 1425)

Alcibiades' bravado speech in favor of the expedition prevailed over the opposition of the reluctant Nicias, but the same qualities of unconventionality that charmed the people on that day made Alcibiades the chief suspect in the affair of the mutilation of the Herms just before the sailing. Although no direct proof was forthcoming that Alcibiades was guilty, allegations were made concerning previous mutilations of other statues "by young men, in childish amusement and wine" and mock celebrations of the mysteries. Alcibiades was (naturally) accused of being the leader in these profanations, Thucydides relates; further, his political opponents, wishing themselves to be foremost *(prōtoi)*, maintained that these were part of a plot to overthrow the democracy:

> evidence for which they found in the unconventional and undemocratic *(ou dēmotikē)* character of his life in general.
>
> (6.27-28)

In other respects, too, Alcibiades was the personification of the aristocratic mentality, which strove to impress the *dēmos* with its superior manner and style while at the same time expressing contempt for their inferior mentality and moral character. When he was in exile from Athens and plotting for his return he reportedly sent word to the most powerful *(dynatōtatoi)* leaders of the army:

> to make his views known to the best people *(hoi beltistoi)* in the army and to say that, if there were an *oligarchia* instead of the *ponēria* which had exiled him, he was ready to return....
>
> (Thuc. 8.47.2; adapted from the Warner translation)

Thucydides records another, earlier, speech of Alcibiades, delivered when under sentence of death *in absentia*. Alcibiades was in Sparta, to which country he had deserted, and was trying to persuade the Spartans to follow his advice on how to defeat Athens. In defending his previous anti-Spartan role as a leader of the people he was at pains to show that in reality he and his fellow aristocrats were different from the Athenian *dēmos* and their democratic leaders. Because a democracy existed at Athens, he says, he had to conform to its institutions:

> However in the face of the prevailing political indiscipline *(akolasia)*, we tried to be more reasonable *(metriōteroi)*. There have been people in the past, just as there are now, who used to try to lead the masses *(ho ochlos)* into evil ways *(ponērotera)*. It is people of this sort who have banished me.... As for *dēmokratia*, those of us with any sense at all *(hoi phronountes ti)* knew what that meant, and I just as much as any ... but nothing new can be said of a system which is a generally recognized foolishness *(anoia)*.
> (Thuc. 6.89.5-6; adapted from the Warner translation)

In every respect Alcibiades' assessment of democracy matches those which we have already examined, from Megabyzus in Herodotus (3.81) to the Old Oligarch; and the attitudinal stance is exactly the same: aristocrats are moderate and possess *sōphrosynē*, the *dēmos* is unbridled, and, being prone to immorality, is easily led by unscrupulous politicians; only aristocrats have sense, the common people (and their form of government) are foolish.[24]

The example of Alcibiades shows that aristocratic life-style entailed difficulties as well as advantages. There was, on the one hand, the need to rise above the mass, to exhibit qualities of flamboyance and unconventionality, which had the effect of making the aristocrat unique and different in a society whose professed ethos was equality, but this very visibility heightened mistrust, envy and suspicion. Nevertheless, despite the "backlash" dangers, the pursuit of a distinctive mode of living was the best means of expressing superiority; hence it was the most prominent feature of the aristocratic image during the fifth century.

It is now easy to understand why Athenian politicians who were not members of the old aristocracy were subjected to vicious attack precisely on the grounds that they did not conduct themselves in the style of aristocrats. Speaking in general terms of the successors of the aristocratic, aloof, Pericles, Thucydides notes that they failed to lead the polis properly because they were "more on a level with each other," and conducted public affairs "to suit the whims *(hēdonai)* of the *dēmos,"* whereas under Pericles Athens was "in name a *dēmokratia,* but in fact the rule of the first man" (2.65.9-10). We recall that Cleon was introduced by Thucydides as "the most violent of the citizens" (3.36.6). His "empty talk" *(kouphologia)* is mockingly contrasted to those of the citizens who were *sōphrones* (4.28.5); his boasting promise of success in the field (which was brilliantly fulfilled) is called "mad" *(maniōdēs,* 4.39.3); his leadership displayed his "ignorance" *(anepistēmosynē)* and "softness (*malakia,* 5.7.2); he died a coward's death (5.10.9); he was an evildoer and an "untrustworthy *(apistoteros)* slanderer" (5.61.1) Hyperbolus, in the one mention accorded him, was a *mochthēros anthrōpos* (8.73.3). In the same way, Cleon, Hyperbolus and other *dēmos* leaders were constantly lampooned by the writers of Old Comedy, not so much because they were ineffectual as leaders but because their attitudes, manner, and style of life were not aristocratic.[25] These men, economically very well-off, could be termed, anachronistically, "middle class entrepreneurs," but Old Comedy consistently degraded them to the level of the lowliest street vendors — loud, coarse, dishonest rascals, who lied and cheated their way to the top, aided by an ignorant *dēmos* which was easily gulled by their cheap flattery and empty promises. In every possible detail they exhibited characteristics exactly opposite to the aristocratic ideal.[26]

Antipathy towards manual labor and petty trade and commerce (the so-called "banausic" pursuits), as opposed to the acceptable occupation of agriculture, was old in Greece. The prejudice stemmed from the deep-rooted cultural conviction that to be forced to labor for another was a form of degradation, and is related to the tenacious survival of tribal egalitarianism. It applied almost as equally to the artisan who sold his own products as to the wage earner who sold his labor, for both worked to satisfy the needs of others, not their own. *Autarkeia* (self-sufficiency, independence) was the ideal; accordingly, the peasant who toiled endlessly in the sun on his own land was "freer" and, in a sense, enjoyed higher status than a smith or potter, who might actually have had a higher standard of living. What counted was not labor itself but the relations of labor, and there can be little doubt that the feeling against banausic pursuits was common to all Greeks, not just to the leisured upper class. And yet, even at times when the majority of free Greeks "enjoyed" the life of a small farmer, a substantial percentage was engaged in manual work or trade.

The fact that no counter-ideology was formulated that put high value on labor *per se* (just as there was never any real effort to put a positive valuation on poverty) was another important psychological advantage for the aristocratic value system. That the leisured life of the wealthy landowning minority represented an ideal that was universally accepted as valid (even if it was resented) demonstrates once again how powerfully persuasive the aristocratic ethos was, even in a period of democratic levelling. It is also significant that, despite the antiquity of the anti-banausic prejudice, its most vehement expression, including the intellectual formulation that the practice of these occupations led to physical and moral degeneration, comes in the period after 450 B.C. It follows that the aristocratic attempt to portray its style of life as the only "proper" one would result in a heightened emphasis of the principle that manual labor and trade were inimical to the realization of a man's potential, whether as citizen or leader. Cleon was no mere "tanner"; he was the owner of a prosperous tannery, and the same is true of other post-Periclean politicians who were not from the old, leading families. But in anti-democratic propaganda they are portrayed as artisans of the lowest class, as proof of their inferiority as leaders (in Aristophanes *Knights* 128-43 they are lumped together as "something-sellers"). If they emulated the life-style of their landowning "betters" they were subject to lampoon as social upstarts; if they chose, as they apparently did, to identify with the aspirations of the poorer elements, they were classed with them.[27]

Nevertheless, the deliberate rejection by these men of the upper class ethos and their consequent success in gaining political hegemony posed a frustrating dilemma to aristocrats, who were certainly not disposed to abandon a style and manner so integral to their claim to be superior; they had no choice but to continue to concentrate on the differences between the *kaloikagathoi* and the masses.

The hardening of attitudes was, in great part, the result of the economic situation. For a variety of reasons (not always clear to us) the differential between rich and poor increased in the last third of the fifth century. For Athens the war itself was a major cause, as has been emphasized recently by a number of scholars.[28] The Periclean policy in 431 of abandoning the countryside to the enemy effected both a sudden spurt of urbanization and the destruction of the land outside. These factors, along with a sharp increase in the volume of trade, the beginnings of a new "market" economy, and the economic dependence of Athens on its empire, produced severe dislocations not only in the economic sphere but in social attitudes as well. The polis was no longer self-sufficient; the traditional autarky of the small farmer was similarly diminished. The growing dependency on a money economy both widened the economic gap and presented the poor with the dilemma of having to resort to banausic activities, which ran counter to the received ideology. The impoverishment of the Athenian citizens in the fourth century had its visible roots in these conditions, and as the fifth century wore on to its bitter, tragic end, a true polarization of the classes had become evident. Income from the empire, redistributed in the form of state pay (pay for jurors and political offices, and for military service), took up some of the economic slack for the poorer classes, but reinforced the feeling among the wealthy that the *dēmos* was using the state revenues as its personal treasury (so the Old Oligarch). For the *dēmos* this was as it should be, just as the rich were supposed to be liberal in the outlay of their own fortunes for the public good—reflecting, once again, the persistent survival of the ancient tribal egalitarianism. The rich, for their part, felt threatened, not just by the people's demands for equitable distribution of the polis' wealth and by their increased control of political power through anti-aristocratic leaders, but also by their doctrinaire insistence on social equality and their resentment of the traditional aristocracy's style of life, criticism of which had steadily grown during the second half of the century.

The defensive reaction of the leisured class in heightened display of their assertions of superiority exacerbated the tensions. As social harmony disintegrated, and as empire slipped away in the face of impending defeat, Athenian aristocrats either withdrew from active political life or plotted revolution. W. R. Connor summarizes the inevitable choices:

> For some the best course seemed to be to withdraw from politics into private circles of like-minded friends, small informal gatherings . . . or the 'narrow circle' of cultured comrades. . . . This form of reaction was essentially apolitical; the other, however, aimed at a new kind of political arrangement in which the 'better' people would again be dominant.[29]

By 403 the democracy, twice restored, was firmly in power. The "backlash" dangers of the unbridled aristocratic life-style (of which Alcibiades' successive rises and falls provide an illustration) became a permanent fact of life. In the restored democracy citizens had to proclaim their faith in the levelling ideal of democracy and to play down expressions and manifestations of class superiority. The case of Alcibiades, son of Alcibiades, is an example of the dominant sentiment in Athens after the War.

In 395 B.C. the younger Alcibiades was brought to trial on a charge of deserting the ranks in a minor skirmish against the Spartans. In the speech, written by Lysias, the main target of attack was the *character* of the son, who was, naturally, compared in vice to his notorious father. The speech abounds in the familiar socio-political/moral terminology of fifth-century political rhetoric — except that the positive categories refer to democrats and the negative ones to oligarchs. The military court is told at the beginning that the purpose of the trial is not only to punish wrongdoers, but "to make other disorderly persons *(akosmountes)* more sensible of duty *(sōphronesteroi)*." Therefore, voting against "unknowns" *(agnōtai)* will do no good, but punishing "the most conspicuous offenders" *(hoi epiphanestatoi)* will make the citizens "better" *(beltious)* (14.12).

Many of the character defects of the defendant are related to style of life: Alcibiades should not be let off because of his birth (*dia to genos*, 14.18); he is accused of an unworthy homosexual affair while still a child, and of having a mistress when he was still a minor; he was debauched by a friend with whom he was in alliance against his own father, and was then imprisoned by the same lover; he was released by another lover, gambled away his fortune, tried to drown his own friends, seduced another man's wife, and so on and on (14.25-29). The prosecutor links the evil character of the son with that of the father, concluding:

> You must ask yourselves, gentlemen of the jury, why anyone should spare men like these — because though unfortunate in their public life they have otherwise been orderly *(kosmioi)* and restrained *(sōphronōs)*? Have not many of them consorted with prostitutes, while some have lain with their own sisters, and some have had children by their own daughters, some have performed mysteries, mutilated the Herms, dishonored all the gods, offended against the whole polis, acted unjustly and unlawfully against others and themselves, holding off from no act of daring, unversed in no deed of horror? They have suffered and done every possible act; for such is their character that they are ashamed at *ta kala* and give honor to *ta kaka*....
>
> (14.41-42)

What we have here, in the early fourth century, is one example of many attacks on individuals, in which the style of life and the norms of behavior of the upper class are discredited.

The new hero is the *sōphrōn politēs*, the "law-abiding citizen," who is above all a fervent democrat and a hater of oligarchy. Claims of superiority are muted; now the emphasis is on the citizen as an aid to the community. Service to the polis, modesty and self-effacement in public life, morality in private life, are now the ideal; and this ideal is attainable by all citizens, not only by a small group. As North says, "All the familiar aristocratic values have been thoroughly 'democratized' in fourth-century Athens."[30] Word usage has come full circle; now it is democrats who are *agathoi, sōphrones* and *chrēstoi*, while oligarchs are *kakoi, ponēroi* and *anandroi*. Thus, by the middle of the fourth century the orator Aischines can compare the "nature" *(physis)* of the man who is *dēmotikos kai sōphrōn* with that of the man who is *oligarchikos* and *phaulos:* freeborn on both sides (in order that he may not, by any misfortune of birth, be disloyal to the "laws which save the *dēmokratia*"); have a legacy of "some good work from his *progonoi* to the *dēmos* (so that he may not harm the polis by attempting to avenge the misfortunes of his family); be *sōphrōn* and *metrios* in daily life (in order that he may not take bribes to feed expensive tastes); have good judgment and ability in speaking; be brave (3.168). Every one of these qualities is possible for the ordinary citizen (except, perhaps, ability in speaking, which must be acquired by expensive education; but Aeschines, even here, explicitly places *eugnomosynē* "reasonableness," "sensibleness," above speaking ability). Naturally, an aristocrat could be all of these things too, but distinguished birth, wealth and education are not essential, while aristocratic pride and style of life are distinct hindrances. The traditional aristocratic virtues have been made available to all men of good will towards the state. In short, *agathos* and *aretē* had been redefined: ". . . it is now *agathos* to be a democrat *per se;*" and the scope of *aretē* had become restricted to a somewhat passive spirit of public fostering of equality, justice and the good of the polis, and a private demeanor of sobriety and moderation.[31]

◊

Thus the events of the final years of the fifth century forced aristocrats to yet another revaluation of the aristocratic ideal. How their class adjusted to the social changes is beyond the scope of this discussion; but the main directional thrust of the newest form of the ideal has been foreshadowed, for it had been a part of the aristocratic ideal for over a century, and it already held a central position in the aristocratic scheme of values. Class superiority will be increasingly stated in terms of the inner excellences: intelligence, wisdom, moderation, personal morality. If these qualities are now successfully proclaimed by non-aristocrats (the struggle over who could be called *agathos* is over), aristocrats will have them to a greater degree, or will exhibit a higher form of these virtues or they will comprehend them in an idealized, transcendent form: they will possess and control the excellences of mind and spirit and alone will be able to understand their deeper nature and to teach them to others. Plato, of course, is to be the classic conveyer of these ideas. For him

> The philosopher-ruler contemplates the values as they actually are (*phusei*, 'in their nature') in the Forms, and cannot resist trying to reproduce them in his own soul. Thus he becomes as well ordered (*kosmios*, a significant epithet) and godlike as a man can be. . . . Then he turns, however reluctantly, to his duty as statesman and stamps these same characteristics on the citizens, who thus possess *dēmotikē aretē* — the result, not of *epistēmē* on their part, but merely of right opinion.[32]

◊

The Greek aristocratic ideal, which we have traced from its earliest manifestation at the end of the Dark Age through the fifth century B.C. was not a static model. The permanent core of its conceptual frame was the conviction that the dominant class was superior in all respects to other elements of the community and should be accorded the privileges and deference due them by reason of their superiority. Operationally, the ideal was a series of flexible "stances," which could be adapted to changing conditions and pressures. Certain aspects of the ideal remained unaltered from beginning to end; others were added as they were needed or eliminated as they proved inadequate or counter-productive to the central purpose of continued recognition of superiority. Because most of the "changes" in the ideal took the form of subtle shifts of emphasis, in response to socio-historical developments, modern observers have often accepted as true the surface impression of a pattern of aristocratic values unaltered from the time of Homer to the end of the fifth century. That impression is misleading. The remarkable staying power of the cultural attitudes of the Greek nobility over a long period of time, even in political situations where those principles were in direct opposition to the expressed values of the mass of people, was the result of an ability to conform to changing social realities.

The impression of an aristocratic ideology unaltered over time and the corresponding inability of non-aristocrats to formulate a coherent and positive counter-ideology have also led to the belief that aristocratic values were not seriously questioned and to the equation of the elitist value system with the cultural ideal of all Greeks.[33] In reality, there was, from the beginning, constant pressure from below which forced aristocrats to make defensive alterations in the images of superiority which they projected. No element of the dominant group's spectrum of values — birth, wealth, mental and moral capacity, habits, and style of living — escaped serious challenge. Although that challenge issued as a formal expression of lower class values only sporadically and inconsistently, it significantly shaped the evolution of upper class behavior until, by the end of the fifth century, the whole network of traditional claims to class superiority had become politically and socially invalid.

The underlying impulse of the erosion of class pretensions was the profoundly rooted legacy of egalitarianism from the tribal past; it was that inheritance, in fact, that was never seriously challenged. The Greek aristocratic ideal had its formation in the tribal chiefdoms of the Dark Age, and its historical development was intimately related to the emergence of the polis, the complex expression of Greek tribal life. The tribal nature of the polis, which was never perceived as anything but a community of all the citizens, insured that political, economic and social stratification within the body of fictive kinsmen could never advance to a true class system. The few wealthy, well-born and influential — those we have termed "aristocrats," "nobles," "upper class" — found themselves, from the beginning, in a constant struggle to maintain (or to regain) their positions as the "rightful" and "natural" leaders of the people. The many, who stood outside the small and jealously exclusive top layer, never permitted the élite to solidify into a true hereditary, ruling class, but forever chipped away at old assumptions and prerogatives.

Finally, the points of identification between the "aristocratic ideal" and the wider cultural ideal were not the results of the filtering down and acceptance by the many of the values of the few, but the reflection of a culture-wide homogeneity of values and attitudes which all Greeks shared. We can accept as correct Starr's conclusion that:

> Fundamentally, the Greek upper classes shared the values and ethical standards of Hellenic civilization as a whole, though they voiced and exemplified those views in a more conscious manner. . . . Those

historians who explore the lower classes and begin with the premise that their culture is essentially different from that of the elite do not stand in full accord with anthropological studies of peasantries.[34]

The aristocratic assertion that their group was the sole possessor of the qualities of mind, body and spirit that made a man good was psychologically persuasive, especially in a culture which put a premium on competition and success, because "noble" ancestry and landed wealth easily translate into political power and social prestige in small, pre-market societies. Because aristocratic claims to exclusive excellence were founded on the potent twin supports of birth and wealth, and their material consequences of a visibly grander style of life and conspicuous display — none of which could be imitated — non-aristocrats found it difficult to formulate a competing ideology, except in negative terms.

Nevertheless, the very nature of the polis had a moderating influence on social discord; the polis idea was the centripetal principle which thrust the complex of contradictory social impulses into the frame of "the common good." The nobleman may have considered himself to be above and apart from the common people, but never apart from the polis; aristocrat and non-aristocrat alike agreed that a man existed to serve the community. The disagreement was over who did this best, which element should hold which relative position. True class conflict would have destroyed the very framework within which both sides were competing — hence the restraint and the reluctance to choose radical alternatives. Both groups shared equally a fear of the *monarchos*, the single ruler (thus hatred of the *tyrannos* was a common element in both democratic and oligarchic propaganda); but, in addition, the upper class often rejected too narrow oligarchies, and the *dēmos*, to a surprising degree, had misgivings about too extreme democracies.[35]

By the dawning of the fourth century the precarious balance had become eccentric; despite the frequent appeals to *homonoia*, "concord," by fourth-century orators, attitudes had begun to rigidify, the spirit of compromise and give-and-take waned as the polis ideal ceased to be the central focus of human activity. Political theorists like Plato and Aristotle reflect the loss of the ideal and the narrowing of interests, as they construct highly rational, static political systems based on a hierarchical social order (and, anachronistically, project these attitudes backwards into the previous centuries).[36]

The Greek aristocratic ideal evolved during the period of benign tension; the ideal was pragmatic, functioning on both the conscious and unconscious levels to preserve the nobility's position at the top of the social pyramid, to create and to foster a gulf between themselves and the rest of the people. Its means, as we have seen, were fundamentally persuasive, not coercive, exploiting every natural advantage and evolving new combinations as necessary. In the process of challenge and reaction the whole of Hellenic society absorbed and benefited from the creative energies generated.

Ω

NOTES TO THE TEXT

CHAPTER ONE

1. Although some scholars still maintain that Homer's "background" is Mycenaean, the decipherment of the Linear B tablets and the accumulation of archaeological research make that possibility more and more remote. Most debate centers about a Dark Age milieu, the poet's own time, or an "amalgam" theory. The question is a difficult one and will not be answered definitively in the near future. M.I. Finley, in *The World of Odysseus*, 2nd ed., rev. (New York 1965) proposed that the *Iliad* and *Odyssey* reflected the social institutions of the tenth and ninth centuries B.C. (p. 43; see his eloquent restatement in "The World of Odysseus Revisited," *PCA* 71 [1974] 13-31). M.M. Austin and P. Vidal-Naquet, *Economic and Social History of Ancient Greece: An Introduction*, trans. and rev. by M.M. Austin (Berkeley and Los Angeles 1977), in a judicious survey of the problem, reach the same conclusions (pp. 37-40). By and large it is archaeologists, who, recognizing the tripartite layering of the material background of the epics, label the social culture as an amalgam. A most forceful expression of this view is A.M. Snodgrass, "An historical Homeric society?" *JHS* 94 (1974) 114-25. The most fruitful approach, in my opinion, is the kind essayed by J.M. Redfield, *Nature and Culture in the Iliad* (Chicago 1975), who sees the historical culture embedded, of necessity, in the poems – the poem had to make sense to a contemporary audience – regardless of specific anomalies. Akin to this point of view is the insight of E.A. Havelock, *Preface to Plato* (Cambridge, Mass. 1963), that the Homeric epics constituted a "tribal encyclopedia," a paradigm of accepted contemporary norms (and of deviations from these norms), representing the "general state of mind."

Finally, that the norms of heroic behavior in the *Iliad* and *Odyssey* were the basis of the later aristocratic "code," is to me a fact beyond dispute. To what extent this (very loose) "system" of beliefs and attitudes became the property of all Hellenes, not just of the upper class, is disputable. A premise of this study is that non-aristocrats did not so much rebel against or reject this set of attitudes; rather, that as this ideal became more and more self-consciously (and defensively) the "property" of aristocratic groups, non-aristocrats formulated other values, more compatible with their own social reality.

2. On the chiefdom form and its relationship to tribal society see M.D. Sahlins, *Tribesmen* (Englewood Cliffs, NJ 1968); idem, *Stone Age Economics* (Chicago 1972); E.R. Service, *Primitive Social Organization. An Evolutionary Perspective* (New York 1965). Especially interesting are Sahlin's comments (*Tribesmen*, 32-39) on the tendency of pastoral nomads to develop "disorderly" chiefdoms, based partly on a corporate descent system (e.g. clans, lineages) and partly on "contractual" relations (e.g. clientage, blood-brotherhood), and the endemic nature of warfare in such groups (cf. the Bedouin saying: "Raids are our agriculture"). The causal role of warfare in the rise of social ranking is hotly debated by anthropologists. For our purposes it is sufficient to point out that externally directed aggression was highly regarded in Homeric society, and that those who placed high on the political, social and economic scales were outstanding fighters. Austin and Vidal-Naquet (above, note 1, 40-47) give a sound, short description of the role of the *oikos* and of other characteristics of the Homeric world. For recent, detailed accounts of Dark Age material life see A.M. Snodgrass, *The Dark Age of Greece*

(Edinburgh 1971), esp. ch. 7; V.R. d'A. Desborough, *The Greek Dark Age* (New York 1972); and J.N. Coldstream, *Geometric Greece* (New York 1977). What makes the Greek Dark Age "dark" is the lack of material evidence from which to reconstruct the society. If Homeric society is to be placed roughly between 1000 and 800, then the society, as revealed by archaeology, is one that is slowly, but with sure direction, emerging from stagnation, isolation, depopulation, nervous movement, to settled village life, rising population, increased vitality and prosperity — not uniformly, and not always steadily, of course, but the trend is evident.

3. The best exposition of this tool is found in the valuable study by A.W.H. Adkins, *Merit and Responsibility: A Study in Greek Values* (Oxford 1960) 30-31 (cited hereafter as *M&R*). See also a more recent treatment by Adkins, *Moral Values and Political Behaviour in Ancient Greece* (New York 1972) 1-9, 12-13 (cited hereafter as *MV&PB*). I disagree with many of Adkins' conclusions concerning the usage of these key words, but his methodology is sociologically sound and makes possible the extraction of valuable information from our often inadequate source material. For a complete analysis of every occurrence of these terms from Homer to Pindar see my unpublished dissertation, *Agathos-Kakos: A Study of Social Attitudes in Archaic Greece* (Northwestern University 1968). Two older studies are often very useful: J. Gerlach, *Aner Agathos* (Munich 1932) and M. Hoffman, *Die ethische Terminologie bei Homer, Hesiod und den alten Eligikern und Jambographen* (Tübingen 1914).

4. E.g. the formula *boēn agathos* (good at the war-cry) occurs 47 times in Homer. For *esthlos* see *Il.* 4.458; 15.283; 17.590.

5. E.g. *agathos*: *Il.* 10.559; 13.238, 284, 314; 17.632; 21.280; *Od.* 18.383. *Esthlos*: *Il.* 5.581; 6.444; 9.319; 11.673; 16.600; 20.383, 434; 22.158. *Kakos*: *Il.* 2.365; 4.299; 5.643; 6.443; 8.94, 153; 9.319; 11.408; 13.279; 16; 570; 17.180, 632; *Od.* 3.375; 4.199; 21.131.

6. The selling of slaves and the ransoming of prisoners was also a source of income for the high-ranking warrior; cf. *Il.* 21.34ff.

7. Significantly, only twice in Homer is a word for wealthy *(aphneios)* coupled with *agathos* (*Il.* 13.664; 17.576); the very epithet *agathos* subsumed the notion of a wealthy man. For a broader discussion of wealth and its uses in the Homeric world see M.I. Finley, *The World of Odysseus* (cited hereafter as *WO*) 128-30; cf. 58-59, 61-63, 66, 102. It was Finley, who, following the lead of M. Mauss and K. Polanyi, first brought to the attention of Hellenists the proposition that in prestate societies the economy is "embedded" in the social structure. S. Humphreys, "History, Economics, and Anthropology: The Work of Karl Polanyi," *History and Theory* 8 (1969) 165-212, has an excellent summary and analysis, with extensive bibliography, of the important concept of reciprocity. For a brief account of "the controversy over the ancient economy," and of Polanyi's contributions, see Austin and Vidal-Naquet (above, note 1) 3-11.

8. E.g. *Il.* 8.139-50; 11.401-10; 17.90-105. See W.K.C. Guthrie's characterization of the "emotional and mental instability" of the Homeric heroes in "The Religion and Mythology of the Greeks," published as a separate fascicle of the revised vol. II of the *CAH* (Cambridge, Eng. 1964) 42-43.

9. E.g. *Il.* 4.370-400; 8.90-96; 12.244-47; cf. *Il.* 17.325ff.

10. *M&R*, 49.

11. *Il.* 22.38-130; cf. *Il.* 6.440-46.

12. E.R. Dodds, *The Greeks and the Irrational* (Berkeley and Los Angeles 1951) 17, 28ff. On failure see Adkins, *M&R*, ch. 3. Redfield (above, note 1) 116, says that "the heroes do not distinguish personal morality from conformity," and emphasizes that the Homeric Greeks "make no distinction between propriety and morality."

13. *Il.* 3.170 (Agamemnon); *Od.* 17.416 (Antinous); 20.194 (Odysseus); 24.253 (Laertes). Cf. also *Il.* 3.158; 24.630; *Od.* 4.27. See B. Fenik, *Studies in the Odyssey*, Hermes Einzelschriften 30 (1974) 61.

14. In *Od.* 13.297ff. Athena changes Odysseus into an old man. Very significant in the transformation is his clothing — vile and filthy — which stamps him obviously as a beggar (434-38). When Athena restores his heroic appearance, in order that he might be recognized by Telemachus, clothing plays an important thematic role (16.172-76, 199-200, 209-12, 456-5). In Book 23, when the logical "proof" of his identity should have been the slaying of the suitors, Penelope still refuses to recognize him because of his rags (94-95). A few lines later Odysseus explains this strange behavior to an angry and bewildered Telemachus:

> Now because I am filthy and wearing vile clothing, for this she dishonors me and does not yet say I am her husband

15. *Il.* 2.216-19. See below, pp. 20-22. As Albin Lesky, *A History of Greek Literature*, 2nd ed., trans. by J. Willis and C. de Heer (London 1966) 111, says: "To the world of Homer the outer and the inner man were inseparably linked."

16. The description of the relatively minor hero, Thoas, may be taken as an expanded paradigm of this advice:

> skilled in the spear's throw and brave in close fight. In assembly few of the Achaians, when the young men contended in debate, could outdo him.
> (*Il.* 15.282-84)

Here, and elsewhere, I have adopted the translations of Richmond Lattimore, *The Iliad of Homer* (Chicago 1951), *The Odyssey of Homer* (New York 1965) and have so indicated in the text. Lattimore's line divisions have not been retained.

17. Cf. *Il.* 13.726-34.

18. It is obvious that mere physical beauty, unaccompanied by strength or valor, is not prized at all in the heroic scale of values. The phrase "admirable in *eidos*" (*Il.* 5.787; 8.228) becomes a term of reproach when unconnected with other excellences of body and mind. Paris is despised because he is merely beautiful, but without warlike spirit (*Il.* 3.39-57; 13.769ff.); cf. *Il.* 10. 316; 24.261-62.

19. Odysseus asks: "at least take pity on all the other Achaians who are afflicted along the host, and will honour you as a god. You may win very great glory *(kydos)* among them" (*Il.* 9.301-303, Latt.). Here the appeal is to pity and to personal glory. In his long reply (lines 308-426) Achilles does not deign even to mention Odysseus' appeal. Phoenix' cautionary tale of Meleager (529-99) implies a claim of responsibility to the larger group. Ajax' blunt response to Achilles' obduracy focuses on the hero's excessive pride and on his betrayal of friendship: "nor does he care for the friendship *(philotēs)* of his companions" (630). It is this appeal, by the way, which touches Achilles most directly (644-45). When

Patroclus sets out to fight in Achilles' armor, his exhortation to the Myrmidons is not that they should save the Greeks but rather give *timē* to Achilles and spite Agamemnon (*Il.* 16.269-74).

20. Cf. *Il.* 16.830-33; 18.265, 514-15. A similar appeal to wives, children, parents, possessions can also be made by the Greeks (*Il.* 15.662-64).

21. As the dead Hector is called "a great joy to the polis and all the *dēmos*" (*Il.* 24.706).

22. *Il.* 22.38-89, 416-36, 477-514; 24.725-75. But in 22.46-55 the possibility of Hector's death is seen as a great sorrow to the *laoi* of Troy.

23. *WO*, 125. See P.A.L. Greenhalgh, "Patriotism in the Homeric World," *Historia* 21 (1972) 528-37, who corrects the exaggerated view of some scholars that *no* sense of community responsibility can be found in the epics. Still, true patriotism and a self-transcending idea of community responsibility must wait until the emergence of the city-state.

24. An example is the treatment of the captured Trojan spy, Dolon, who was implicitly promised his life if he told the truth about the Trojan encampment, yet was cooly dispatched by Diomedes when he did (*Il.* 10.378ff.). A defeated warrior may beg for mercy, invoking "religious" sanctions, but the victor apparently feels free to listen or not (e.g. Achilles and Lycaon in *Il.* 21.74-77). The gods do have a regard for pity; they are angered at Achilles' mistreatment of Hector's body (*Il.* 24.33ff.); they are opposed to the use of poisoned arrows (*Od.* 1.262). In contrast the Cyclopes have no "assemblies for council," no "custom laws" *(themistes)*, nor any reciprocal relations beyond the nuclear family (*Od.* 9.112-15). For Homer the absence of civic association and of religiously sanctioned rules for the treatment of strangers are equally the sign of uncivilized beings.

25. Compare the "proper" response by the very civilized Phaeacians to a suppliant stranger (*Od.* 7.155-66).

26. Cf. *Od.* 24.351-52: Laertes' prayer that Zeus has punished the suitors for their *hybris*. In the same way Troy's destruction is seen as a punishment from Zeus for breaching the laws of hospitality (*Il.* 13.62-32; cf. 3.351-54) and for the breaking of oaths (*Il.* 4.155-68). Homer indulges in moralizing disapproval of Heracles, who slew Iphitus when he was a guest at his table (*Od.* 21.24-28).

27. See Finley, *WO*, 63, 103-108, 133-36; Austin and Vidal-Naquet (above, note 1) 43. For representative descriptions see *Il.* 11.769-79; *Od.* 3.34-74 4.26-67; 15.72-159). *Xeniē* is "foreign policy" in its tribal form. The intertribal marriage alliance in Homer, by which "strangers" are turned into kin, had the same instrumental purpose, the increase of one or both *oikoi* (e.g. *Od.* 7.311; 14.211). Throughout the archaic and classical periods both the *xeinos* relationship and marital alliances between families from different *poleis* continued to be important mechanisms by which aristocratic *oikoi* increased their sphere of influence, often in contradiction to communal solidarity.

28. It is assumed in the epics that Greek and Trojan speak the same language just as they worship the same gods. Homer *is* aware that different peoples speak different languages; *Il.* 2.803-806; 4.436-38: Trojan allies speak mutually unintelligible languages; *Il.* 2.867: the Carians are *barbarophonoi; Od.* 19.172-77: differing tongues among the peoples of Crete. Cf. also the Homeric hymns to Apollo (162-63) and Aphrodite (113-14).

29. See C.M. Bowra, *Tradition and Design in the Iliad* (Oxford 1930) 170; W. K. Lacey, *The Family in Classical Greece* (London 1968) 37-38. Aeneas claims seven generations, Glaukos six, Antilochus five, Diomedes and Idomeneus four. The original ancestor is usually a god or a shadowy eponym.

30. G.M. Calhoun, in an important article, "Classes and Masses in Homer," *CP* (1934) 192-208, 301-16, noted that despite the wealth of genealogical material available to Homer surprisingly little attention is centered on it. It is introduced "in moderate amount and for definite reasons of art" and is focused primarily on "kings" and "kingly families" (pp. 207-208).

31. Cf. *Il.* 6.207-210; *Od.* 24.506-509.

32. *Od.* 1.386-87, 402-404; 16.383ff.

33. Eumaeus the swineherd was the son of a *basileus* in his own land, kidnapped and sold as a slave (*Od.* 15.403-84). The women Chryseis and Briseis were both well-born spear prizes of Agamemnon and Achilles (*Il.* 1.11ff.; 19.291ff.).

34. Finley, *WO*, 86ff.; C.G. Thomas, "The Roots of Homeric Kingship," *Historia* 15 (1966) 387-407.

35. *Od.* 14.199ff.

36. The one (and only) exception to this is *Il.* 2.198-206, where, in the aftermath of Agamemnon's abortive "test" of the army's morale, there is a general rush of high and low to the ships. Odysseus restores order, and whenever he came upon a "man of the *dēmos*" he struck him with the sceptre, calling him "unwarlike and weak, of no account in war or in counsel." It is possible, as Calhoun says (above, note 30) 304 that "it is not one of the heaven-born flogging common clay, but the *de facto* commanding officer stemming a rout which may at any moment bring disaster." Clearly, however, there is real significance in this isolated statement of inferiority – the man of the *dēmos* is said to lack precisely those qualities of body and mind which belong to the warrior-aristocrat.

37. E.g. *aristoi: Il.* 2.577-78; 5.780; 12.89, 197; 13.128; heroes: *Il.* 2.110, etc. 12.165; 15.230, 261; 19.34.

38. E.g. *Od.* 9.60, 63; 10.134; 12.281, 309.

39. E.g. *Il.* 1.374-77; 2.149-54, 333-35; 9.50-56; 23.539-40, 822-23; *Od.* 3.149-50; 16.375-82, 424-29. See also *Il.* 18.497-502; *Od.* 2.239-41; 3.214-15; 14.238-39.

40. Apparently, although we are not told this explicitly.

41. For an analysis of Thersites and his place in Homeric society see H.D. Rankin, "Thersites the Malcontent, A Discussion," *Symbolae Osloenses* 47 (1972) 36-60.

42. E.g. Adkins, *M&R*, 34, maintains that even Thersites accepts the epic scale of values. In *MV&PB* he says sweepingly, "the *kakoi* agree with the *agathoi* about the evaluations of Homeric society" (pp. 13-14).

43. *WO*, 19.

44. Finley's assertion (*WO*, 102) that this passage is "anachronistic" and that here Homer "permitted a contemporary note to enter, carefully restricting it, however, to a harmless simile and thus avoiding any possible contradiction in the narrative itself," is an example of the unwillingness of many modern scholars to admit the possibility of anything but acceptance of the aristocratic value system in Homeric society.

45. C.G. Starr, *The Economic and Social Growth of Early Greece: 800-500 B.C.* (New York 1977) 120; see also Starr, *The Origins of Greek Civilization: 1100-650 B.C.* (New York 1961) 123-38.

46. Translations of Hesiod are by H.G. Evelyn-White in the Loeb Classical Library (Cambridge, Mass. and London 1967), except as noted.

47. See *Works and Days* 80-89; *Theogony* 585-602. See S.C. Humphreys, *Anthropology and the Greeks* (London, Henley, Boston 1978) 216: "The story of Pandora sums up in a single image the rejection of two essential values of the Homeric world, women and gifts. A gift to Hesiod is either a bribe, a debt, a tax, or a trap. Women are a necessary evil."

48. *The Livelihood of Man,* ed. by H.W. Pearson (New York 1977) 152.

49. See E.A. Havelock, *The Liberal Temper in Greek Politics* (New Haven and London 1964) 36-40.

50. *Works and Days* 190-91.

51. *Kakos anēr* in *Works and Days* 240-41 (see above, p. 28) has no parallel in Homer and can only be taken in an ethical sense of a man (in a position of leadership) who commits injustice. Adkins insists that *kakos* here still decries the absence of "prosperity and social status," i.e. that the usage of these words is the same in Hesiod as in Homer (*MV&PB*, 30).

52. *Works and Days* 286-92. See W. Jaeger, *Paideia: The Ideals of Greek Culture,* vol. I, trans. by G. Highet (New York 1945) 70-71 and Adkins *M&R*, 71. More recently Adkins has modified his conception, and sees Hesiod and Perses as *déclassé agathoi (MV&PB,* 25ff.).

53. Examples of Hesiod's peasant values in the *Works and Days:* appreciation of simple things (40-41); praise of common sense (293-97); industriousness (238-309, 381-82, 398-413, 493-503); thrift (361-71); social cooperation (342-51); peasant view of women (60-105, 373-75, 695-705). Also, Zeus as protector of the weak (5-8); distaste for violence and strife (12-16, 161-66, 182-94, 213-16, 320-22); violence, greed, injustice of the leaders (38-39, 202-212); primacy of justice (225-35); divine retribution for injustice (217-24, 238-73, 333-34). In the strictly formal anthropological sense, a "peasant" is a rural producer who is in a relation of dependence on others in the society, who use the surplus for their own means. It is permissible, however, to employ the term more loosely to describe Hesiod and others of his economic class – small to middling independent freeholders – in a society which is in the process of structural change. Cf. Starr, *The Economic and Social Growth of Early Greece* (above, note 45) 162-67.

54. See A.M. Snodgrass, *Archaeology and the rise of the Greek state. An inaugural lecture* (Cambridge, Eng. 1977); Austin and Vidal-Naquet (above, note 1) 49-69; Starr, *Economic and Social Growth of Early Greece,* 21-117. For a general discussion of the interrelationship among economic, political and ideological structures see L.A. White, *The Evolution of Culture* (New York 1959) 308ff.

55. White (above, note 54) 220. For an exposition of this theory see G.E. Swanson, *The Birth of the Gods. The Origin of Primitive Beliefs* (Ann Arbor 1968) 153-74.

◊

CHAPTER TWO

1. For a somewhat different point of view, see Starr, *Economic and Social Growth*, 82-83, who speaks of "the great technological upsurge in the Aegean world" after 900. Although Starr admits that most of these skills were borrowed, he insists that Greek craftsmen surpassed "their Near Eastern sources in matters of technique." The most important technological advance made by the Greeks was the ability to work iron, which became common after 800 B.C. This (borrowed) technique was certainly significant for agriculture and warfare and may even qualify as a "revolutionary" step (see Polanyi, *The Livelihood of Man*, 149-50).

2. Starr, *Economic and Social Growth*, 40-41. See also Austin and Vidal-Naquet, *Economic and Social History*, 53ff., who correct the earlier, exaggerated, theories about large-scale production, manufacture and commerce.

3. White, *The Evolution of Culture*, 220, 221.

4. For recent discussions of the origin and nature of the early polis, see Starr, *Economic and Social Growth*, 31-34, 98ff., and Austin and Vidal-Naquet, *Economic and Social History*, 49-53. Still valuable are the 1937 and 1943 articles by V. Ehrenberg, reprinted in *Polis und Imperium* (Zurich 1965) 83-97, 98-104. L.H. Jeffery, *Archaic Greece. The City-States c. 700-500 B.C.* (New York 1976) gives useful summaries of the constitutional histories of the most important *poleis*.

5. For an excellent brief account of the age of tyranny in Greece see A. Andrewes, *The Greek Tyrants* (London 1956); cited hereafter as *Tyrants*.

6. The technical stages from the old style of fighting to the new hoplite tactics, the connections between the tactical revolution, the emergence of the polis and the rise of the tyrants are still matters of great controversy. A brief, plausible reconstruction of these events may be found in W.G. Forrest, *The Emergence of Greek Democracy* (New York 1966) 88-93, 104-105 (cited hereafter as *Greek Democracy*); see also Andrewes, *Tyrants*, 31-38. For a more detailed analysis of weaponry and tactics consult A.M. Snodgrass, *Arms and Armour of the Greeks* (Ithaca 1967).

7. Many historians find a causal link between the formation of the hoplite style of fighting and the rise of the tyrants − i.e. the *dēmos* which was championed by the early tyrants was the "middle class" of hoplite infantrymen (Andrewes, *Tyrants*, 34-38). Forrest, *Greek Democracy*, 105 cites "a growing sense of independence among ordinary men; an awareness of a sort among the hoplites; a shift of power inside the aristocracy itself . . ." It is impossible to know what percentage of the (male) population possessed sufficient wealth to take the field as hoplites during the archaic period. Some scholars insist that the number was small and, therefore, that the "hoplite revolution" was not in any real sense a democratizing influence − the number of *agathoi* was merely being increased. But the very essence of the phalanx is numbers and it is difficult to imagine that in times of danger any large number of able-bodied men from any polis would be ignored. In any case we must consider that more than a third of the men of fighting age were hoplites (Forrest, *Greek Democracy*, 94).

We must be careful above all not to import the modern concept of Klassenkampf into the picture. The Greek tyrant was no popular revolutionary, leading his people against an oppressive aristocracy. Tyrants, most of them aristocrats themselves, were motivated by concern for their own prestige and position. In the absence of a true "class system," class warfare is not possible. The number of recorded incidents of bloody violence between the upper and lower classes during the Archaic period is quite small, and none of these appears to have had the character of a popular uprising. See Starr, *Economic and Social Growth*, 178-80. M.T. Arnheim, *Aristocracy in Greek Society* (New York and London 1977) 121-29, asserts that the tyrants "were genuinely popular leaders of anti-aristocratic revolutionary movements" (p. 121), who capitalized on the "combination of growing hope and growing frustration" of the lower classes, and that "tyranny was not only an alternative to aristocracy. It was *the* alternative to aristocracy" (pp. 128-29).

8. Cf. fr. 6.7.15-32D. The fragments of most of the lyric poets are taken from the Teubner text of E. Diehl (ed.), *Anthologia Lyrica Graeca*, 3rd ed. (Leipzig 1949-52). The translations are mainly my own, with occasional reliance on those of J.M. Edmonds in the *Loeb Classical Library*. What follows conforms in most essentials to the perceptive analysis of the Tyrtaean poems by W. Jaeger in *Paideia*, I, 87-98. For a more complete treatment see Jaeger's "Tyrtaeus on True *Arete*," tr. A.M. Fiske, in *Five Essays* (Montreal 1966) 103-42.

9. H. Fränkel, *Early Greek Poetry and Philosophy*, trans. by M. Hadas and J. Willis (New York and London 1973), cited hereafter as *EGPPh*, sees in Callinus' thought implications of transition from Homeric concern with personal glory, honor and shame to the polis-concept of community reaction (pp. 152-53). Snodgrass (above, note 6) 64, notes in fr. 1 (lines 5, 14) evidence of a transition from the old style of fighting to the phalanx.

10. *Paideia* I, 90. In reducing the whole complex of heroic qualities to the one essential of savage valor (*thouris alkē*, a Homeric term, see *Il.* 15.250), Tyrtaeus implies that none of the concomitant qualities so prized by the epic hero was required for a man to be *agathos* or to win *timē*. It should be stressed that the Sparta of the Tyrtaean poems is a special case, for he wrote during a period of grave external danger to the Spartan state; accordingly, these are crisis poems. Elsewhere in the fragments Tyrtaeus urges his compatriots to honor and obey their aristocratic leaders. Fränkel, *EGPPh*, 337-39, maintains that fr. 9 is not by Tyrtaeus, but belongs to the time of Xenophanes, about 100 years later.

11. Fränkel, *EGPPh*, 137, says: "Archilochus seriously balances the value of life against an exaggerated notion of honor, draws a realistic conclusion, and acts accordingly; and at once, in a tone of aggressive challenge, he proclaims to all the world what he has done." See also Jaeger, *Paideia* I, 119. Another point of view, shared by many modern scholars, is that although Archilochus may have been "un-Homeric," he was not "anti-Homeric" (G.M. Kirkwood, *Early Greek Monody* [Ithaca and London 1974] 32-33). Despite differing opinions about the degree of Archilochus' divagation from the traditional epic norms of behavior, there is almost universal agreement that he expressed new attitudes to old values.

12. E.g. *Od.* 9.27: Ithaca is "rough, but a good nurse of young men."

13. A rather large portion of the fragments has to do, in one way or the other, with the polis and its citizens: frgs. 7, 9, 19, 52, 54, 60, 64, 70, 79, 85, 88, 109D. The point that Archilochus, despite his hardbitten cynicism, was essentially a patriot, is made well by P. Green, *The Shadow of the Parthenon* (Berkeley and Los Angeles 1971) 132-69.

14. The fears of old age and death voiced by later archaic poets (see below) is another manifestation of this mood. Hesiod's obsessive religious scrupulosity (or "superstition," if you will) in *Works and Days*, so starkly different from Homer's "un-miasmic" version of divine-human relations, is mirrored in archaic art's preoccupation with fearsome beasts and monsters. On this and other manifestations of "general stress" see Starr, *Economic and Social Growth*, 170-72; also 136-37.

15. H.D. Rankin, *Archilochus of Paros* (Park Ridge, NJ 1977) 36.

16. Cited and translated by Rankin (above, note 15) 11.

17. E.g. fr. 1.54D.

18. See C. Gallavotti, "Il tiranno di Archiloco," *PP* 4 (1949) 69-71: Leophilos is a tyrant, and Archilochus is delivering a moral judgment. Cf. G.L. Huxley, *The Early Ionians* (London 1966) 60, who suggests that Leophilos was an archon in Paros or Thasos.

19. See Jaeger, *Paideia* I, 102 and note 11. Green (above, note 13) emphasizes the similarity of outlook among Hesiod, Archilochus and Thersites, whom he calls "the voice from the ranks, the snarling apostle of self-help and common sense, the deft puncturer of epic pretensions" (p. 152).

20. Hesiod, *Works and Days* 202-212. See Jaeger, *Paideia* I, 121-23; Lesky, *History of Greek Literature*, 154-56; M. Treu, *Archilochus* (Munich 1959) 230-35. Kirkwood, *Monody*, 45, says: "The fable from its beginning in Greek literature suggests earthiness, simplicity, the non-heroic, non-Homeric."

21. See above, Ch. 1, pp. 15-17.

22. E.A. Havelock, *The Greek Concept of Justice* (Cambridge, Mass. and London 1978) 196, renders *deilos* as "down and out," and *esthlos* as "noble," "distinguished." V. Ehrenberg, *Polis und Imperium*, 92, translates them as "poor man," and "the wealthy."

23. Starr, *Economic and Social Growth*, 166. See Starr's discussion of "The Agricultural World," pp. 147-67.

24. J.D. Beazley, *The Development of Attic Black-Figure* (Berkeley and Los Angeles 1951), esp. pp. 22, 38, 49-50, 61; T.B.L. Webster, *Potter and Patron in Classical Athens* (London 1972) 297-300. For grave *stēlai* and bronze figurines depicting warriors and horsemen, see Starr, *Economic and Social Growth*, 121, 132-33. Cf. Jeffery, *Archaic Greece*, 30-31, 90.

25. Translated by Rex Warner. According to A.W. Gomme in his *Commentary on Thucydides*, I (Oxford 1956) *ad loc.*, the adoption of these fashions took place in the sixth century and continued through 480 or 470 B.C.

26. H.I. Marrou, *A History of Education in Antiquity*, tr. by G. Lamb (London and New York 1956) 366, note 5, asserts that there are no homosexual allusions at all in Homer. Cf. D.M. Robinson and E.J. Fluck, *A Study of Greek Love Names* (Baltimore 1937) 18-19, who list possible oblique references to homosexuality in the epics. Some, e.g. Finley, *WO*, 138, are willing to see the absence of overt mention as another example of Homeric "expurgation," but it is hard to see why, if male homosexuality was part of the early warrior ideal, Homer would not have given it a prominent place.

27. A.W. Gouldner, *The Hellenic World. A Sociological Analysis* (New York 1965), has made the interesting suggestion that Greek pederasty was partly the result of a "crisis of intimacy" occasioned by the decline of the kinship system (reliance on relatives) — hence the need for friends. But within a highly

competitive culture there is an inevitable ambivalence in friendship, and, therefore, a need for relationships which provide a basis for trust and security. Accordingly, "pederasty must be most common among the males most deeply involved in the contest system, and thus most common among the upper classes or aristocracy" (pp. 60-62).

28. C.M. Bowra, "Xenophanes, Fragment 3," in *CQ* 35 (1941) 119-26, details other examples of luxury during this period. Bowra also maintains that the chief concern of Xenophanes was that this luxury was both useless and harmful to the polis. See also Starr, *Economic and Social Growth*, 134-35, 139-46 on aristocratic leisure activities and luxury.

29. E.g. *Il.* 6.161; *Hom. hymn* 10.2; cf. *Il.* 15.32.

30. Actually *aischros* is found only once in Homer pertaining to persons (Thersites in *Il.* 2.216); otherwise it refers to actions. *Aischistos* (the superlative), used of Thersites, seems to mean "ugliest," in which case the aesthetic reference predates Mimnermus' usage, and also shows the genesis of the important aristocratic notion that lack of physical beauty is an indication of lower class status.

31. Contrast this with Tyrtaeus, fr. 9.39-42D, where the old, brave warrior is honored by his fellow townsmen.

32. Cf. fr. 4D, where Tithonous' immortality is "an old age chillier than painful death," and fr. 6 where he prays to die in his sixtieth year without disease or care.

33. E.g. frgs. 10, 12a, 13, 14D.

34. The fragments of Anacreon and Ibycus are from D.L. Page, *Poetae Melici Graeci* (Oxford 1962).

35. Athenaeus 13.600d (8 Diehl) preserves a poem by Critias in praise of Anacreon, in which the poet is represented as completely devoted to wine, women and song. For some acute observations on Anacreon's psychology see C.M. Bowra, *Greek Lyric Poetry*, 2nd ed. (Oxford 1961) 272, 282-84 (hereafter cited as *GLP*). Anacreon was not, of course, devoid of civic sense. Like all Greeks of the period he was a man of the polis and some of his fragments attest his patriotism and awareness of the citizen's duties; but very few of the surviving poems speak of fighting and glory, and there is a very definite sense of withdrawal from the simple heroic code of prowess and valor. Cf. frgs. 382, 391, 401, 419 Page.

36. For further citations and fuller discussion of these themes see Fränkel, *EGPPh*, 291-303, and Kirkwood, *Monody*, 150-77. Thus Fränkel speaks of Anacreon's "lightly jesting tone," "light, bantering manner," "softness and delicacy," and his "admirable occasional poetry, like pieces of fine goldsmith's work," with their "late archaic prettiness." On his part, Kirkwood calls Anacreon an "ironist" and "satirist"; his "sophisticated intellectual verse" lacks "passion and earnestness." What characterizes "the sophisticated playfulness of his poetry of love and wine" is its "limpid and graceful phraseology," and "graceful self-mockery." Kirkwood notes especially the "theme of moderation" and "strong feeling for civilized behavior" in Anacreon's poetry.

37. In Sparta, where all activity was singlemindedly channeled towards the interests of the state, there were severe restrictions on social differentiation among the citizens, who proudly called themselves "equals" *(homoioi)*. All Spartiates, including their "kings," ate the same food in common messes; luxury was forbidden, softness despised. Unwieldy iron spits were used in place of coinage to

discourage economic disparity. That the vaunted Spartan equality soon ceased to be true in fact means simply that the urge for social differentiation and superior prestige was ultimately stronger.

38. Fränkel, *EGPPh*, 283. On the channeling "into public contexts" of choral songs, displays and distribution of wealth, funeral and marriage processions, sacrifices, religious festivals, see S.C. Humphreys, *Anthropology and the Greeks* (London, Henley, Boston 1978) 219.

39. Fragments of Alcaeus are quoted from E. Lobel and D. Page (edd.) *Poetarum Lesbiorum Fragmenta* (Oxford 1955). I have adapted the translations of D. Page, *Sappho and Alcaeus* (Oxford 1955).

40. See Page, *Sappho and Alcaeus*, 176. For a capsule description of the political strife in Lesbos see Andrewes, *Tyrants*, 92-99.

41. Page, *Sappho and Alcaeus*, 177. See also W. Donlan, "Changes and Shifts in the Meaning of Demos in the Literature of the Archaic Period," *PP* 135 (1970) 391-392, 394.

42. *Sappho and Alcaeus*, 211. Cf. the comments by A.J. Podlecki, "The Language of Heroism from Homer to Pindar" in *Classics and the Classical Tradition* (University Park, Pa. 1973) 159.

43. Interestingly, it is about this time that the custom of burying arms with the corpses of warriors ceased to be prevalent. M. I. Finley, *Early Greece. The Bronze and Archaic Ages* (New York 1970) 102, comments, "it is tempting to link the disappearance of arms from the graves with the development of the hoplite phalanx since arms no longer signified exclusive social status." If this is so, then Alcaeus may be seen as attempting to memorialize the past glory of the individual warrior. His statement, "For it is noble *(kalon)* to die in Ares" (fr. 400 L-P), appears more a romantic glorification of the warrior's role (un-Homeric as the sentiment is) than a reflection of similar Tyrtaean expressions.

44. *GLP*, 139. The fragments of Alcaeus' poetry contain numerous references to mythological events and heroic legends, expressed in Homeric language. Cf. Kirkwood, *Monody*, who notes Alcaeus' "affinity for the Homeric tradition" (pp. 85ff.); see also 71-72.

45. *Kakopatridēs* (literally, "son of a *kakos* father") is found three other times in Alcaeus. In frgs. 75.12 and 106.4 L-P there is not enough context to establish who is meant. In 67.4-5 L-P the word is in the plural, a clear indication that Alcaeus lumped his enemies together as a group of "low-born" men.

46. See Page, *Sappho and Alcaeus*, 169-75; Andrewes, *Tyrants*, 94-95; Bowra, *GLP*, 151. Two facts alone – that Pittacus had been a sworn companion of Alcaeus' circle and had married into the noblest family of Lesbos, the Penthilidae (fr. 70 L-P) – make a "plebeian" Pittacus difficult to imagine.

47. Fr. 429 L-P; cf. frgs. 129.21, 70, 72. On Alcaeus' descriptions of Pittacus see H. Martin, Jr., *Alcaeus* (New York 1972) 30-31.

48. Frgs. 129, 167, 306(9) L-P.

49. For the meaning of *aisymnētēs* and the character of Pittacus' ten-year office see Andrewes, *Tyrants*, 96-99; Martin, *Alcaeus*, 29-31; Bowra, *GLP*, 136 (with notes). Pittacus instituted sumptuary legislation which limited the amount that could be spent on funerals and imposed double fines on crimes committed in drunkenness.

50. Andrewes, *Tyrants*, 55, 118. G. Busolt, *Griechische Staatskunde*, 3rd ed.,

vol. 1 (Munich 1920) 211, gives the ancient sources for the names. These are not the same as subjected native populations who tilled the soil as kinds of serfs; e.g. *helots* in Sparta, *klarōtai* in Crete, *penestai* in Thessaly, although there may be some identification or overlapping.

51. On Alcaeus' rather fierce dedication to wine and his erotic poetry see Page, *Sappho and Alcaeus*, ch. 13, "Women and Wine" (pp. 291-301) and Bowra, *GLP*, 157-63. Page, for some reason, wishes not to believe that Alcaeus wrote of homosexual attachments, but the later tradition, which had all the poetry available to it (e.g. Quintilian 10.1.2; Cicero *Tusc.* 4.33.71, *De nat. deorum* 1.28.79; Horace *Odes* 1.32.6 ff.) is unequivocal. For a discussion of these ancient references see Martin, *Alcaeus*, 114-15.

52. *Alcaeus*, 52. Sappho, the great female poet of Lesbos, and a contemporary of Alcaeus, was herself obsessed with love (homosexual), beauty and style. "I love luxury . . ." she once said (fr. 58.25 L-P); another time she castigates her rival Andromeda for being enamored of some "countrified" woman in a "countrified" gown, who "does not even know how to draw her dress about her ankles" (fr. 57 L-P). Fränkel, *EGPPh*, 187, speaks of the concern of Sappho and her circle with "sense, consistency, order and propriety, over dullness, disorder, accident, and coarseness."

53. Cf. fr. 37D and Bowra, *GLP*, 276; also frgs. 412, 416 Page, and Fränkel, *EGPPh*, 299-300: Anacreon's "party poems" preach "moderation and propriety."

54. See Bowra, *GLP*, 297-300. Artemon is called *ponēros* ("worthless," "low," line 5). This is the first recorded instance of class usage of a word which later became part of the arsenal of aristocratic social vocabulary. Before this time *ponēros* meant simply "oppressed by toil."

55. In fr. 353 Page he says that "rebels" or "talkers" *(mythiētai)* rule Samos as *stasiōtai* – and these are identified by a scholiast as seamen or fishermen.

56. Cf. also frgs. 16, 17, 24b, 25, 39, 42D.

57. Jaeger, *Paideia*, I, 121, makes the point that "the rise of the lampoon in the early city-state is a symptom of the increased importance of the demos, the common people." Hipponax follows the tradition of Archilochus and Semonides (a seventh-century Ionian, who wrote a scathing indictment of womankind in a popular vein: fr. 7D). In all respects Semonides' is a peasant's view of women – their defects are qualities contrary to a common man's ideal of the practical and useful: neglect of household duties, intellectual pretensions, lack of common sense, instability, gluttony, promiscuity, love of luxury. The portrait he draws of one type (the "mare's daughter") is especially interesting: she shuns menial work, will not grind, sift, or carry out the filth, refuses to sit before the oven because of the soot, bathes two or three times a day, keeps herself perfumed, combed and wreathed with flowers – a *kakon* to her mate unless he is a *tyrannos* or king *(skēptouchos)*, "the kind that takes delight in things like that" (57-70). Cf. a similar poem by Phocylides (fr. 2D).

58. Fr. 3D. See above, pp. 53-54.

59. See Fränkel, *EGPPh*, 228-30; C.M. Bowra, *Early Greek Elegists* (Cambridge, Mass. 1938) 126-27 (cited hereafter as *EGE*). In other respects Xenophanes broke with tradition, especially in his search for a universal conception of the divine as opposed to the anthropomorphic and anthropocentric vision of the gods inherited from Homer and Hesiod.

60. The line is also found in the aristocratically oriented corpus of poems which has come down to us under the name of Theognis (see below, Ch. 3, pp. 93-94), the next line of which goes: "and every man is *agathos* if he is *dikaios*" (lines 147-48). Adkins, who discusses this as Theognis' sentiment, calls it "amazing" and "startling" (*M&R*, 78). But in the light of Phocylides' other pronouncements, and in the context of the anti-aristocratic tradition, it is not at all startling that those to whom the upper-class notions of *aretē* were not significant would see man's highest accomplishment as justice.

61. This is evident both from the fragments and from the somewhat schematic description of Solon's accomplishments by Aristotle (who had all of the poems available to him) in the *Constitution of the Athenians* (Chs. 2-13). Some scholars persist in viewing Solon as an unregenerate aristocrat; others see him as a spokesman for a newly rich middle class. A.W. Gomme, "Interpretation of Some Poems of Alkaios and Sappho," *JHS* 77 (1957) 257, somewhat overstates the democratic position: "There was undoubtedly a democratic movement, that is, one of the many, the poor, against the few rich, in Athens; and Solon led it and guided it." Andrewes' assessment that "In the crisis which called him to power there is no doubt that he stands on the side of the poor," and that Solon "came forward primarily as the champion of the poor against their oppressors" (*Tyrants*, 84-85) is more balanced.

62. A commonplace of Greek ethical thought (cf. Hesiod, *Works and Days* 320ff., Theognis 197ff., Pindar, *Nem.* 8.17), but more strongly expressed here.

63. At least in frgs. 23.21 and 24.18D. It is important to note that otherwise, when Solon speaks of the dominant group, he uses terms which connote possession of power and wealth (frgs. 3.7; 5.3, 7; 10.3; 25.4; 27; cf. 1.72; 4.6). The majority of the population is described in terms denoting poverty or oppression (frgs. 3.23; 24.8-15). He also uses *dēmos* in the narrow class sense (frgs. 5.1, 7; 24.22; 25.1,6). Solon never employs birth words to indicate either group, and, in general, we may conclude that with the exception of class usage of *agathos/esthlos, kakos* and *dēmos*, his terminology is factually descriptive rather than qualitatively judgmental.

64. Cf. fr. 14D, in which the simple pleasures of life are favored over the possession of wealth and luxury.

65. Plutarch, *Solon* 21.5, 23.3; cf. Diog. Laert. 1.55; Diodorus 9.2.5. Tradition records other legislation by Solon, the apparent purpose of which was to strengthen the economic position of the poorer or the landless element; e.g. laws stating that every father had to teach his son a trade and encouraging the export of olive oil and prohibiting the export of other agricultural products. See Starr, *Economic and Social Growth*, 184-86, with notes.

66. For Fränkel, *EGPPh*, 232, this fragment "implies considerable enlightenment that in Solon's opinion goodness has nothing to do with wealth and that it attaches to its bearer permanently." This "emerging view" was a harbinger of the later distinction between "'inward' and 'outward' goods."

67. Starr, *Economic and Social Growth*, 190.

68. *Livelihood of Man*, 168.

CHAPTER THREE

1. Controversy over the authorship of the collection, specifically which lines are by Theognis himself, and their dates of composition, seems never to be finally resolved. For the sake of simplification the author will be referred to as Theognis. Citations are from D. Young (ed.), *Theognis* (Leipzig 1961). The translations are mine, with frequent reliance on the Loeb translation of J.M. Edmonds.

2. *Agathos* is found 76 times in the *Theognidea;* in the *Iliad,* which is ten times longer, the word occurs 87 times. There are 41 instances of *agathos* used of persons, 20 of *esthlos,* 53 of *kakos,* 21 of *deilos* in Theognis.

3. G. Cerri, "La terminologia sociopolitica di Teognide: I," *Quaderni Urbinati* 6 (1968) 7-32, attempts to reconcile the apparent contradictions between Theognis' social and ethical usage of these terms. Cerri correctly sees that *agathos/esthlos, kakos/deilos* combine both spheres of meaning in Theognis; the unifying element is the complex of aristocratic "presuppositions" (birth, wealth, etc.) and aristocratic "qualities" (loyalty, justice, etc.) which are produced only by a particular kind of upbringing. See P.A.L. Greenhalgh, "Aristocracy and Its Advocates in Archaic Greece," *G&R* 19 (1972).

4. This is not a universal change in fashion, of course. *Agathos* and *deilos* in Solon (fr. 1.39) mean "brave," "coward," and the words are so used frequently by fifth-century authors.

5. To these we may add fr. 100D (of uncertain ascription); also frgs. 382, 391, 419 Page (see above, Ch. 2, note 35). The inward-turning quality of Anacreon's poetry is described by Lesky, *Hist. of Greek Lit.,* 176-77. The fragments of Stesichorus (a Sicilian poet, who died in the 550's) contain similar sentiments. One begins: "O Muse, thrusting away wars and celebrating with me the marriages of gods, the feasts of men and the festivities of the blessed . . ." (fr. 210 Page). The *Theognidea* is firmly in this tradition, as we can see in some tamperings with the martial poetry of the Spartan Tyrtaeus. After quoting the rousing quatrain which urges martial valor (fr. 9.13-16D), Theognis adds a hedonistic postscript, which essentially subverts the Tyrtaean lines (1003-12). For this and other changes see D. Young, "Borrowings and self-adaptations in Theognis," *Miscellanea Critica* I (Leipzig 1965) 309-11.

6. Cf. lines 535-38, 1109-14.

7. M.I. Finley, *The Ancient Economy* (Berkeley and Los Angeles 1973) 41. The destitute man, "altogether without resources," was called *ptōchos,* "beggar." Starr, *Economic and Social Growth,* 123, has estimated that the largest landholdings in Attica were about 30 hectares of farmland, while the smallest plots, minimally sufficient to support a family, might range from two to four hectares (about five to ten acres). Starr further estimates that the Solonian class of *zeugitai* at Athens (those who served as hoplites) possessed an average of 12 hectares per family (pp. 154-55).

8. Starr, *Economic and Social Growth,* 123ff., coins the term, "semi-aristocrats," to identify a "much larger group, not so well-to-do, probably not so wellborn," who, "together with men of ancient lineage . . . helped to form the upper classes of historical Greece" (p. 124). These are the *kakoi* of Theognis and Solon. The "semi-aristocrats" were not a commercial and industrial urban middle class (although some traders and artisans might be included, p. 125); rather, they were

the "middling farmers," landowners of some substance, also identified by Starr as the "hoplite class." They "shared the cultural patterns of men of ancient blood and wealth rather than upholding a distinct social code" (p. 128). Starr's invention of a specific group of this kind strikes me as an attempt to layer Greek society too precisely. And there is an inherent difficulty in Starr's distinction. If, as he maintains, this group "sought to imitate the aristocrats socially," but were regarded by them as *kakoi*, that is, were completely disdained by the élite for their "social assertiveness" (p. 128), where could they have stood in ideological relationship to the aristocrats, so jealous of their own position – except in an adversarial posture? There *was* a middle group (composed of medium farmers and a lesser number of trader/artisans), but it had more the character of a "middle mass" in a society which, by all the evidence we have, recognized only two social strata – aristocrats and the rest – or, in economic terms, "the rich" and "the poor." However much (or little) social and economic gradation there may have been among non-aristocrats, the Greeks themselves never conceptualized it beyond vague references to "the middle." It is true that at the upper level of the middle group distinctions will have blurred somewhat (thus Theognis' complaints about intermarriage), and that the decline of the aristocracy's political power was met by a greater degree of civic participation on the part of non-nobles, resulting (by the fifth century) in a broadening of the power base, and consequently some identification of interest. Nevertheless, despite a certain convergence, the consciousness, on both sides, of the distinction between aristocrats and non-aristocrats remained a fundamental fact of life through the period studied in this book. From this it follows that the value systems of the two groups not only remained distinct (aside from the sharing of a collective body of cultural assumptions), but as the political and economic gap between them narrowed, the socio-psychological differences increased.

9. More traditional statements are 561-62, where he hopes that he may have some of his enemies' wealth and much to give to his friends. He prays that Peace and Wealth may possess the city (885), that he may warm his heart with youth and riches (1122), that he may live "rich, apart from evil cares" (1153).

10. E.g. Tyrtaeus fr. 6.7.8D; Archilochus fr. 58.5D; Mimnermus fr. 2.12D.

11. See also lines 321-22, 523-24, 751-52, 865-66, 1061-62.

12. See 465-66, where the embracing of *aretē* and *dikaia* is contrasted to being overcome by gain, "which is *aischron*."

13. E.g. 42-52, 1147-50. Greed is also a universal vice, of course; e.g. 83-86, 401-406.

14. J. Ferguson, *Moral Values in the Ancient World* (London 1958) 20: "Theognis, presented with the spectacle of impoverished aristocrats, cannot equate *arete* with wealth."

15. B. Snell, *The Discovery of the Mind* (Cambridge, Mass. 1953) 171: "For Theognis material gain has, in contrast with earlier views, become an enemy of virtue." E.L. Highbarger, "Literary Imitation in the *Theognidea*," *AJP* 50 (1929) 350-51, notes that Theognis has changed the meaning of *aretē* from that which is purely physical to the sphere of the moral and intellectual. Jaeger, citing lines 149-50: even the *pankakos* man can have wealth, but only the few have *aretē* (see above, p. 83), says, "Theognis holds that arete is the quality which characterizes the true nobleman when the presence or absence of wealth is left out of account:

namely the very rare quality of spiritual nobility" (*Paideia* I, 203).

16. Simonides: Aristotle, in Stobaeus, *Anth.* 86.25; Aristotle: *Pol.* 1293b 10; cf. 1272b 36; 1273a 23, 26; *Ath. Pol.* 1.1; 3.2; Euripides: *Phoen.* 439-42. Arnheim, *Aristocracy in Greek Society*, 170, calls primacy of birth the "bedrock of aristocracy," and of the aristocracy's assertion of its pre-eminence; but, "with the growth of trade new opportunities opened up to the non-noble, and the resultant social mobility made the old equation of birth and worth seem less self-evident than before."

17. Lines 39-52 (cf. 1081-82b) imply power in the hands of aristocratic leaders *(hēgemones)* who have "turned to plunge into great evil-doing." These nobles (to whom Theognis applies the epithet *kakoi*), by aiming at tyranny will ruin the polis. Like all Greek aristocrats what Theognis feared and hated even more than the gradual usurpation of political power by the lower class was the sudden seizure of absolute power by one man. This was the basis of Alcaeus' hatred of Pittacus, and Solon's most pressing concern. The *dēmos*, of course, is despised for being easy prey (they are *philodespotos*, 849). Thus it is never a crime to lay low a "tyrant who devours the *dēmos*" (1181-82); he will not mourn a *tyrannos anēr* any more than a tyrant would grieve at his death (1203-06; cf. 891-94, a reference to Euboea and the Cypselid dynasty). Since the would-be tyrant is usually a fellow aristocrat there is something of an ethical dilemma:

> Neither raise up a man to be a *tyrannos* in hopes, yielding to gain; nor kill him if you have sworn an oath to him by the gods
>
> (823-24).

18. Above, p. 83.

19. The neglect of patriotism is consonant with the few references to war and martial zeal in Theognis and other sixth-century aristocratic poets. Lines 541-42, 603-04, 667-82, 757-68, 825-30, 855-56, 865-68, 947-48, 1003-06, 1043-44 (some of which have been discussed above) are all the references to patriotism or to concern for the polis. Cf. 549-54, 887-90, a war going on. As Fränkel notes, in addition to a lack of "patriotic feeling" in the *Theognidea*, there is "little indication of a feeling of responsibility for others or of service to a cause. Family relationships are very seldom mentioned and there is no mention of the duties of office" (*EGPPh*, 413, and notes 27, 28, 29).

20. See also 35-38, 563-66, 792, 1165-66: associate with the good; 59-60, 65-72, 613-14, 1025-26, 1167-68: the counsel of the *agathoi* is superior, that of the *kakoi* is inferior and untrustworthy.

21. In 979-82 a true friend is one who acts as well as says, and who proves himself *agathos* in deed. Cf. 83-86, 115-28, 1049-54, 1087-90.

22. Other statements that an *agathos* is a good friend, the *kakos* a bad one: 105-14, 853-54, 955-56, 1083-84, 1151-52, 1377-80.

23. E.g. 295-98, 309-12, 323-30, 399-400, 409-14, 467-98, 509-10, 627-28, 841-44, etc. See Bowra, *EGE*, 161-62, for further examples.

24. Cf. lines 355, 395-98, 445-46, 555-56 (=1178 a-b), 591-92, 1029-30, 1162 a-d.

25. According to Fränkel, *EGPPh*, 421, what Theognis means by *tolmān* is "a strong and composed attitude of mind; a spirit of resistance which sets the oppressed on his feet again; a kind of active patience which strengthens those who

have been weakened . . . based upon a peculiar elasticity which is produced by simultaneously recognizing and disregarding the ugly truths . . . for in the behavior of the self-controlled man the dark depths of sorrow are concealed behind calmness."

26. H. North, *Sophrosyne* (Ithaca, N.Y. 1966) 17. Cf. lines 39-42, 377-80, 753-54, 1081-1082 (*sōphrosynē* opposed to *hybris*).

27. See North, *Sophrosyne*, 18-19 on this passage. North also points out that *sōphrosynē* in Theognis 699-718 has a specific intellectual connotation, another new direction.

28. Phocylides' fr. 12D, in which he expresses a wish to be *mesos* in the polis, relates to the ordinary man's lack of pretension (see above, Ch. 2, p. 68. Solon's keen interest in the mean has no "class" significance (North, *Sophrosyne*, 15). It is at this time that the doctrine of "nothing in excess" *(mēden agan)* becomes associated with the aristocratically oriented shrine of Apollo at Delphi.

29. Lines 233, 847. Other lines on intellectual capacity and their moral implications are 59-60, 279-82, 369-70, 453-56, 625-26, 631-32, 1037, 1167-68. See Bowra, *GLP*, 334 (citing lines 279-82): "The nobles arrogated the name of wise to themselves, and thought their democratic adversaries fools."

30. Cf. lines 29-30, 53-60, 289-90, 393-98, 547-48, 749-52. In 39-52 the (aristocratic) leaders are *kakoi* and *adikoi;* see above, note 17.

31. *Paideia* I, 203. Cerri (above, note 3) 14, note 13, gives a summary of the controversy. Adkins, in his discussion of this "amazing" couplet (*M&R*, 78-79) says that this notion "smashes the whole framework of Homeric values," but that it did not become generally accepted and only reemerges as a result of the interior moral speculation of the late fifth and fourth centuries. Arnheim, *Aristocracy in Greek Society*, 164-67, attacks Adkin's position. On Phocylides' maxim, see above, Ch. 2, note 60.

32. In these examples *aretē* still retains its essential sense of "ability," "achievement," "success." Other instances of *aretē* in the collection have this meaning: 129, 317, 402, 624, 654, 904, 971, 1062, 1074. Cerri (above, note 3) 31, note 36, asserts that in the frequent opposition between "few" and "many," these words signify *agathoi* and *kakoi* for Theognis.

33. Fränkel, *EGPPh*, 401; see Fränkel's summary, pp. 422-25, in which he contrasts Theognis' attitude ("aristocratic" in a social sense, but intellectually and spiritually "bourgeois") with Pindar's loftier aristocratic vision.

34. The poems of Pindar are cited from the Teubner text of B. Snell, *Pindarus*, 2 vols. (Leipzig 1964, 1971). The chronology of the odes is that of C.M. Bowra, *Pindar* (Oxford 1964). The translations are my own, with frequent reliance on those of J.E. Sandys in the Loeb edition of Pindar, and R. Lattimore, *The Odes of Pindar* (Chicago 1947). The games were held at regular intervals at Olympia, Delphi, Nemea and the Isthmus of Corinth. The traditional date of the founding of the most prestigious festival, the Olympian, is 776 B.C.; the others were regularized in the early 500's, coinciding with the heyday of aristocratic ostentation.

35. The usage of *agathos* in Pindar reflects this: the *agathoi* are a group set apart from the rest of the citizenry (*Pyth.* 2.81, 96; 3.71, 83; 4.285; 10.71); the *agathoi* are fittest to rule (*Pyth.* 10.71); they are wise (*Ol.* 7.91; *Pyth.* 3.83). Pindar's usage of *eslos* is similar, but somewhat more general.

36. *Cheirōn* occurs twice; in *Isth.* 4.34 it means "inferior" in a physical sense and in *Nem.* 8.22 it is opposed to *esloi* in a generalized ethical sense.

37. Cf. *Pyth.* 1.84; *Nem.* 3.40-41; *Parth.* 1.8-10. The same idea is found in Theognis 797-98: "One man blames, another praises the *agathoi*, but of the *kakoi* there is no mention at all."

38. *Ol.* 2.10-11; 10.20; 11.19-20; 13.13; *Pyth.* 5.17-19, 76; 8.44-45; 10.12; *Nem.* 1.27-28; 5.40-41; 6.8, 15-16; 11.12, 33-38; *Isth.* 1.39-40; 3.13-14. Pindar's insistence on "the genealogical principle" is well demonstrated by P. W. Rose, "The Myth of Pindar's First Nemean," *HSCP* 78 (1974) 151-55.

39. A. Andrewes, *The Greeks* (New York 1967) 201. The numerous local festivals, on the other hand (like the Panathenaea at Athens, a pet project of the tyrant Pisistratus), were more consciously civic and patriotic and gave greater scope to the religious, athletic and cultural expressions of the populace.

40. See above, Ch. 2, p. 65.

41. D. Kagan, *The Great Dialogue. A History of Greek Political Thought From Homer to Polybius* (New York 1965) 54. Greenhalgh (above note 3) 204-207, shows that while the concept of the aristocracy's "hereditary capacity" and their "hereditary fitness to rule" is stated with little reservation in Pindar, the *Theognidea* recognizes the "problem of noble failure" (e.g. lines 305-308), a significant difference in outlook.

42. V. Ehrenberg, *From Solon to Socrates* (London 1967) 175ff.; cf. also p. 123.

43. Other Pindaric statements on wealth are consistent: wealth must not be hoarded but enjoyed and distributed (*Nem.* 1.31-32; *Isth.* 1.67-68); greed is dangerous, but is regarded as a universal vice and not connected with the *kakoi* (*Pyth.* 3.54; 4.139-40; *Nem.* 11.47-48; cf. *Pyth.* 1.92; 8.13; *Nem.* 7.18; 9.33).

44. E.g. *Ol.* 9.70ff.; *Nem.* 3.36-37; 10.73ff.; *Isth.* 6.35ff. See Bowra, *Pindar*, 386-88.

45. *Ol.* 2.86; 7.91; 9.100; 11.10; *Pyth.* 1.42.

46. In *Pyth.* 5.107-15 the "understanding" *(synetoi)* praise the victor, who is wise, courageous, strong and skilled in poetry and athletics; and in *Nem.* 8.41 the *sophoi* are linked with the just *(dikaioi)*. Cf. *Isth.* 5.11; *Nem.* 6.4-5.

47. In *Ol.* 2.83-86 Pindar says that his shafts are aimed at the "understanding" *(synetoi)* but the crowd *(to pan)* needs interpreters; and in *Ol.* 5.16 those who are successful and prosperous "seem *sophoi* even to the citizens *(politai)*."

48. Cf. *Ol.* 13.11-12, where the poet speaks of his unerring boldness *(tolmā eutheia)*. In *Nem.* 7.59 the victor's father has "a daring spirit for noble deeds" *(tolmā kalōn)*, and in *Nem.* 10.30 *tolmā* is opposed to a "toil-avoiding heart." See also *Pyth.* 5.117.

49. North, *Sophrosyne*, 24-26.

50. See W. Donlan, "The Origin of *Kaloskagathos*," *AJP* 94 (1973) 365-74.

51. J.D. Beazley, *The Development of Attic Black Figure* (Berkeley and Los Angeles 1951) 64; D.M. Robinson and E.J. Fluck, *A Study of the Greek Love-Names* (Baltimore 1937) 66-69.

52. The lines which follow this couplet (935-38) provide a good example of the change in values. They are obviously adapted from Tyrtaeus (fr. 9.37-42D), but Tyrtaeus is referring to honor won only in battle, while for Theognis it is the combining of (now generalized) *aretē* and *kallos*. Other erotic references in the

Theognidea to beauty are 994, 1017-19, 1259-62, 1279-82, 1319-22, 1327-28, 1335-36, 1341-44, 1345-50, 1365-66, 1369-70, 1377-78. At the beginning of the *Theognidea* the Muses and Graces are made to say, "whatever is beautiful *(kalon)* is dear *(philon)*, and what is not *kalon* is not *philon*" (17). Here beauty, as Fränkel says, is "at once physical and moral beauty" (*EGPPh*, 402; cf. 418).

53. In *Nem.* 11.11-14 Pindar praises the victor's father, the victor's beauty and his "inborn fearlessness," and ties together wealth, good looks, and might in the games. See also *Ol.* 10.99-105; *Isth.* 2.3-5. Homosexual love and the pleasures of conviviality are occasional themes in Pindar's poetry (e.g. frgs. 123; 124 a.b).

54. Fränkel, *EGPPh*, 490-91, and note 8.

55. He could, then, praise democratic Athens and write odes honoring tyrants while condemning tyranny at home. Even here, as Ehrenberg points out, "Pindar stresses the old family descent of the tyrants; thus he can see their states as examples of *eunomia*, as though they were aristocracies" (*From Solon to Socrates*, 177, note 122).

56. A.G. Woodhead, *Thucydides on the Nature of Power* (Cambridge, Mass. 1970) 68; a fault also shared by the democratic factions in the fifth century, as Woodhead points out.

57. Fränkel, *EGPPh*, 337, 487-96.

58. B.R. English, *The Problem of Freedom in Greece From Homer to Pindar* (Toronto 1938) 100. Pindar attempted to recreate the easy and natural aristocratic panhellenism of the Homeric epics, but achieved it only by ignoring the realities of quarreling city-states and narrow class interest.

59. Fränkel, *EGPPh*, 426. Cf. pp. 428, 432, 460.

Ω

CHAPTER FOUR

1. Citations of Simonides are from E. Diehl, *Anthologia Lyrica Graeca;* the translations are my own. For a perceptive analysis of the Scopas fragment see Fränkel, *EGPPh*, 307-12; the poem corrects "the system of norms and values then in force," and initiates ideas that are "entirely new and revolutionary," namely the abandonment of the archaic way of thinking in antitheses and the substitution of a "relative mode of thinking." Another poem, preserved in a papyrus fragment first published in 1959 and believed to be by Simonides, contains similar ethical thought. See W. Donlan, "Simonides, Fr. 4D and *P. Oxy.* 2432," *TAPA* 100 (1969) 71-95.

2. In his article on Theognis' language (see above, Ch. 3, note 3), G. Cerri contrasts the outlooks of Simonides, Theognis and Pindar and concludes that in the two Simonidean poems there is a conscious repudiation of "the aristocratic ethic" (pp. 31-32).

3. *From Solon to Socrates,* 173; cf. fr. 106D.

4. See Pindar fr. 110 Snell; Ehrenberg, *From Solon to Socrates,* 173-77; Bowra, *Pindar,* 110-117; P. Green, *Ancient Greece, An Illustrated History* (New York 1979) 102-03.

5. *Kakos* here has not a social but a moral meaning. Other statements of Simonides reflect a shifting of focus away from conventional aristocratic ideas; e.g. fr. 55D: "Appearance *(to dokein)* forces even the truth"; fr. 37D on *aretē*, reminiscent of Hesiod, *W&D* 289-92, but more speculative; fr. 8D: "For all things come to one horrible Charybdis, both great achievements *(aretai)* and wealth *(ploutos)*." See also frgs. 6, 9, 10.3-4, 11, 26, 48D. The message is that life is difficult, mortal achievement is illusory, all is in the hands of the gods. Other sentiments are more traditional (e.g. 57D, on pleasure), but in general Simonides' poetry is grounded in realism and in common-sense morality — hard work, piety, cooperation — which, translated into the political realm, means that "the new democratic man is fully responsible for his actions" (T.B.L. Webster, *Political Interpretations in Greek Literature* [Manchester 1948] 24).

6. The "modernity" of Simonides sometimes makes us forget that he was an almost exact contemporary of Xenophanes *(ca.* 570-475). Fränkel, *EGPPh*, 325, calls both of them relativists, apostles of enlightenment, fighting for "a rational ordering of values and for a practical code of ethics." Simonides is "the clever and lucid advocate of a rational revision of prevalent modes of thought and behavior .... the arrogance of self-conscious nobility must be replaced by bourgeois propriety" (p. 400).

7. Citations of Bacchylides are from *Bacchylidis carmina cum fragmentis,* ed. H. Maehler post B. Snell (Leipzig 1970). The translations are my own.

8. Bacchylides' emphasis on virtues which are both civic and pious is also seen in Ode IV.3, where Hiero, the tyrant of Syracuse, is called "just ruler of the city" *(astythemis),* and in Ode III. 83-84, where Hiero is advised to "make glad his heart by doing pious deeds *(hosia)*, for this is the highest of gains."

9. Bacchylides was not opposed to wealth, of course, and he displays none of the bitterness on the subject often seen in Theognis; his general attitude is conventional: wealth is a good thing (fr. 4.61-62; V.53; III.81-82); greed is bad, moderation is good (XV.57ff.; fr. 1; I.165-68).

10. It should be noted that for Bacchylides *esthlos* and *chrēstos* were probably synonymous terms — the *esthlos* is the man "useful" in the community. Aristocrats and non-aristocrats in the fifth century both claimed title to the words.

11. Lesky, *Hist. of Greek Lit.*, 203; W.C. Greene, *Moira. Fate, Good and Evil in Greek Thought* (Cambridge, Mass. 1944) 81.

12. P.W. Rose, "The Myth of Pindar's First Nemean," *HSCP* 78 (1974) 152-53; see above, pp. 97-98.

13. Bowra, *GLP*, 373ff., discusses the background and the historical problems of the various *scolia*. The Attic *scolia* are cited from Page, *PMG*. The translations are my own.

14. See also frgs. 892, 903 Page.

15. Four fragments (893-896 Page) which, taken together, are called the "Harmodius Song," celebrate the slaying of the Athenian tyrant Hipparchus, son of Pisistratus, by two aristocratic lovers, Harmodius and Aristogeiton. There are many problems of dating and interpretation of these poems, in which the word *isonomos* ("with equal laws") first occurs, a word later to be a democratic catchword. See Bowra, *GLP*, 391-96 and M. Ostwald, *Nomos and the Beginnings of the Athenian Democracy* (Oxford 1969) *passim*. But, aside from these historical questions, the central fact is that they commemorate a tyrannicide by two aristocratic lovers. The poems thus indicate aristocratic hatred of one-man rule, pederastic friendship, and, very significantly, early employment of propaganda to enhance the aristocratic image.

16. Similar are frgs. 901, 904, 905 Page.

17. Thuc. 2.40.2. The translation is adapted from Rex Warner, *Thucydides. History of the Peloponnesian War* (Baltimore 1972).

18. G.E.M. de Ste. Croix, *The Origins of the Peloponnesian War* (Ithaca 1972) 349.

19. *Ibid.* 35.

20. *M&R*, 207.

21. The practice of "liturgies" was established in Athens in the fifth century; individual wealthy citizens were required to fit out a warship (trireme) or to bear the expense of a public chorus, as well as other, less costly, functions. This form of taxation was an excellent way for the author to manifest his dedication to the community, and most men of wealth with political ambitions made the most of the opportunity.

22. E.g. *gennadas* (noble), *agenēs* (of no birth), *dysgenēs* (of low birth) are found (apparently) first in the fifth century. For a fuller analysis, with contextual citations, see W. Donlan, "Social Vocabulary and its Relationship to Political Propaganda in Fifth-Century Athens," *Quaderni Urbinati* 27 (1977) 95-111.

23. Other valuative designators which appear either for the first time or with frequency include *sōphrōn* (prudent, moderate), *dexios* (clever), *ponēros* (wicked), *mochthēros* (wretched, knavish), *phaulos* (insignificant). One of the most interesting of the aristocratic words is *chrēstos* (useful, worthy), an old word, used during the archaic period with political force but in the context of civic usefulness, opposed, often, to aristocratic luxury. But in the fifth century it was appropriated by oligarchs who proclaimed *themselves* the useful members of the polis.

24. See R.A. Neil, *The Knights of Aristophanes* (Cambridge, Eng. 1909), App. II, "Political Use of Moral Terms."

25. See W. Donlan, "Changes and Shifts in the Meaning of *Demos* in the Literature of the Archaic Period," *PP* 135 (1970) 381-95; "The Origin of *Kaloskagathos,*" *AJP* 94 (1973) 365-74. Also de Ste. Croix (above, note 18) 871-76. *Dēmos* and its derivatives had negative connotations only in aristocratic usage, of course. Similarly, *kaloskagathos*, by the early fourth century, had been taken over by non-aristocrats and we find the orators using it proponents of the radical democracy. Subsequently it, and most of the other social terms, lose their social bite and become general designations of ethical behavior without regard to social status.

26. See Neil (above, note 24) 209, who translates *hoi pacheis* as "the bloated." Neil notes that in Attic the word is found mainly in Herodotus and Aristophanes.

27. *EGPPh*, 321. The following description of the political attitudes of the sophists is drawn from E.A. Havelock, *The Liberal Temper in Greek Politics* (New Haven and London 1957). See also W.K.C. Guthrie, *The Sophists* (Cambridge, Eng. 1971).

28. Havelock, *Liberal Temper*, 342-43.

29. See Guthrie, *The Sophists*, 153. The translations are from K. Freeman, *Ancilla to the Pre-Socratic Philosophers* (Cambridge, Mass. 1966).

30. It is of no matter really whether or not the author himself held these sentiments to be true; the point is that they represented to the reading or listening audience the kinds of statements that proponents of particular views would be likely to make. The translations of the Athenian dramatists are my own.

31. The fifth-century Athenian dramatists often state vehemently the democratic doctrine that the *people* decide the destiny of the state, not a single ruler. See, e.g. Aeschylus, *Suppliants* 356-75, 517-18, 600-24, 698-703, 942-49; *Persians* 234-42; *Agamemnon* 1348-65; Sophocles, *O.C.* 75-80, 907-30, 1032-33; *Antigone* 726-39; Euripides, *Heraclidae* 422-24; *Suppliants* 399-454. Very explicit are Euripides, *Suppliants* 352-53 and *Phoenissae* 535-45, on equality.

32. Compare Euripides, *Helen* 1678-79: "For the gods do not hate *hoi eugeneis*, but their sufferings are greater than the mob's *(hoi anarithmētoi)*."

33. The paradox of the "noble slave" was a favorite of Euripides, e.g. *Ion* 854-56: "For one thing brings shame *(aischynē)* to slaves – the name. In every other way a slave is no more inferior *(kakiōn)* than the free, as long as he is *esthlos.*" Cf. *Helen* 1640-41; frgs. 511, 831 (Nauck). For other statements by Euripides on slaves see Guthrie, *The Sophists*, 156-58.

34. Impoverished nobles: Euripides, *H.F.* 588-92 and V. Ehrenberg, *The People of Aristophanes* (New York 1962) 110, and note 8. The upper class was naturally ill-disposed to men of no family who had become wealthy; cf. Aristophanes, *Wasps* 1309-10, Euripides, *Suppliants* 741-44. See also W.R. Connor, *The New Politicians of Fifth-Century Athens* (Princeton 1971) 155-56. The term *neoploutos* (newly-rich), found first in Aristophanes, seems to have been a pejorative (cf. Cratinus, fr. 208, *neoploutoponēroi*).

35. See Ehrenberg, *People*, 247-48, with notes. Ehrenberg's ch. 9, "Money and Property," is a measured exposition of the complex of attitudes towards wealth in the fifth and fourth centuries B.C. at Athens.

36. The date, authorship and purpose of this political pamphlet is much disputed. It may have been written as early as the 440's or as late as the 420's. See G. Bowersock, "Pseudo-Xenophon," *HSCP* 71 (1966) 33-55; also H. Frisch, *The*

Constitution of the Athenians (Copenhagen 1942). For a discussion of the socio-economic terms in this work see G.E.M. de Ste. Croix, "The Character of the Athenian Empire," *Historia* 3 (1954) 24-25. The author groups *poneroi, penetes, demos* in opposition to *gennaioi, plousioi* and *chrestoi* (1.2). In 1.4 *poneroi, penetes, demotikoi, demotai, cheirous* are opposed to *chrestoi*, while in 1.9 *dexiotatoi* and *chrestoi* stand in contrast to *mainomenoi* (the mad) and *poneroi*, and in 2.18 *demos, plethos, penetes, demotikoi* are ranged against *plousios, gennaios, dynamenos*. See also 1.13, 2.14 (*demos* opposed to *plousioi*), 2.19 (*demos* equivalent to *penetes*), 2.10 (*demos, ochlos* opposed to *plousioi, oligoi, eudaimones*).

37. Cf. Euripides, *Electra* 37-38, frgs. 22, 95, 247, 249, 326 Nauck. At the same time, the opposite point of view can be maintained: e.g. Eur. fr. 232;cf. 235. This represents a kind of "fall back" position, and demonstrates the confused welter of opinion regarding the relative weight of birth and wealth in the fifth-century's treatment of a volatile social issue.

38. Nor, as a matter of fact, does he refute the claim to superiority based on the wisdom of the upper class — the many are implicitly contrasted with the wise counsellors, their role is merely to listen and to vote.

Although Pericles in the Funeral Oration naturally minimizes class distinctions, when he does allude to the subject he implies differences of wealth and poverty (Thuc. 2.37, 40, 42, 43). Ehrenberg, *People*, 250-51, comments on *Suppliants* 238ff. that this is a "purely theoretical" exposition, and that there "never existed any distinct social groups or classes to correspond to those three types." Ehrenberg is doubtless correct, but the point is that increasingly in the latter half of the fifth century the upper class pressed hard its natural advantage in this area and succeeded in keeping democratic apologists on the defensive, even forcing them to employ rhetorical categories which favored the wealthy few.

39. Cf. de Ste. Croix, *Origins of the Peloponnesian War*, 35, 90.

40. Which is precisely the point made by the Old Oligarch: the democracy is conducted for the benefit of the useless poor against the *chrestoi* wealthy; the contributions of the rich in the form of liturgies are a ploy by the poor to impoverish the rich.

41. The arguments *for* democracy were also couched in the rhetoric of moral right. Theseus' defense of democracy in the *Suppliants* was that under written laws *(gegrammenoi nomoi)* "the weak and the rich have equal *dike*," and it is possible for the weaker to speak up against the fortunate when attacked: "Armed with *dikaia* the lesser *(meion)* may overcome the mighty *(megas)*." Anyone at all may bring forward some "useful counsel" *(chreston bouleuma)* and thereby gain fame (433-41; cf. *Phoenissae* 531ff.). Otanes' plea for democracy against monarchy in Herodotus 3.80 is also based on moral arguments. He speaks of the *hybris* of the monarch, the lack of self-restraint caused by unrestricted power, the envy, jealousy, injustice and savagery that necessarily follows from one-man rule. But the rule of the *plethos* "has the fairest name of all, equality before the law *(isonomia)*." So too, in *Suppliants* 238-45, while the divisions are economic the judgments are moral; the rich are useless and greedy, the poor are envious, beguiled by *poneroi* politicians; those "in the middle" guard the *kosmos* of the polis.

42. Cf. *Electra* 253, where Electra calls the peasant "a poor man *(penes)* but *gennaios* and reverent *(eusebes)* to me." Also, fr. 53 Nauck.

43. See also 473-75, 489-98, 502-504, 627-30, 750-73, 779-81, 860-70.

44. Compare 510-16: Poverty is the reason why men perform necessary and useful work; 593: all good things *(agatha)* come from Poverty; Euripides fr. 327: a poor man is often more pious than a rich man.

45. In tone Cleon's remarks are similar to those of the Sicilian Athenagoras (above, p. 142). The chorus in Euripides' *Ion* (834-35) prefers a friend who is "an ordinary man but upright" *(phaulos chrēstos)* to one who is "wiser but evil" *(kakos sophōteros)*.

46. Thucydides is a prime example. It is not correct to term him a doctrinaire anti-democratic (like the Old Oligarch), but for him, as for the aristocratic authors of the sixth century, qualities like *sōphrosynē* and *gnōmē* were pre-eminently characteristics of the upper class. He consistently applied these to statesmen whom he admired, like Themistocles and Pericles, and denied them to men like Cleon and other leaders of the "extreme democracy." See Woodhead, *Thucydides on the Nature of Power,* 44-46; North, *Sophrosyne,* 102; P. Huart, *Gnōmē chez Thucydide et ses contemporains* (Paris 1973).

47. Examples of this kind of "self-consoling" argument are frequent in Euripides; e.g. the powerless lower class is really better off than the upper class with all its troubles: *I.A.* 16-19, 446-50; birth, wealth, and power are not what determine loyalty, friendship, honest character: *Orestes* 1155-57; *Andr.* 639-41; *H.F.* 633-36; *Heraclidae* 1-5, 743-47; *Ion* 621-47; *Phoenissae* 531-67; the noble slave whose body is in bondage but whose soul is free: *Helen* 726-33; *Ion* 854-56. Cf. *Andr.* 695-705; *Ion* 834-41.

48. *Aristocracy in Greek Society,* 170-72. For lines 367-72 see above p. 213. Adkins discusses these passages at some length *M&R,* 177-78, 195-96; *MV & PB,* 115-117). Orestes, he says, "has been shocked into questioning traditional assumptions." He continues, ". . . nowhere else in the extant complete plays of Euripides is any male character commended as *agathos* for self-control or for any cooperative excellence" *(MV&PB,* 116). This is an oversimplification (see e.g. *Orestes* 902-31, *Hecuba* 592-602, and above pp. 136-37). Adkins preserves his thesis that only the success standard counted, even in the fifth century, by interpreting lines 386ff. to mean "self-control renders a man *agathos,* because men who are self-controlled are good at administering both their cities and their households." That is, if *sōphrosynē* is effective in terms of the success standard, it will be valued *(MV&PB,* 117). Adkins errs in insisting that the upper class (and hence Greek society as a whole) simply did not value highly the "cooperative" virtues. We have seen, to the contrary, that the upper class did, in fact, and by claiming them as specifically their own, aristocrats maintained their edge of superiority. The non-noble argument presented here by Euripides is an attempt at counterclaim and is not some new impulse.

49. Electra's peasant husband displays the same kind of common-sense wisdom in *Electra* 404-30 (his final appearance in the play) where he cleverly parries with her on the subject of wealth and poverty. Cf. Euripides, frgs. 168, 377 on bastards.

50. *Sophrosyne,* 75. Cf. Sophocles, *Philoctetes* 874.

51. In a variation of the *physis/nomos* dichotomy Euripides presses for equality by contrasting good qualities that are available to all men "by nature" with the appearance of such. For example, in the Electra passage "appearance"

CONCLUSION OF NOTE ON PAGE 153

(dokēsis), "empty opinions" *(kena doxasmata,* repeated in the *Melanippe* fragment), "hulks of flesh, empty *(kenai)* of mind, statues," are opposed to *physis*. Euripides implies that the mere appearance of excellence is what the upper class uses to intimidate and deceive the lower class. This is given more explicit utterance by an old slave in the *Electra,* who muses to himself on seeing Orestes and Pylades (550-51):

> *Eugeneis* it seems, but this may prove false, for many who are *eugeneis* are *kakoi,*

and by Andromache, who says to Menelaus:

> Oh, reputation, reputation *(doxa)*, you have raised to mighty honors countless mortals who were nothing. I call blessed those who have good fame *(eukleia)* based on truth *(alētheia);* but to those whose fame is from lies *(pseudē)* I grant only the chance appearance of wisdom *(tychēi phronein dokein).*
> (*Andromache* 319-23)

Cf. *Electra* 394-95; *Phoenissae* 531-58. It is clear that Euripides has not worked out the problem completely; the formula *ouden ōn* (being nothing) is applied both in the aristocratic sense, applicable to the lower class, and in the moral sense of nobles who are, in reality, nothing. The focus on appearance vs. reality must be connected with the upper-class emphasis on style of life, calculated to impress the lower class.

Ω

CHAPTER FIVE

1. See above pp. 140-41 and Frisch (Ch. 4, note 36) 211-14. The Old Oligarch also says that the *dēmos* are exploiting the rich, who pay for choral performances, athletic contests and the equipping of triremes; the poor have the enjoyment of these things, for which the rich expend their money, the purpose being the impoverishment of the rich. On Greek education in general see Marrou, *A History of Education in Antiquity*.

2. Ehrenberg, *People*, 99; for a full discussion of the social effects of education, with citations from Old Comedy and other fifth-century sources, see *People*, Chs. 10 and 13.

3. See J.H. Oliver, *Demokratia, the Gods and the Free World* (Baltimore 1960) 134.

4. See C.R. Beye, *Ancient Greek Literature and Society* (Garden City 1975) 168-69. On the "cult of masculinity," see Starr, *Economic and Social Growth*, 130-33. The red-figured vases of the period after the Persian Wars, like those of the archaic period, continue to concentrate on the leisured pursuits of the upper class: athletics, hunting, drinking parties, pederasty. In his short treatise *On Hunting (Kynēgetikos)* Xenophon extols the virtues of this manly art; it makes the body healthy, improves sight and hearing, retards old age, and is the best training for war. "For men who are sound in body and mind *(psychai)* are always at the edge of success" (12.5). Again, "A good education *(paideusis kalē* = physical training) teaches a man to observe the laws and to talk and listen about *ta dikaia*" (12.14).

5. Guthrie, *The Sophists*, 50.

6. In 1450ff. the chorus congratulates Philokleon on his adaptation to a life which is "dainty and soft."

7. E.g. of a cavalry officer in *Lysistrata* 561 and of a homosexual aristocrat in *Clouds* 100; cf. *Knights* 1121. See *Knights* 1331-32, *Clouds* 984 on the (by then) old-fashioned custom of wearing the *tettix* or "cicada" in the hair-knot.

8. Compare *Clouds* 545; *Ploutos* 170-71, 571-74; *Birds* 1280-83.

9. The word is *Komētamynia*. Amynias was an aristocrat, general in 423/2, suspected of Spartan sympathies, notorious for his long hair, effeminacy and foppishness. K.J. Dover, *Greek Homosexuality* (Cambridge, Mass. 1978) 142, notes that "long hair was regarded as characteristic of wealthy and leisured young men," and that the slighting references to long hair were expressions of "class antagonism." The verb *komaō* "is used in comedy in the sense 'give oneself airs,' 'think oneself a cut above other people'" (p. 78).

10. The proposal that the latter be given precedence in mating with Athenian women is seen as "a democratical notion" *(dēmotikē gnōmē)* and a "mocking" of the former.

11. Compare *Clouds* 872ff., 985ff., 1002ff., 1045ff.; Pherecrates frgs. 2, 29; Plato Comicus fr. 208; Cephisodorus fr. 3; Phrynicus fr. 3; Cratinus frgs. 98, 100; *Adespota* 56; Lysias 4.7-8, 16.11. See Ehrenberg, *People*, 104-105, 243.

12. Cf. 74, 243. Hunting was another of the aristocratic pursuits that made distinctions of class so visible. See *Knights* 1382-83 and *Wasps* 1202-04.

13. *Wasps* 1025-28; *Peace* 762-63.

14. *Knights* 732-40, 867-77; *Clouds* 973-83, 1022-23, 1088-1100; *Acharnians*

716; *Wasps* 686-91; *Ecc.* 102ff.; Lysias 3 *(passim);* 14.26. See Ehrenberg, *People,* 100-102.

15. See W.K. Lacey, *The Family in Classical Greece* (Ithaca 1968) 157-58. Cf. Aristophanes fr. 338 (from *Thesmophoriazusae* II) where *lakōnizein*, "to play the Spartan," is glossed by ancient commentators as "to be a pederast."

16. Dover, *Greek Homosexuality*, 151; see pp. 194-96.

17. Dover, *Greek Homosexuality*, 198.

18. Dover, *Greek Homosexuality*, 151. Dover states that the central characters (and bulk of the audience) of comedy were more heterosexually oriented. Prerequisites for homosexual courtship were "impressive gifts" and "leisure," not available to the non-wealthy (p. 150).

19. Dover, *Greek Homosexuality*, 201-02. Cf. P. Slater, *The Glory of Hera* (Boston 1968) 59. Beye (above, note 4) 157, identifies upper-class homosexuality with imitation of Sparta and the desire for an aristocratic exclusiveness which had overtones of kinship affiliation. A.W. Gouldner's discussion (*The Hellenic World*, 60-64) is enlightening in this regard. He concludes that "pederasty must be most common among the males most deeply involved in the contest system, and thus most common among the upper class or aristocracy. This, in fact, appears to be the case. In particular, the section of the aristocracy that affects the Spartan manner, the *Lakōnizontes* (or Spartan sympathizers), view pederasty as a Spartan and hence noble tradition."

20. Certainly it is not the teaching of Socrates that is parodied in the *Clouds*, nor does Aristophanes give an accurate portrayal of the instruction furnished by the sophists to the wealthy young men of Athens. Aristophanes, as artist and moralist, is constrained to fix concrete blame for what he and others saw as dangerous departures from older and more socially productive ideals. By concentrating on Socrates and the distorted popular image of the sophists (few in his audience had ever heard one teach) the poet confounds, perhaps purposely, cause and effect. Aside from the moral and philosophic "messages" put in the mouths of the two Arguments (Wrong Argument disclaiming, for example, the existence of justice, utilizing "sophistic" methods), the picture of upper-class manners and lifestyle that emerges conforms exactly to our other information on the subject. See K.J. Dover's Introduction to his edition of the *Clouds* (Oxford 1968).

21. Brasidas was the most prominent Spartan general of the time; the clothing and beard-style described here are Spartan.

22. E.g. Thuc. 8.48.3; 854.4; 8.81.2; cf. Aristophanes, *Lysistrata* 577.

23. *Knights* 257. For other citations see Ehrenberg, *People*, 98, note 9 and 109-10. In Old Comedy partisans of the democracy seem positively paranoid about the possible subverters of the constitution. For a recent, brief discussion of the political clubs see Connor, *New Politicians*, 25-29.

24. To the modern mind Alcibiades' defection, which actually included plotting the military destruction of his own country, is unspeakable treason (every American school child remembers the awful lesson of Benedict Arnold); yet Alcibiades' behavior is but another illustration of the precedence of the claims of class over all other appeals. Alcibiades gives an *apologia* in the same speech (6.92.2-4) saying that he was an exile because of the *ponēria* of those who drove him out, he was a lover of his country *(philopolis)* when he held his citizen's rights, but not when he was wronged; he is, in fact, a true *philopolis*, because he is striving to

recover a country he has lost. Alcibiades' sophistic argument perfectly represents the aristocratic tendency to separate themselves from the rest of the community. We are not surprised to learn that Alcibiades had previously re-established himself as *proxenos* (public representative) to the Spartans and that he was an hereditary guest-friend *(patrikos xenos)* to a Spartan ephor. The name Alkibiades was, in fact, as Thucydides tells us (8.6.3), a Spartan name.

25. Examples abound; see Ehrenberg, *People (passim)*, and for a recent discussion see de Ste. Croix, *The Origins of the Peloponnesian War*, App. 29, "The Political Outlook of Aristophanes." De Ste. Croix notes that Aristophanes treats two very prominent politicians of the day, Alcibiades and Nicias, quite gently, and that the rich (except for "demagogues" who are accused of getting rich from politics) are seldom satirized (pp. 360-62). The negative portrayal of democratic politicians acting in a democratic manner has often beguiled modern observers. Thus Jaeger can say of Cleon: "Athenians who were accustomed to the magnificent manners and intellectual nobility of Pericles turned with disgust from the common tanner whose vulgarity brought discredit on the whole nation" *(Paideia* I, 366).

26. Connor, *New Politicians,* 171ff., offers an explanation for Old Comedy's prejudice against Cleon and other demagogues: they were attacked precisely because they consciously repudiated the old values and the old style: "He offended not because he was contemptible, but because he showed contempt for a system that others had accepted" (p. 174).

27. The Greek attitude towards banausic occupations brings up the subject of slavery, which, along with attitudes towards race, has hardly been mentioned, despite their importance to a full understanding of social ideology. Equality of individuals for the Greeks was restricted to those who shared real or fictive kinship; and, despite sporadically expressed feeling that slaves and barbarians ought to be regarded as equal, this attitude persisted throughout antiquity. Because of a number of complex factors – among which was technological stagnation, which necessitated slave labor as the only means of increasing production – slavery was an apparent economic necessity for the Greeks. Since chattel slaves (in contrast to the various forms of helotage) were totally outside the framework of civic rights and obligations, they did not constitute a "social class," and hence do not figure at all in discussions of social problems.

28. Austin and Vidal-Naquet, *Economic and Social History*, 131-41; S. C. Humphreys, "Economy and society in classical Athens," in *Anthropology and the Greeks*, 136-58. De Ste. Croix, *Origins of the Peloponnesian War*, sees the war itself as a struggle between oligarchy and democracy, extended to the dependent states of each power (pp. 34-49).

29. *New Politicians,* 196-97. See the whole discussion on pp. 175-98. Alcibiades represents a third alternative, by appealing alternately to the $d\bar{e}mos$ and to the oligarchs; but his *style* was never anything but purely aristocratic. See also P. MacKendrick, *The Athenian Aristocracy: 399 to 31 B.C.* (Cambridge, Mass. 1969) 3-27, who details the careers of aristocrats and *nouveaux riches* in the "unaristocratic fourth century."

30. *Sophrosyne,* 137. One of the charges against the younger Alcibiades was that he had fraudulently served in the (less dangerous) cavalry instead of the infantry. In his defense of Mantitheus (see above, p. 161) Lycias is at pains to

show that Mantitheus, although enrolled as a knight, preferred hoplite service (16. 13), and that his private and public life were free from the vices of drinking, dicing, etc., that he was a true democrat and aided the polis as much as his means would allow.

31. Adkins, *M&R*, 210-13. See Humphreys, *Anthropology and the Greeks*, 233: "Attic society was becoming more complex and more mobile; the old aristocratic conception of *aretē*, in which class attributes, status obligations, and more abstract moral qualities were inextricably mingled, was no longer adequate. Virtue had to be democratic, the same for all men; at the same time it had to be rational, adaptable to all circumstances."

32. North, *Sophrosyne*, 174. This same kind of argument can be found in fourth-century orators who were unfriendly to the democracy. See North, *Sophrosyne*, 146, on Isocrates' *Niocles* (46), where the *sōphrosynē* and *metriōtēs* which are present by means of reasoning and good judgment are superior to the same qualities which come through nature and chance. Otherwise the old fifth-century arguments on the primacy of birth, wealth, life-style, muted to some extent, and given a bourgeois flavor, are duly produced by Isocrates and other *laudatores temporis acti*.

33. Arnheim's conclusion, *Aristocracy in Greek Society*, 159, is typical: "... the dominant ideology amongst the ancient Greeks was an aristocratic one." Cf. Austin and Vidal-Naquet, *Economic and Social History*, 16: "... aristocratic values were by and large not seriously challenged."

34. *Economic and Social Growth*, 130.

35. Terms like "social revolution," "class struggle," "class warfare," are much too extreme to describe the internal strife *(stasis)* of Greek *poleis*. The actual extent of bloody class war was limited in Greece until well into the fifth century, when economic differentiation became sufficiently severe to produce a true polarization of interests. A case in point is the restraint of the restored democracy in Athens in 403. After the crude excesses of the oligarchical "Thirty" in 404, which included executions and banishments on a large scale, the democratic regime did not retaliate in kind but reacted with remarkable mildness and moderation. Cf. Aristotle *Ath. Pol.* 50.3.

36. Andrewes, *The Greeks*, 192-194.

Ω

INDEX

- Abdera, 131.
- Achaeans, 8.
- *achreios*, 32, 117, 122.
- *achrēstos*, 170.
- *adikia*, 145.
- *adikos*, 71, 91, 93, 199.
- Aeschines, 176.
- Aeschylus, 204.
- Aesop, 49.
- Africa, 104.
- *agathos*, 4, 15, 16, 32ff., 41, 72ff., 77ff., 86, 87, 89ff., 104f., 107, 109, 110, 113, 114, 116, 119, 120, 126, 127, 131, 144, 148, 163, 176, 177, 184, 187, 189ff., 190, 195, 196, 206.
- *agenēs*, 203.
- *agnōmosynē*, 92.
- agriculture, 22, 26, 33, 36, 70, 74.
- *aidōs*, 47, 92, 93.
- *aischros*, 54, 79, 94, 114, 135, 137, 140, 145, 192, 197.
- *aischynē*, 204.
- *aisymnētēs*, 62, 193.
- *akolasia*, 171.
- Alcaeus, 59-63, 65, 81, 104, 120, 198.
- Alcemeonids, 119, 123, 164.
- Alcibiades, 168ff., 173, 175, 209, 210.
- Alcibiades, son of Alcibiades, 174f.
- *amathēs*, 146, 148, 157, 160.
- *amathia*, 145, 148ff.
- Anacreon, 55ff., 63ff., 67, 79f., 92, 120, 196.
- Ananius, 67.
- *andreia*, 120.
- *andreios*, 151, 152, 159.
- *anepistēmosynē*, 172.

- 213 -

- *anoia*, 170, 171.
- Antiphon, 131.
- *aphneios*, 184.
- *aphrōn*, 80, 90, 93.
- *aphrosynē*, 117.
- *apistos*, 172.
- *aporoi*, 128.
- *apragmōn*, 122.
- *apragmosynē*, 122.
- Archaic period, 35ff., 57f., 63, 67, 81, 86, 95, 109, 119, 155.
- Archilochus, 44-49, 53ff., 61, 65, 81, 90, 100, 194, 197.
- *archōn*, 66, 69, 132.
- *aretē*, 6, 7, 18, 23, 33, 34, 41ff., 66ff., 74, 81, 83, 84, 91ff., 100, 102, 103, 105, 106, 107, 109ff., 114, 116, 117, 118, 125, 145, 157, 176, 177, 197, 199, 200, 202, 211.
- Argives, 10.
- Aristophanes, 133, 145-59, 157, 159, 161, 163, 164, 166, 167, 173, 204, 209, 210.
- *aristos*, 19, 23, 32, 127, 135, 143, 144, 150, 151, 156, 187.
- Aristotle, 39, 48, 85, 179, 195, 197.
- Ascra, 46.
- Asia, 2, 104.
- Asius, 54.
- Athenagoras, 142, 206.
- Athens, 68ff., 106, 113, 123ff., 131, 136, 140, 156, 158, 166, 168ff., 196, 200, 201, 209, 211.
- Attica, 69, 119.
- *autarkeia*, 172.

- Bacchylides, 116ff., 202, 203.
- *basileus*, 2, 6, 16, 20, 22, 24, 25, 27ff., 31, 34, 50, 69, 122, 187.
- *beltiōn*, 127, 142, 145, 148, 170, 175.
- *bdelyros*, 157.
- birth, see lineage.
- Boeotia, 26.
- *boulē*, 6, 124, 156.
- Brasicas, 209.

- Callinus, 42, 44, 50, 65, 114.
- Ceos, 113, 116.
- *charis*, 56, 91, 125.
- *cheirōn*, 16, 128, 200, 205.

INDEX

- chief, 17ff., 25, 26ff., 38, 69; see *basileus*.
- chiefdom, 2, 9, 13, 17ff., 25, 31, 33, 69.
- *chrēstos*, 66, 117, 136, 137, 138, 145ff., 148, 152, 157, 176, 203, 205, 206.
- Cicero, 57, 194.
- class, social, 9, 18ff., 23, 32ff., 36f., 38, 39f., 44, 47, 48, 49ff., 57, 59, 62, 64, 65, 69, 71f., 75, 78, 81, 84, 86, 88, 89, 90, 94ff., 107, 109, 115, 117ff., 122, 126ff., 136, 142, 144f., 148f., 152, 156ff., 161ff., 177f., 190, 205ff., 210, 211.
- Classical period, 7, 35, 95, 113ff., 155ff.
- Cleisthenes, 123, 124.
- Cleon, 133, 148ff., 168, 172, 172, 206, 210.
- colonization, 33, 37.
- Crete, 119.
- Critias, 47, 158.
- Cylon, 70, 161.
- Cyrene, 105.

- Dark Age, 1ff., 20, 25, 58, 177, 178, 183.
- *deilos*, 50, 77, 78, 89, 90, 93, 95, 96, 107, 118, 120, 128, 191, 196.
- *dēmagōgia*, 146, 157, 210.
- democracy, 48, 108f., 115, 122ff., 130, 131, 133f., 140ff., 156, 158, 168, 174, 176, 205, 209ff.
- Democritus, 131.
- *dēmokratia*, 123, 124, 129, 142, 171, 172.
- *dēmokratikos*, 129.
- *dēmos*, 8, 12, 18, 24, 29, 41, 42, 47, 59f., 71, 73, 75, 84, 86, 87, 93, 122, 123, 124, 126, 129, 141ff., 148, 149, 153, 156ff., 168, 170ff., 174, 176, 179, 186, 187, 189, 195, 198, 205, 208, 210.
- *dēmotēs*, 132, 205.
- *dēmotikos*, 129, 170, 176, 177, 205, 208.
- *dexios*, 156, 159, 203.
- *dikaios*, 10, 32, 90, 93, 94, 146, 147, 148, 152, 157, 167, 195, 197, 200, 208.
- *dikaiosynē*, 68, 93.
- *dikē*, 10, 11, 27ff., 48, 50, 71, 93, 116, 205; see justice.
- *dokēsis*, 207.
- *doxa*, 43, 87, 90, 92, 207.
- Draco, 70.
- *dynamis*, 85, 86, 105.
- *dynatos*, 128, 170.
- *dysgeneia*, 135, 140, 147, 203.
- *dysgenēs*, 138, 140, 147, 203.

- economy, 4, 22, 26, 33f., 25ff., 51f., 66, 68f., 70, 74, 81ff., 142, 172ff.
- education, 145, 156ff., 166f., 176.
- Egypt, 11.
- *eidos*, 6, 7.
- Ephesus, 42, 64.
- Ephialtes, 125.
- *epieikeis*, 127.
- epinicians, 95.
- *epiphanēs*, 175.
- *epistēmē*, 177.
- *esthlos*, 4, 32, 50, 61, 72, 77ff., 81, 83, 87, 89, 90, 92, 93, 96, 113, 117, 118, 120, 127, 134, 137, 147, 184, 191, 195, 196, 199, 200, 203, 204.
- *ethos*, 83, 138, 150.
- *euandria*, 138, 150.
- *eudaimōn*, 205.
- *eugeneia*, 133, 134, 136ff., 141, 147, 152.
- *eugenēs*, 68, 80, 85, 97, 127, 132, 134, 135, 140, 141, 146, 147, 150, 152, 157, 207.
- *eugnomosynē*, 176.
- *eukleēs*, 114.
- *eukleia*, 118, 207.
- *eunomia*, 11, 65, 72, 100, 105, 116, 145, 201.
- *eupatridai*, 62, 70, 71, 119.
- Eupolis, 140.
- *euporoi*, 128.
- Euripides, 85, 135-39, 144, 147, 150ff., 158, 198, 204ff.
- *eusebēs*, 205.
- *exochoi*, 25.

- *gennadas*, 163, 203.
- *gennaios*, 49, 127, 136, 138, 144, 150ff., 205.
- *genos*, 38, 68, 137, 140, 141, 175.
- *gēomoroi*, 62.
- *geras*, 4, 19.
- *gnōmē*, 92, 93, 138, 148.
- *gnōrimoi*, 127.
- Gyges, 48.
- *gymnastika*, 156.

- Heraclitus, 143.
- Hermippus, 163.

INDEX 217

- Herodotus, 124, 132, 144, 161, 171, 204.
- Heroic Age, 1ff.
- heroic ideal, 2ff., 40ff., 44ff., 54, 57, 59ff., 134, 190.
- Hesiod, 14, 26-34, 36, 39, 44, 46, 48ff., 53, 68, 83, 93, 102, 106, 165, 191, 194, 195.
- *hetairia*, 168.
- *hetairos*, 23, 88.
- Hiero, 102, 202.
- *hippeis*, 62, 162.
- *hippobotai*, 62.
- Hipponax, 64f., 67, 82.
- Homer, 1-8, 14, 18-29, 32f., 42ff., 49, 52ff., 60f., 80, 92, 100, 106, 108f., 161, 165, 191, 194, 201.
- *homoioi*, 192.
- *homonoia*, 179.
- homosexuality, 53, 63, 89, 120, 129, 164ff., 175, 194, 200, 203, 209.
- hoplite, 39f., 44, 60, 70, 74, 116, 160, 196, 197.
- Horace, 194.
- hospitality, 10ff.
- Hybrias, 121.
- *hybris*, 11, 28, 48, 50, 71, 72, 84, 93, 117, 186, 189.
- Hyperbolus, 172,

- Ibycus, 57, 65, 92.
- *Iliad*, 1f., 6ff., 12ff., 20ff., 27ff., 39, 48, 50, 55, 196.
- Isagoras, 124.
- *isēgoria*, 159.
- Isocrates, 211.
- *isonomia*, 205.
- *isonomos*, 203.
- Ithaca, 9, 13, 17.

- justice, 12f., 27ff., 48ff., 68, 78, 94; see *dikē*.

- *kakopatris (idēs)*, 61, 62, 80, 82, 193.
- *kakos*, 4, 11, 16, 27, 28, 32, 54, 72ff., 77ff., 93ff., 107, 113, 117, 128, 132, 134, 136ff., 144f., 147, 176, 184, 187, 188, 193ff., 198ff., 202, 204, 207.
- *kakotēs*, 93.
- *kallos*, 94, 106, 200.
- *kalos*, 106, 107, 121, 129, 134, 137, 147, 156, 175, 193, 201.
- *kaloskagathos*, 129, 133, 134, 146, 157, 160, 173, 204.

- kinship, 8f., 13, 31f., 38, 70, 124, 191; see lineage.
- *klarotai*, 194.
- *kleos*, 92, 114.
- *komaō*, 161.
- *komētēs*, 161, 164.
- *kompsos*, 161.
- *koros*, 84, 103.
- *kosmios*, 175, 177.
- *kouphologia*, 172.
- *kydos*, 4, 23, 58, 108, 117.

- *laos*, 8, 18, 25, 28, 41, 42, 186.
- law, 70, 73, 130.
- Leonidas, 114.
- Lesbos, 81.
- life-style, 22f., 52ff., 56ff., 62f., 65f., 73, 75, 89, 91, 100, 106, 126, 143f., 146, 155ff., 207, 208, 209, 211.
- lineage, 2, 9, 12, 15f., 38, 49, 61f., 68, 69f., 75, 78, 80, 81, 85, 93, 97ff., 119, 127f., 131f., 133ff., 143, 144ff., 140f., 155, 158, 159, 168, 178f., 183, 196, 206, 211.
- liturgies, 126, 203.
- lyric poets, 35ff., *passim*.
- Lysias, 161, 175, 210.

- Macedon, 115.
- *malakia*, 172.
- *maniōdēs*, 172.
- manufacture, 33, 36f., 189.
- Marathon, 116.
- Megacles, 164.
- Megara, 77.
- *megas*, 50, 150, 205.
- mental qualities, 90, 92f., 95, 104f., 126ff., 139, 143ff., 170f., 178, 199, 205.
- *mesos*, 72.
- metic, 156.
- *metrios*, 171, 176, 211.
- Miletus, 66.
- Mimnermus, 54f., 57, 63, 65, 67, 72, 77.
- *misthioi*, 128.
- *misthophorioi*, 128.
- *mochthēros*, 128, 172, 203.
- *moira*, 94.

INDEX

- *monarchos*, 179.
- moral qualities, 78, 83ff., 87ff., 95, 103ff., 113f., 118ff., 126ff., 136, 139, 143ff., 170f., 175, 178.
- *mousikos*, 157.
- Myrsilus, 61.
- Mytilene, 60, 61, 148.

- Nebuchadrezzar, 60.
- Nicias, 169, 210.
- *nomos*, 130, 138, 158, 206.

- *ochlos*, 127, 136, 141, 144, 171, 205.
- *Odyssey*, 1f., 6ff., 10ff., 17ff., 23f., 26, 28f., 49, 50, 87, 90.
- *oikos*, 2, 4, 9, 13, 14, 23, 38, 183, 186.
- *olbios*, 94, 128, 141.
- *olbos*, 102.
- "Old Oligarch," 141, 144f., 156, 171, 174, 205, 206, 208.
- *oligarchia*, 123, 170.
- *oligarchikos*, 176.
- oligarchy, 123f., 142, 144, 158, 168, 176, 210.
- *oligoi*, 94, 125, 127, 205.
- Olympic games, 169, 199.

- *paideia*, 166, 167.
- *paideusis*, 167, 208.
- *panaristos*, 32.
- Paros, 44, 46.
- *parrhēsia*, 159.
- *pauroi*, 94.
- peasant, 26, 36, 51, 66, 121, 162, 188.
- *penēs*, 82, 85, 128, 140, 141, 147, 152, 205.
- *penestai*, 194.
- Penia, 148, 149.
- *penichros*, 81.
- Pericles, 122, 125, 140, 148, 171ff., 205, 206, 210.
- Persia, 155.
- phalanx, 39f., 74, 79, 190.
- *phaulos*, 148, 203, 206.
- *philodespotos*, 198.
- *philopolis*, 209.
- *philotēs*, 9, 185.
- Phocylides, 66f., 93, 94, 194, 199.
- *phyā*, 97, 98.

- *physis*, 130, 135, 137, 138, 150, 152, 153, 158, 176, 177, 206, 207.
- Pindar, 58, 77, 95-111, 113-19, 131, 199ff., 202.
- Pisistratids, 119, 203.
- Pisistratus, 70, 123, 200, 203.
- Pittacus, 59ff., 73, 75, 198.
- Plataea, 115f.
- Plato, 47, 158, 165, 177, 179.
- *pleistos*, 108.
- *plēthos*, 85, 127, 205.
- *plousios*, 81, 85, 128, 142, 147, 162, 205.
- *ploutos*, 102, 103, 140, 202.
- *poinē*, 12.
- polis, 3, 8, 9, 37ff., 42, 43, 44, 51, 52, 57, 59, 60, 65, 69, 70, 71, 74, 75, 87, 100, 108, 109, 116, 121, 122ff., 129, 131, 132, 134, 141, 142, 145, 156, 157, 171, 173, 174, 176, 178, 179, 186, 190, 205, 211.
- *politeia*, 125.
- *politēs*, 8, 38, 51, 52, 67, 123, 170, 200.
- *polloi*, 127, 142ff., 150, 169.
- *polymathēs*, 159.
- Polycrates, 56, 57, 132.
- *polypragmosynē*, 122.
- *ponēria*, 145, 170, 209.
- *ponēros*, 128, 137, 141, 144, 145, 147, 148, 156, 171, 176, 194, 203, 205.
- population, 32, 33, 37, 156.
- poverty, 64, 81ff., 140, 147, 156, 173f., 197, 205, 206, 208; see *penia*.
- *prostatēs*, 141, 142.
- *ptōchos*, 196.
- *prōtoi*, 118, 140, 170.
- Pythermus, 66.

- Quintilian, 194.

- religion, 20ff., 29, 38, 68, 69, 99f., 123.
- Rhegium, 57.
- *rhētōr*, 158.

- Samos, 50, 132.
- Sappho, 194.

INDEX

- *scolion*, 119ff., 160, 203.
- Scopas, 114, 116.
- *semnos*, 162, 164.
- Semonides, 194, 198, 202.
- Sicily, 104, 169.
- Simonides, 85, 113-16, 118f., 202.
- slavery, 204, 210.
- Socrates, 161, 166, 209.
- Solon, 68-75, 77, 81, 84, 87, 100f., 123, 165, 196, 198, 199.
- *sophia*, 92, 95, 108, 145.
- sophists, 130f., 138, 158f., 166, 204, 209.
- Sophocles, 131, 133ff., 204.
- *sophos*, 104ff., 108, 117, 148, 153, 159, 200.
- *sōphrōn*, 80, 90, 93, 105, 138, 145ff., 150, 157, 172, 175, 176, 203.
- *sōphrosynē*, 90, 91, 93, 95, 105, 138, 148, 149, 152, 167, 171, 206, 211.
- Sparta, 36, 41, 149, 157, 168, 171, 190, 209.
- *stasis*, 38, 66, 70, 73, 211.
- Stesichorus, 196.
- *synoikismos*, 69.
- *synomotai*, 168.
- Syracuse, 96, 202.

- technology, 35f.
- Thasos, 46.
- Thebes, 30, 105, 115.
- *themis*, 116, 186.
- Themistocles, 206.
- *Theognidea*, 77-80, 82-97, 106ff., 109ff., 113f., 117ff., 131, 196ff., 202.
- Theognis, 77-80, 82-97, 106ff., 109ff., 113f., 117ff., 131, 196ff., 202.
- *Theogony*, 26, 28f.
- Thessaly, 115.
- Thrace, 131.
- Thucydides, 53, 106, 122, 125, 140, 142, 148ff., 158, 169ff., 206.
- *timē*, 4, 13, 23, 54, 58, 78, 87, 90, 102, 117, 118, 120, 186, 190.
- *timios*, 55, 81.
- *tlēmsoynē*, 90.
- *tolmā*, 105, 198, 200.
- trade, 33, 36f., 51, 74, 140, 196.
- tribal culture, 2ff., 9. 13, 18ff., 29f., 38, 42, 75, 124, 178.
- Trojan War, 1, 14.

- Troy, 9, 17, 30.
- *tyrannos*, 39, 62, 70, 123, 179, 194, 198.
- tyranny, 39, 51, 53, 56, 61f., 70, 75, 115, 123, 132, 149, 179, 189, 198, 201; see *tyrannos*.
- Tyrtaeus, 40-44, 47, 54, 59, 65, 77, 84f., 92, 100, 114, 190, 196, 197, 200.

- vase painting, 52f., 66, 107, 208.

- *wanax*, 2.
- wealth, 4f., 19, 23, 26, 32ff., 38, 51ff., 58, 64, 66, 71ff., 78, 79, 80ff., 94f., 101f., 109, 117, 118, 127f., 139ff., 143, 146ff., 150ff., 155, 158, 159, 168, 173f., 178f., 196, 197, 200, 202, 204ff., 208, 211.
- *Works and Days*, 26-32, 49f.

- *xenios*, 186.
- Xenophanes, 53, 65f., 100, 202.
- Xenophon, 140, 208.
- *xynesis*, 148, 150.
- *xynetos*, 142, 148, 151, 200.